The Idaho Four

For a preview of upcoming books and information about the author, visit JamesPatterson.com or find him on Facebook, X, Instagram, or Substack.

The
Idaho
Four

An American Tragedy

James Patterson
and Vicky Ward

Little, Brown and Company
New York   Boston   London

Little, Brown and Company
Hachette Book Group
1290 Avenue of the Americas, New York, NY 10104
littlebrown.com

First Edition: July 2025

Little, Brown and Company is a division of Hachette Book Group, Inc. The Little, Brown name and logo are trademarks of Hachette Book Group, Inc.

The publisher is not responsible for websites (or their content) that are not owned by the publisher.

The Hachette Speakers Bureau provides a wide range of authors for speaking events. To find out more, go to hachettespeakersbureau.com or email hachettespeakers@hbgusa.com.

Little, Brown and Company books may be purchased in bulk for business, educational, or promotional use. For information, please contact your local bookseller or the Hachette Book Group Special Markets Department at special.markets@hbgusa.com.

ISBN 9780316572859 (hc) / 9780316580816 (large print)
LCCN 2025932205

Printing 1, 2025

LSC-C

Printed in the United States of America

I couldn't wrap my head around—there can't be this kind of evil in our midst...I just couldn't bring myself to do it, to think that. There's no way. This person *can't* be amongst us.

—Evan Ellis, *Morning News,*
Pullman Radio (Washington)

Authors' Note

This book reads like fiction, but none of it is made up. Every detail in these pages has been meticulously sourced through interviews or has been factually documented.

Bryan Kohberger has been charged with murdering Ethan Chapin, Xana Kernodle, Maddie Mogen, and Kaylee Goncalves, who became known as the Idaho Four, on November 13, 2022. His criminal trial is set to begin in August 2025. Of course, he is innocent until proven guilty.

The book does not offer a view on what the verdict will be. Rather, it is the story of four tragic murders and the impact of the crimes on a small American town.

This book could not have been written without the help and support of hundreds of people, including the 320 individually interviewed (some many times) by Vicky Ward.

We'd especially like to thank the victims' friends and family for giving us so much precious time, hospitality, and insight: the Chapin family and

Hunter Johnson for sharing about Ethan; the Goncalves family for sharing about Kaylee; Ben Mogen and Kim Cheeley, aka Deedle, for sharing about Maddie; and the Alandt family—Karen, Matt, and Emily, Xana's best friend—for sharing so much about Xana.

Moscow, Idaho, police chief James Fry, now retired, generously gave his time and shared his insights on dealing with the most horrific crime of his career amid worldwide media scrutiny. Importantly, he did this without discussion of any of the specifics of this case and investigation, per the gag order put in place by a local judge. The supporting details are drawn from public documents, including court records—and from elsewhere.

Thanks also to Cathy Mabbutt, the Moscow coroner, and retired police officers Paul Kwiatkowski and Brannon Jordan.

At the University of Idaho, thank you to dean of students Blaine Eckles as well as to Kelly Quinnett and Bruce Pitman.

Thank you also to these University of Idaho Vandals: Ava Wood, Josie Lauteren, Linden Beck, Emma Tyger, David Berriochoa, Alejandro Salvador, Ben DeWitt, Claire Qualls, Lexi Pattinson, Haadiya Tariq, and Daniel Ramirez. And to the guys at the Sigma Chi fraternity, especially Gus Elwell, Tim DeWulf, and Kyle Frei.

Above all for introductions to Moscow, Idaho, residents and culture, thanks go to psychologist Dr. Rand Walker. Without him, none of this would have been possible.

Much appreciation to those who opened the doors of the city of Moscow: Mayor Art Bettge; Pat Greenfield, owner of Bucer's coffeehouse; Christ Church pastor Doug Wilson and his son Nate Wilson; Marc Trivelpiece, owner of the Corner Club; and attorneys Mike Pattinson and Wendy Olson.

* * *

For invaluable insight into the Pullman, Washington, perspective, thank you to Washington State University police chief Gary Jenkins; former Pullman mayor Glenn Johnson; Pullman Radio host Evan Ellis; and WSU alumni Ben Roberts, Cassie Handziak, and Deola Adetunji.

For a sense of Kohberger's life in the Poconos, thanks to Mark and Jack Baylis, Connie Saba, Josh Ferraro, Chad Petipren, Brittany Slaven, Jesse Harris, John Gress, Bob Himes, and Casey Arntz.

And for taking us into the online community of their University of Idaho — Case Discussion Facebook group page, thanks to Kristine Cameron and Alina Smith.

Here is the story of the Idaho Four, their young lives cut short by unspeakable violence. It's an exploration of a complex criminal investigation — and a timeless portrait of the worst and best in us.

—James Patterson and Vicky Ward

PROLOGUE

One

C hief, we've got a bad situation."
James Fry, the God-fearing chief of the Moscow, Idaho, Police Department, picks up the call from Captain Tyson Berrett informing him of a mass homicide: four murders at 1122 King Road.

Berrett has the inside track. Ava and Emily, two of the kids in the group sitting outside the rental house, work at the football stadium. The Kibbie Dome is under Berrett's purview, so he knows them well.

It's Sunday, and Fry is about an hour into the four-hour drive back from an overnight visit with a friend in Wenatchee, Washington, 150 miles east of Seattle. Whatever has happened, whoever the victims are, it already feels too close for comfort.

In the passenger seat, listening, is Julie Fry. The chief's whip-smart wife of thirty-odd years also happens to be the newly elected Latah County clerk. Chief Fry will later say he should have let Julie drive, but now it's all he can do to absorb what Berrett tells him.

Four young people, likely UI students, stabbed in their bedrooms? In their beds? In a residence that's part of a large cluster of student housing right on the campus line? And no one heard a thing?

Fry's put in thirty years on the force. The common assumption about small-town police chiefs is that they have no experience with murder, but this is not Fry's first brush with homicides on campus.

In 2007, when he was still a sergeant, he worked on three homicides in just one year. One involved a University of Idaho student, David Boss, who was shot by a former classmate. In 2011, as a lieutenant, Fry oversaw the investigation of another university tragedy. That summer, psychology professor Ernesto Bustamante, who had a history of mental illness, fatally shot Katy Benoit, a twenty-two-year-old graduate student he'd previously dated, outside her home, then later turned the gun on himself.

Even so, Fry already knows that this one is different.

He knows this is going to test the department in an unprecedented way. He also knows that this is too big for Moscow to handle without help. In a rural area like this, there's a general view that it's all hands on deck.

He's going to need support from the state. Probably the FBI.

But first things first . . .

It's not his job to run point at the scene of the crime. When he was a detective, which was not so long ago, he headed up investigations, but now he's chief, and chiefs who get in the way of their teams can really screw things up. His role today is to stay in close touch with his officers, provide whatever support is needed.

Part of leading, Fry believes, is trusting and delegating. But Fry knows that when adrenaline is running high, anyone can forget things, so he rattles off a punch list to Tyson Berrett, realizing from experience that his captain is out in front of him.

"Have you reached Bill?" he asks, referring to veteran county prosecutor Bill Thompson, who has never lost a case. In their parallel careers, the chief and the prosecutor have worked every crime scene together. They meet every single day at eight a.m. Fry's belief in Thompson—the only prosecutor in Idaho who has ever won a murder conviction in the absence of a dead body—is unwavering.

"On his way," Berrett says.

"Forensics?" The two forensics officers, Lawrence Mowery and Andrew Fox, are Fry's appointments. "State?" A scene as big as this needs help from the Idaho State Police forensics team, based in Lewiston, about thirty miles south of Moscow.

"On their way."

"Who have you got there?"

Berrett tells him that Mitch Nunes was the first officer on scene.

And at this, Fry blanches. "My heart broke," he said later. His thirty-seven-man department runs like a family. Twenty-two-year-old Nunes is like a son to Fry, a baby.

He knows that his youngest officer will never be able to erase from his mind the horrific crime scene that he's just witnessed. That he will be forever altered. And Fry will need to find Nunes—and his wife—the resources to cope with the trauma.

Mental health is not something that was discussed when Fry was a rookie, and he believes that was a mistake. PTSD, according to Fry's longtime ride-along partner and best friend, Paul Kwiatkowski, lingers as he sorts through memories that won't dim.

Fry is going to take care of his young officers and their families. Make sure they feel supported.

Speaking of . . .

"Has the university been notified?"

"Affirmative."

"Where's Brett Payne?"

Two months prior, Fry promoted Brett Payne, a thirty-two-year-old cop and military veteran whom he hired in 2020, to detective corporal—a new position in the department that Fry created for a reason.

Ordinarily, detectives are the higher rank of sergeant. But Fry had been faced with a specific set of challenges—he had to run a small department at a time when applications for jobs in law enforcement were dwindling (this was shortly after an officer in Minnesota had been convicted in the death of George Floyd). The chief decided to free up some of the sergeants to learn the administrative part of police work—how to actually run a department, pay bills, budget, and so forth.

Which means today, Fry realizes, Payne will be the one to lead this investigation. Organize the department into teams.

Talk about diving into the deep end.

Tyson responds that yes, Payne is on his way to the crime scene. He'll get there at around four p.m.

Which will be ahead of Fry. He presses harder on the gas. And dials a number.

"Rand," he says into the phone to Dr. Rand Walker, a local therapist who has counseled his officers before. "I need you to be on standby."

The rest of the drive is a blur of staccato calls.

Chief Gary Jenkins—the head of the Washington State University police over in Pullman and former chief of the Pullman PD—phones.

"Do you need backup from us?" Jenkins asks.

The two departments often tag-team. Moscow's last convicted murderer, John Lee, had in fact been caught on the run by the officers in Pullman.

But Fry is cautious. In 2015, they knew who the murderer was.

This time they have no idea.

Fry is aware of the importance of locking down an investigation, keeping information on a need-to-know basis to stop leaks that could jeopardize it.

He and Bill Thompson are completely in sync on this. Thompson never speaks to anyone about an investigation until he gets to sentencing—and even then, he keeps it short.

And there are too many unanswered questions right now. It's not safe or prudent for Fry to involve another team.

"Not yet," Fry tells Jenkins. "I'll keep you posted."

Berrett's shared with Fry that a knife sheath was found in one of the rooms. It's imperative this doesn't get out.

Somewhere, there's a maniacal murderer on the loose who is almost certainly watching their every move.

Who in God's name could have done this? Fry wonders.

And again he presses harder on the gas.

One good thing about being the police chief is that no one is likely to arrest him for speeding.

Two

One hour later

The notifications about death are the thing Chief Fry dreads most in this job. It takes seconds to give or receive the news. Yet the needlessly lost lives haunt his dreams. He can recall each and every one as he hurtles toward Moscow.

Take January 22, 2013—nearly a decade ago. He'd been a lieutenant. A couple had shown up at the station, wondering anxiously where their son was.

A Latah County sheriff's deputy had found a body the next day and called it in. The corpse had been on the ground for two days. It looked like the kid, a college student named Joseph Wiederrick, had frozen to death. He'd been intoxicated.

The department spread out, trying to piece together what had happened, and Fry became the point person for the kid's parents.

Notifying parents of the loss of their children is something you never get better at. And tragically, student deaths are not that unusual. There's one practically every semester. Typically, it's the result of a car accident that occurs during the long drive most of the kids take to cross the state in treacherous conditions in winter.

One year Fry taught a class up at the university, and right before

Thanksgiving break, he told his students: "Remember, drive extra-slow. Your parents don't care what time you get there. They just want you there."

Fry may be a cop, but he's also a husband and the father of four kids — three daughters and a son. "I understand what that's like as a parent, to drop a child off," he'll say. He knows that parents expect their kids to be safe in college.

And he also knows that sometimes, they aren't.

The tragedy with young Joseph Wiederrick was a double whammy for Fry because it seemed like no one in the community helped the kid out by notifying law enforcement that he was in trouble on the night he ended up dying.

His body was found two miles from town. *Two miles.* Fry knew that *someone* must have spotted the drunk kid while he was walking.

Sure enough, when all the details about Wiederrick's final night were in, and when Fry put together a map for Joseph's mom, Michelle, it emerged that Joseph walked a circuitous *eight* miles before lying down to rest one last time.

Various people in the town *did* see the kid. They *could* have helped him by calling the MPD when he stumbled into their backyards or, in a few cases, into their homes.

Instead, they just watched him or sent him on his way. One lady later said: "I just didn't want to get him in trouble."

Joseph *would* have been in trouble. He would have been locked up and most likely given a criminal citation. But nothing more.

Fry tells everyone he works with that the key to serving the community is respect, respect, respect.

"You ever see the movie *Road House* with Patrick Swayze?" he'll ask people. If they haven't, he tells them to watch it.

The movie's message is *his* message, the one he instills in his officers: "Be nice, be nice, be nice, and until it's time not to be nice... be nice. If you treat people with respect even when you arrest them, they'll thank you."

But in 2013 the town's residents seemed unaware of the chief's message of police compassion.

The tragic story of Joseph Wiederrick that he put together went something like this:

On January 20 at two a.m., a Moscow woman hears a noise downstairs. She goes to take a look. Is it an animal?

It's a human. A drunk human. An eighteen-year-old man, clearly disoriented, smelling of alcohol, his blond hair disheveled, is stumbling around in her basement. She doesn't know how he got in. He's lost.

"Safe, safe," he mumbles to her. It's clear he wants to stay, sleep it off.

But she asks him to leave. He'll figure it out. No need to call the police.

It's black outside. Snowdrifts piled high. But students often wander drunk, a nuisance with their noise and their parties.

Joseph shuffles off down Highland Drive.

Three a.m. *Bang, bang.* He's knocking on another door, this one on Mountain View Road.

The owner looks through the window. "Go home," he says to the kid.

Again, there's no call to the police. The townsfolk think they're protecting him.

It's a mistake.

Four a.m. *Bang, bang.*

A third homeowner looks out the window, shrugs, and goes back to bed.

Joseph wanders away. He's trying to get back to his dorm but has no idea where he's headed.

Somehow, he ends up near Paradise Creek. Two miles north of the city.

Joseph trips and falls. He hits the frozen creek. His body sinks like a dead weight through the ice into the frigid water.

He fights. He climbs out. He crawls under a nearby bridge. And rests. And rests.

His body is discovered by police two days later. It emerges that Joseph Wiederrick had drunk too much at a Saturday-night party given by the Sigma Alpha Epsilon fraternity.

* * *

Fry doesn't like to toot his own horn, but he reckons that since he became chief in 2016, attitudes in town have changed about a lot of things, including over-the-top college drinking. He isn't stupid enough to think you can stop college kids from drinking. But he believes you can take steps to keep it in check.

You can, for example, go, as he does, to Rosauers, look at the keg list, and figure out where each keg is. If a keg is somewhere it isn't supposed to be—if, say, it's with a group of underage kids—you take it away. Nicely, but that's what you do.

One time Fry and the guys took forty-two cases of Keystone Light away from a fraternity party because they saw a nineteen-year-old pushing the cart. So, yes, you've got to teach them that the law is the law.

If Fry and his ride-along partner Captain Paul Kwiatkowski had been called to deal with drunk Joseph Wiederrick, sure, they might have locked him up, but he'd have still had his life ahead of him.

Fry is upset that people in Moscow don't get that. "What else can we do?" he asked Paul one time.

"Keep going," his friend and colleague said. "Don't give up."

The two guys had looked at the framed quotations on Fry's wall. The chief knows them by heart, but he still reads them every day.

The first is from Philippians 4:7: *And the peace of God, which passeth all understanding, will guard your hearts and your minds.*

The second is from a Theodore Roosevelt speech on citizenship. In April 1910, after finishing his second term as US president, Roosevelt delivered "The Man in the Arena" speech at the Sorbonne in Paris. He was on his way to Oslo, Norway, to officially accept the Nobel Peace Prize, which he had been awarded in 1906 for his efforts to end the Russo-Japanese War.

> The credit belongs to the man who is actually in the arena, whose face is marred by dust and sweat and blood; who

strives valiantly; who errs, who comes short again and again…who at the best knows in the end the triumph of high achievement, and who at the worst, if he fails, at least fails while daring greatly, so that his place shall never be with those cold and timid souls who neither know victory nor defeat.

Fry thinks about those words: *Who at the worst, if he fails, at least fails while daring greatly.*

So as the chief reaches the city's outskirts, he takes a deep breath. He knows that with this startlingly awful and strange case, now more than ever he needs to get a critical message through: The Moscow police, on his watch, are to be trusted, not feared.

Three

1122 King Road
Moscow, Idaho
Two hours earlier

Officer Nunes radios the police station and reaches Sergeant Shaine Gunderson, who's been taking advantage of his quiet Sunday-morning shift to plan a hiking trip to Mount Borah, on the other side of the state.

"This is serious," Nunes tells him.

Gunderson snaps out of his boredom, leaps into his car, and heads for King Road.

As he rides, he phones Tyson Berrett. His boss, the commander of the campus police, is on call that day.

Berrett says he's already sent patrol officers Smith and Warner to join Nunes, who's taping off the area around the house.

Berrett knows what to do, and not just because he's an experienced cop. He was the sergeant assigned to Moscow's previous famous homicide, the case of John Lee, a mentally ill man who went on a shooting spree in January 2015, killing three people, including his adoptive mother.

But Berrett has another advantage here. He's a Vandal (the name of the school's athletic teams, a nickname that comes from a long-ago U of I basketball team said to have "vandalized" its opponents). He knows the school, the students, the faculty, the administration, the culture. He's been attached to the university on and off for years. He worked it years ago as a sergeant. His daughter is a student.

When Berrett arrives, he recognizes Ava Wood, a neighbor who rushed out with blankets for the group of students sitting in front of the house at 1122 King Road.

"Do you know the people inside, Ava?" Berrett asks.

She nods and Berrett looks at her, eyes filled with sympathy.

And then he turns to the front door.

All those years of training and experience kick in. He runs through his checklist.

    1.   Clear the residence and run tape around the perimeter.

Check.

    2.   Call for medical assistance if needed.

There is no need.

    3.   Secure the scene.

Check. Nunes has put up the tape. Berrett assigns one cop to watch the front of the house, another the back.

    4.   Call in the detectives who will lead the investigation.

There'll be five detectives: John Lawrence (who is about to retire); Dani Vargas; Brett Payne, detective corporal; and forensics detectives

Lawrence Mowery and Andrew Fox. Berrett knows it's important to call only those cops who will play essential roles. With each body comes the risk of contaminating evidence.

5. Notify the police chief.
6. Notify the county prosecutor, Bill Thompson.
7. Notify the other Moscow PD captains, Anthony Dahlinger and Roger Lanier.
8. Call the sergeant running the Idaho State Police detectives.

Moscow is going to need the state police's forensics team, at a bare minimum. This is too big for the MPD to handle alone. State has a forensics lab; Moscow does not.

9. Call the university's president, provost, and dean of students.
10. Call the coroner, but not until all the evidence is collected. Someone might accidentally move something and contaminate the scene.
11. Notify the public if there is a threat.

Berrett knows not just from his years of experience but from common sense that the probability of some random stranger knifing four people to death in their bedrooms is almost nil. There's a connection somewhere between whoever did this and at least one of the victims. There always is. That's what the police are going to have to find.

The patrol officers correctly begin with the people in front of them. Why is this young student, Hunter Johnson, holding a kitchen knife? What happened here?

Hunter sits with the patrol officers and tells them what happened as best he knows. They let him go.

Sirens start to wail.

But the first emergency vehicle that arrives is unnecessary. It's the volunteer ambulance, the medical responders to the 911 call. It stays a couple of minutes, then, at the cops' request, leaves.

It's much too late for anyone to need medical attention.

PART ONE

The Innocents

Chapter 1

It's Bid Day at the University of Idaho.

Kaylee Goncalves and Maddie Mogen chose the University of Idaho precisely because of its strong Greek life. Nearly one-quarter of UI students take part.

The two look-alike, blond (Maddie's is natural; Kaylee's is dyed) best friends, both freshmen, take their seats in the auditorium. They glance nervously at the throng of women packed around them like canned sardines, all clutching envelopes. Inside each is the name of the sorority the student has gotten into.

Kaylee's and Maddie's top choice is Alpha Phi — or APhi, as it's known, pronounced "ay-fee." As one of its members described the sorority, it's a place "for blondes, for homecoming queens, for popular girls, leaders, girls who like to party — and to get ready to party."

Last night, to help the newcomers make up their minds, the sororities invited the women to so-called preference ceremonies at their top choices. At APhi, one of the sisters told a sad but moving story: Her boyfriend, a football star, had tragically lost his battle with cancer, and the support of the house was what got her through.

Both girls know that Greek life isn't just about parties. The friendships and networks and bonds formed in each house are an important factor in most students' social and, later, professional lives. Maddie wants a career in marketing, Kaylee in IT.

Kaylee and Maddie drove to campus together and spent the past few days rushing together.

And the past six years doing everything together.

Maddie has been entering Kaylee's house without knocking just like she's part of Kaylee's noisy, happy, hectic, vast family since they were both twelve years old. Maddie is more of a girlie-girl than Kaylee, who used to be a bit of a tomboy. Kaylee is more of an extrovert than Maddie and maybe more of a hustler. She's had to be to get what she wants, given the size of the Goncalves household. Kaylee has four siblings. Maddie is an only child, and her home, by contrast, is quiet.

Since their early teens, these two shared summer boat rides on the lake in Coeur d'Alene, winter bathing in the nearby hot springs, trips to Seattle, beach vacations in Puerto Rico, in Grand Cayman, in Hawaii. They've never spent more than a few days apart.

Maddie recently heard that UI sororities like to separate girls who know each other well. Apparently, the point of Greek life is to make new friends, not cling to old ones.

Here in the auditorium, Maddie waits to learn if APhi will choose Kaylee over her.

It's a daunting moment as the clock ticks on.

Twenty seconds to go. The hundreds of freshman girls in the auditorium count down together. Ten seconds. Five seconds. Four. Three. Two...

Maddie and Kaylee tear open their envelopes.

There are screams all around, women sobbing, running. Maddie's eyes blur with tears.

She didn't make APhi.

And Kaylee did.

The slip of paper in Maddie's envelope tells her she's been picked by

Pi Beta Phi, known as Pi Phi (pronounced "pie-fie")—a perfectly respectable sorority but not generally considered a top house on campus.

Within seconds, there's a stampede for the exit as the women race out to the lawn to find their new sorority sisters, standing out there under signs.

Here, now, isn't the time to say goodbye. But for Maddie and Kaylee, it's an ending. And it's a beginning.

Chapter 2

Moscow, Idaho
August 20, 2019

Maddie's a talented photographer, and she's done some modeling, so she knows how to make her Instagram seductive. The Pi Phi sisters want to build up their house's reputation so they can be more competitive with the top ones like APhi.

Maddie does her part, creating a scene befitting a Disney movie. Seven beaming, modern-day Cinderellas, Maddie among them, pose on the steps of the Pi Phi sorority house in matching white tank tops. The four older sisters have on matching pink miniskirts, and the three younger girls wear matching denim shorts. The archway behind them is covered with pink balloons.

Maddie captions it: **I ran home! #pibetaphiUI**.

Kaylee comments: **THATS MY BEST FRIEND!!!! I love you so much!!! 4LIFE BABY!!!!**

Of course Kaylee knows how disappointed Maddie is. And she hurts because Maddie is hurting. Showing wisdom beyond their years, the friends accept the idea that widening their respective social circles will be good for both of them.

In other words, they'll play the game of Greek life.

Kaylee can't fail to express her own unmitigated joy about her acceptance into APhi.

Which is why she posts a photo of herself smiling with two new sorority sisters in front of the Alpha Phi house with the caption **What flo rida said #welcometomyhouse** (referencing the rapper's 2015 hit "My House").

Maddie comments: **So happy for you bestie.** 😍 😍

Their public Instagrams, TikToks, and Snapchats tell the story of their growing closeness with their new sisters and new best friends. Privately, Kaylee and Maddie remain as tight as ever, quietly maintaining their lifelong bond IRL (in real life), as the expression goes.

Maddie's posts reflect her new friendship with sorority sisters Sophia Whitehead, who is in the year above her, and Ashlin Couch, who, like her, is from Coeur d'Alene.

Kaylee's posts show weekend activities: attending U of I football games on campus, traveling to Seattle with her APhi sorority sisters, and nuzzling her boyfriend, Jack DuCoeur.

What they *don't* post is pictures with each other.

The two keep up this illusion of separateness well into the next semester... when the balloon of unreality surrounding them is abruptly pierced.

In March 2020, COVID strikes.

Chapter 3

Rathdrum, Idaho
March 2020

At the end of spring break, Kaylee and Maddie both receive emails containing the same instructions: Don't come back to the sorority house. School is going remote.

The girls are home in Rathdrum and the neighboring town of Coeur D'Alene, Idaho, and for them, it's like old times. They have each other. And given the stress surrounding the virus, they decide that pretense, even on social media, is no longer important.

The day after Maddie's birthday, May 25—"Maddie May Day"—Kaylee posts the first Instagram photo of the two best friends together since their arrival at UI. The two of them are hugging, wearing pretty summer dresses, standing by the lake. **The easiest person to celebrate,** Kaylee writes, **here's to you my sweet maddie may!!** 🌿✌🏻

Later that summer, Kaylee gives Maddie a shout-out: **@maddiemogen thanks for always being my personal photographer.** 🤍

It's a source of pride to Kaylee that Maddie has been asked to run the official Instagram account for the Pi Phis. It's a huge honor.

It's also an irony. Maddie, initially disappointed to be joining Pi Beta

Phi, is now responsible for attracting recruits and making the house look as appealing as Alpha Phi.

She's good at this.

Thanks to her pretty pictures, despite the isolation of COVID, the number of freshmen women interested in joining is climbing.

Few people in the Goncalves family think COVID is the big deal that UI administrators believe it is. The Goncalves children have been raised not to trust the government or institutions. They are libertarians. They live to bet on themselves.

Kaylee's dad, Steve, works in IT at the hospital in Coeur d'Alene, an hour and a half north of Moscow. Over dinners at home, he tells his family that the only people who are dying in the hospital are those who have preexisting conditions. Mostly, they're obese.

He thinks the university is making a mistake not letting the kids back.

So does Kaylee. As the weeks stretch on, her frustration grows. Paying to take college classes over Zoom is bad enough, but bills keep coming in from APhi. She's livid that she and her APhi sisters are paying live-in dues for the house they're not allowed to occupy.

Following orders unquestioningly is not a Goncalves thing to do.

So Kaylee queries the chapter president. Why are they paying for nothing? If they can't get some of that money returned, Kaylee says, she doesn't want to go back to the house in the fall.

The rules are the rules, the president tells Kaylee. The house won't negotiate, especially with a new sister. None of the sisters can move out of the house until they're juniors and have accumulated a certain number of service points. Even then, the APhi admins add another hurdle: Sisters need to pay for both living in *and* living out.

So in late August, Kaylee's stuck returning to the APhi house and its litany of COVID health and safety protocols.

Kaylee doesn't want to do the physical distancing or the regular testing or the mandatory quarantine procedures. Not any of it. But she's Kaylee, so she faces the reset head-on, posting: **Now let's get back to it!** ⚡ 🤍

This year, the girls who are rushing sororities have their smiles hidden behind masks. Coffee meetings are held on Zoom. Hugging is not allowed.

Still, Kaylee takes a liking to two of the freshmen: Emma Tyger, a beautiful brunette from Vancouver, Washington, whose soccer career was sidelined by an injury, and Jaden Anderson, a blonde from Spokane.

One of the most important rituals among sorority sisters is choosing Bigs and Littles. A Big mentors her chosen Little through college, academically and socially.

Emma and Jaden are eager to become Kaylee's Littles partly because of her extraordinary enthusiasm and can-do attitude. When Kaylee hears there might be an in-house quarantine one weekend, she whisks Emma and Jaden off home with her to Coeur d'Alene. She takes them shopping, to concerts, for drinks, to coffee. She makes them baskets of goodies.

"She also was a girl you don't mess with," Emma recalled. "Nobody would ever say a bad word about me in front of her because she was not okay with it. If there was some guy that was being rude to me at a party, Kaylee was the first one to say something to him."

On Big-Little Night in October, Kaylee surprises the two by waiting for them, shrouded in pink wrapping paper, in the parking lot by a large off-campus apartment building known as the Whites. When the two freshmen find Kaylee and unwrap her, their screams of delight echo several blocks away.

At this point, the two younger girls are still caught up in the excitement and honor of being accepted into APhi. They don't yet know about the pressure that comes with being in the "pretty girls" house.

Darker times are just around the corner.

Chapter 4

Greek Row
Moscow, Idaho
September 2020

I'm Xana, pronounced 'Xanax' without the *-x*" is how the petite brunette introduced herself to the Pi Phis on the first day, and everyone laughed.

Her name is Xana Kernodle, and she's as irrepressible as Tigger in the Winnie-the-Pooh books.

Always smiling when I'm with my Xan, Maddie captions a pair of Instagram posts of the two of them together on September 11.

Maddie tells Kaylee she is impressed with Xana because, despite her freshman status, she is not afraid of anyone or anything.

Xana isn't much used to rules. She grew up in Post Falls, Idaho, pretty much without her mother, Cara, who had been battling drug addiction much of her life and gave up custody of Xana and her sister, Jazzmin, in 2006. Xana adores her dad, Jeff, but he traveled frequently for work, so Xana and Jazzy were often left on their own.

Along with her best friend, Emily Alandt, a pretty, feisty blonde from Boise and a fellow new Pi Phi, Xana regularly busts out of the house at night and on the weekends, even though they've both been told to stay inside — and stay sober.

One evening, Maddie introduces Xana and Emily to a group of Sigma Chi brothers — and she's surprised and amused to discover the two new girls had already met them. On an illicit night out!

"That was pretty cool, actually," Maddie says to Kaylee the next morning.

The two are tiring of the enforced restrictions in this life they had once wanted so badly.

"At APhi, I have a worse deal than you do," Kaylee tells Maddie, who is sympathetic.

Under the stress of the COVID restrictions, Kaylee explains, the bitchiness for which the house is infamous is coming to the fore. APhi is turning into a nightmare version of *Mean Girls.*

"I hear you," says Maddie. "We didn't sign up for this."

They begin to discuss their options for living off campus.

Kaylee finds an apartment in the Whites. Maddie's got her eye on a house right next to it — 1122 King Road — where some older Pi Phis, like Sophia, her Big, and Ashlin, her best friend in the house, are planning to move.

The house sticks up on the hill like a finger. It's got a deck in the back, so it will make a fantastic party space.

Even better, Maddie tells Kaylee, it signifies freedom.

"It's gonna be great," she says.

Chapter 5

Moscow, Idaho
Valentine's Day 2021

"You forgot your wallet?" Maddie asks Jake Schriger.

Maddie is all dressed up, even though it's just breakfast. She's wearing jeans with an oversize beige sweater that falls artfully off her shoulders. It should be obvious to Jake that she's taking this seriously.

It's Valentine's Day. She told Kaylee it was a date. She told Xana and Emily it was a date. They're all eager to hear how it goes.

And Jake has forgotten his wallet!

The guy sitting opposite her in this cute downtown Moscow café called the Breakfast Club is a junior in the Delta Tau Delta fraternity who's been hotly pursuing her — "pining for her" is how some of her friends put it — for over a year.

Maddie always has a lot of admirers. Though Jake is handsome, nice, fun, and a great water-skier, for some reason she's always kept him at bay. Maddie has to give the guy credit, though. He's never given up. He's stuck around. He's grown on her, and she's thinking of relenting.

Now he's stuck her with the bill.

Maddie can already hear the girls shrieking with laughter. She knows they'll make fun of her. Sure enough, when she tells them, they think it's hilarious.

That night, Emily posts a picture of Maddie—all made up, false lashes on, clearly ready to go out—on Snapchat. It's cheekily captioned: **Didn't Even Pay for the Date.**

Still, the handsome upperclassman succeeds in winning Maddie's affections.

Soon after Valentine's Day, Maddie commits to Jake. She stops seeing other guys. And from then on, they're a thing.

Just over a year later, on April 27, she'll post a throwback on Instagram of some of the couple's best times together: Boating in Coeur d'Alene. At the Watershed Music Festival. Hanging out at school.

Maddie captions the post: **One year with my best friend!! Life is so much sweeter with you in it** 🕊️💜 **I love you lots & lots @jakeschriger.**

Jake will soon be graduating and moving to Boise for a job. Maddie wants to move there too, get a summer job, and be with him.

Why? Because Jake, she has decided, is her future.

Chapter 6

Moscow, Idaho
Fall 2021

F"amily breakfast" is Kaylee's conscious effort to maintain her bonds with her four best friends from APhi: Ava, Zoe, Katie, and Phoebe.

Kaylee is cooking in the little kitchen in her off-campus apartment at the Whites. The pan is sizzling as the pancakes she's making turn golden brown. They look and smell delicious. She whips out her phone so she can document the moment with an Instagram post.

Helping Kaylee out in the kitchen is her boyfriend since middle school, Jack DuCoeur. Like Maddie, he came to UI mostly because he wanted to be with Kaylee.

Jack is living off campus in a house close to Kaylee with a bunch of his Beta Theta Pi fraternity brothers. He and Kaylee go to games together. They share custody of a goldendoodle, Murphy. She even includes Jack in her APhi Instagram posts. He's family.

Everyone loves Jack. An Idaho all-state tennis player, he has strawberry-blond hair and freckles. In photos, he bears more than a passing resemblance to the Harry Potter character Ron Weasley, but in real life, he is considerably more handsome.

Jack is as quiet and calm as Kaylee is effervescent. He's a rock for

Kaylee as long as she wants one. And to be sure, her family and friends have always had the impression that Kaylee decides the tempo and terms of the relationship.

Recently, though, there have been small signs of trouble in paradise.

Kaylee's been feeling an itch to do things on her own. Not because she wants to part from Jack but because she likes being independent.

"Jack, I need five hours to get ready," Kaylee will tell him as she sits down at her vanity. That means he needs to go away. And he does.

Kaylee has a lot on her mind now that she's finally won her freedom and is living off campus. She wants to travel, to experience the world, to learn what's out there beyond Coeur d'Alene.

And she wants to make money. COVID helped expand her professional network online, and she's made connections at Extreme Networks, an IT firm in Austin, Texas, doing work she's interested in pursuing full-time. Her dad and her brother are in IT, so it's in the blood. The job would require a big move—and probably leaving Jack behind.

If Jack is serious about her, he might have to play the long game and wait. Which is what he's doing now as she flips pancake after pancake and piles them into a stack.

"Almost ready?" Jack asks her.

Kaylee pours more batter into the sizzling pan.

"It'll be a little while."

Chapter 7

Moscow, Idaho
August 2021

Tomorrow is Bid Day, and Ethan Chapin and his brother, Hunter, have options.

In the freshman dorms, Ethan, all six foot four of him, turns on the shower, stands under the torrent of hot water, and closes the stall door. He wants a moment of privacy. He wants a moment to mull over the choice he's facing.

The Chapin triplets grew up in Mount Vernon, Washington, two hours north of Seattle, and they seem to have it all: looks, height, smarts, athletic ability, likability. Ethan is a superb athlete. He played varsity basketball. Hunter was right there with him, but always one step behind, sometimes on the bench. Their blond sister, Maizie, played varsity soccer. All three of them are first-rate golfers.

And all three of them are as tight as can be. They've shared rooms and meals since they were born. Before, even. During her pregnancy, Stacy Chapin, their mom, used to joke that Hunter, who was born last, was on top in "the penthouse."

It's unsaid but understood that whatever choice Ethan makes, Hunter will follow. That's the dynamic of their relationship. Always has been. So

Ethan is thinking pretty hard about what his decision will be, knowing it affects them both.

The obvious choice is Sigma Chi. It's the fraternity for athletes who have smarts.

And yet he's leaning toward Phi Delta Theta. Which is, by reputation, a dry house, but it's also known as the stoner-gamer house.

Not Ethan's thing. But an older Delt has been persuasive. Over several meetings during rush, Hunter Johnson, who is doing a master's in athletic training, has made an understated yet confident case for Phi Delta Theta by demonstrating qualities that Ethan admires in a brother.

Ethan gets out of the shower still lost in thought. A door bangs open. He looks up.

Emerging from the next shower stall is another freshman, Tim DeWulf, a blond hunk of a varsity basketball and soccer player from Odessa, Washington, a small farming community. DeWulf, who is also six foot four, exudes masculinity.

"Hey, Tim," Ethan says. "What house are you going into?"

Tim looks at Ethan like he's stupid. "Duh. Sigma Chi," he says. It's the natural fit for athletic dudes like them.

"Oh," says Ethan. "Well, I was thinking of Phi Delta Theta. Because of Hunter Johnson."

Hunter Johnson, Ethan feels, has a unique sort of soulful charm. He's a talented guitar player. He's slender yet athletic—but also goofy.

But Tim DeWulf is *it*.

Ethan pauses, then says, "But if you're going to Sigma Chi, then I'm going to Sigma Chi."

And with that, the angst is over. The decision is made.

Chapter 8

Moscow, Idaho
October 3, 2021

The doorbell rings at 1118 King Road. The rectangular house with huge windows—a design that inspired the building's nickname, "Shark Tank"—sits just off campus.

The place might as well be called Party Central, because just a few weeks into the fall semester, its five occupants, especially Xana and Emily, have become known for hosting the best and most frequent parties at UI.

That Sunday morning, a bunch of freshman Sigma Chi brothers are standing there, summoned to get to know the Shark Tank women by playing a game called champagne shackles.

"Come on in," says Xana.

She and Emily grin. They've got the bottles of bubbly ready.

And the zip ties.

The rules of the game are simple: The ties go around the wrists of a pair—a man and a woman—who have to stay tied together until their bottle of champagne is finished. Even when going to the restroom!

The tall, dark Chapin brothers, Ethan and Hunter, are easy to spot among the crowd of Sig Chi freshmen. One of Xana and Emily's housemates, Josie, a pretty brunette from Boise, immediately calls dibs on both of them. Xana cracks up.

"Josie, can you even tell them apart?" she asks.

Excitement builds as they all whip out their phones to take the most embarrassing photos possible for social media. That's part of the fun of this—it's almost the point.

Xana has on an eclectic outfit: a psychedelic sun hat that is a mix of bright pinks, purples, and yellows; a yellow bustier; and black jeans. She's in her element, giggling as Emily photographs her sitting on the toilet while the guy she's shackled to, Peter, is stuck on the floor by her side.

Sitting in the living room, practically immobilized by the ties for hours, Ethan can't help but notice Xana's effortless magnetism.

Xana is the one running the music. "DJ Xan!" her housemates yell as she changes songs. She's the one in charge of the shambolic Wii dancing and making sure everyone has drinks. Xana is the focal point of the party, though she doesn't seem to notice the attention.

When the game's over and the day's finally winding down, Ethan asks Xana about herself. He discovers that Xana is...just Xana. She has no big plans. No idea what her future is. She's in the present. She makes no apologies for this. She's the most real person he's ever met.

He's hooked.

In the next few days and weeks, he often finds himself making the few-hundred-yard trek from Sigma Chi to the Shark Tank.

He and Hunter regularly hoist their massive stereo on their broad shoulders and carry it across the Lower 40, as the field is called, so DJ Xan can play whatever she wants. In the midst of all the music, the dancing, the talking, he notices that Xana gets some work done by passing her assignment book around and insisting each person take a stab at writing a paragraph.

Her spirit is infectious.

He's so smitten he asks Xana to become his Big. According to the esoteric fraternity rules, there can be brothers and sisters in different houses, though dating your Greek sibling is considered sort of incestuous.

But Xana has never cared about the rules.

In early 2022, it starts to become unclear as to when Ethan arrives and when Ethan leaves 1118 King Road. Does he actually go home at night? Or does he sleep over in Xana's room?

"Anything going on I should know about?" Emily asks Xana one morning.

Xana shakes her head.

She'll speak only when she's 100 percent sure what she wants to say.

Chapter 9

Boise, Idaho
April 2022

It's nearly midnight when Karen Alandt wakes to her ringing phone. The caller ID says it's Xana.

Karen's blood runs cold, as any mother's would. Is Xana okay? Is her daughter Emily okay? She picks up, panicked.

"Mama Karen, guess what?" says Xana casually, as if the late hour were completely irrelevant.

"Xana! You scared me half to death! Do you know what time it is?" Karen asks.

Xana just laughs.

Karen relaxes in spite of herself. How distinct and rich and simply full of joy Xana's laugh is.

"I want you to be the first to know: I've got a boyfriend."

Karen giggles at the needlessness of this conversation. It's been obvious to everyone that Xana and Ethan are on the cusp of something, but she plays the game.

"How did the talk go? Did you guys sit down and discuss it seriously?"

Xana spills the details. "No, it was easy. We didn't need a big talk. It just happened naturally."

Xana is a free spirit. Karen sees the relationship as a sign she's growing up. In fact, all the Shark Tank girls are growing up, forming committed attachments. Emily has begun to date Hunter Johnson. Josie is seeing another Delt, Linden Beck.

Karen is thrilled that Xana feels able to share this moment with her. She has developed strong maternal feelings toward this exuberant, effervescent young woman who is so passionate, so resilient, so un-self-pitying, despite a difficult upbringing.

Xana doesn't talk much about having grown up without a mother. But the signs of loneliness are there for them all to see.

Emily could sense that Xana's home life wasn't exactly the most orderly. Sometimes Xana drives over to Pullman, where her older sister, Jazzmin — Jazzy — is studying marketing at Washington State. Jazzy, petite and pretty, is the "sensible" one. Xana idolizes her big sister and wants to follow in her footsteps. Jazzy also has nice stuff, so when Xana and Emily visit her in her dorm room, Emily knows she's supposed to chat with Jazzy to distract her while Xana filches a shirt or whatever she needs from her sister's closet.

In the Pi Phi house, Xana has mismatched bedding, few clothes. Emily teaches Xana how to do her makeup, how to use a curling iron, skills that the other girls learned years ago but that no one has ever taught Xana. Before their first Christmas break, Emily noticed that Xana was the only one not packing.

"Xana," she said, "where are you going for winter break?"

Xana shrugged and said she didn't know. Her dad, Jeff, might not be home. She didn't know his new girlfriend. And she didn't much like her room in the basement.

That first Christmas, Emily invited her home to Boise to hang with her parents: Matt, an army veteran, and Karen, a pretty blonde who was a dead ringer for her daughter.

At first the Alandts didn't know what to make of this free-spirited young woman their daughter had brought home. But Xana, with her expressive hand movements, her open personality, had a talent for winning people over, making everyone laugh.

Now Xana regularly stays with the Alandts during breaks. Karen looks forward to their eleven p.m. phone calls. She comes to visit the girls in the Shark Tank and goes out with them sometimes. Karen starts to consider Xana a second daughter.

After Xana hangs up with Karen, she finds Emily and gives her the news.

"You told my mom first, you bitch!" Emily says with a laugh, then gives Xana a hug.

Chapter 10

Priest Lake, Idaho
Summer 2022

It's four p.m. and Ethan Chapin is finishing up his shift as a server at the Hill's Resort restaurant, nestled on beautiful Priest Lake up in the Idaho mountains. The sparkling water with its snow-crested surroundings got its name from the Jesuit missionaries who once lived near there.

The Chapins have two homes, one in Mount Vernon, near Seattle, and a summerhouse on Priest Lake. His mom came here as a little girl, and he and his family have been coming here all his life. There's nowhere Ethan would rather be.

He yells to Hunter, and the two head to his favorite place within his favorite place: the resort's sand volleyball court, right on the shore, in front of the resort's bar and restaurant. The community is tight. No one locks their doors. People call one another by their first names.

Ethan knocks on the door of cabin 101, which belongs to the Zylak family. It's a running joke that the Zylaks are über-competitive. Ethan's ideal matchup is the six Zylak kids versus everyone else. Whatever the numbers, he finds a way to make a game of it.

Once on the volleyball court, he strips off his shirt and takes his position. He and Hunter hit the ball back and forth over the net while a little crowd, including their parents, Jim and Stacy, and, this summer, Xana, gathers to watch the magnificent sight of Ethan in full athlete mode. He jumps, he sets, he dives, he spikes—a mythic Greek god in action.

Ethan made varsity basketball as a high-school freshman, but COVID restrictions deprived him of crucial competitive seasons that would have prepped him to play at the college level.

Over the summer, the Chapin triplets worked at Hill's Resort, which was full to bursting with people wanting a rural escape. This time together made the trio realize that they wanted to attend the same college, and they needed it to be east of the mountains. And they wanted to be involved in Greek life, to keep the small-family feeling that they were used to at home.

UI was an easy decision. WSU felt vast when they visited. By comparison, Greek Row at UI felt so small and bucolic, it was like a private school.

Their mom, Stacy, a former school principal and a Greek life alum at the University of Puget Sound, was relieved that her children would experience the safety net and type of community that had been such a welcome part of her own college years.

Now, as Stacy watches her son leap around on the volleyball court, she's filled with pride. UI has been exactly the nurturing place she wanted for them. They're thriving. Her husband, Jim—who believes Stacy's judgment is consistently rock solid—agrees.

After the game, Jim, Stacy, Hunter, Maizie, Ethan, and Xana sprint to the boat Jim recently bought to satisfy his kids' love of the water. They turn the music up high, blasting out Morgan Wallen's latest album, and Jim drives the boat while the kids take turns wakeboarding and sipping drinks from the cooler.

Ethan and Hunter love boarding so much that early every morning, they stuff their work clothes into their backpacks and go out on the water, coming back with only five minutes to spare before their shifts. Jim drops them at the dock, and they sprint, barefoot, to their posts.

This summer, Ethan has been inseparable from Xana, who's been staying with the Chapins most of the time. Stacy can see immediately that her son is serious about this carefree young woman. The Chapins happily welcome her as one of their own.

Changes are ahead for the upcoming fall semester. Xana is moving from the Shark Tank into a rental house on King Road. Stacy and Jim have rented Ethan an apartment in Moscow. The Sigma Chi president told Ethan that frat brothers who are double deficient—that is, with a GPA below 2.75 for two consecutive semesters—have to live outside the house.

Stacy's only concern about her oldest triplet is how far his grades have slipped. Though she suspects Ethan will stay most nights with Xana, she knows that the forced separation from his fraternity brothers will motivate him to raise his grades high enough to return to the Sigma Chi house.

In the boat, the wind whips up and the sun slowly starts to redden and sink low into the horizon. Jim turns the boat toward the shore. Ethan turns the volume one notch higher, and they head home listening to Morgan Wallen's "Heartless."

If this isn't paradise, Stacy thinks, *then what is?*

Chapter 11

Coeur d'Alene, Idaho
July 31, 2022

The room is spinning, like it often does when Xana has had one too many White Claws, which she has today, out on the lake.

She falls flat on her face. Feels the pain immediately.

She looks in the mirror. She's chipped her front tooth.

Damn. She turns to Emily. She's upset. And not because it's going to cost money to fix the tooth.

"I don't want to be this person anymore," she tells her understanding friend.

Xana is well aware of her reputation as the free-spirited girl in their core friend group: Xana and Ethan, Emily, Hunter Johnson, Josie, Linden, Peter Elgorriaga, and Ethan's triplet siblings, Hunter and Maizie.

But she wants to change that. Xana wants to grow up. She wants to be someone who fits into the world of Ethan and his parents. The Chapin family is fun, easygoing, but as Xana has seen, their life is different from her hardscrabble existence in her dad's basement.

At Priest Lake, the Chapins all play golf on the local course. Xana has never played golf, but the Chapin triplets are really good. They love it, like they love all sports.

When Xana first joined them on the course, she found that hitting a golf ball was harder than it looked; out of mockery for their passion, she threw a club—then took a swig of her drink. Everyone laughed.

As Karen Alandt—Mama Karen—has noticed, Xana "is someone who is prepared to make a total fool of herself in public if it will put someone else at ease." But Xana doesn't want to be the butt of everyone's jokes forever.

She never thought about the future before. But now she does. She wants to become a person who is taken more seriously.

And she wants to grow old with Ethan.

Chapter 12

Moscow, Idaho
June 2022

Maddie can hardly believe it when Kaylee walks through the front door of 1122 King Road. She's pulled it off!

Their freshman-year Bid Day, when the best friends were accepted by different sororities, feels like a distant dream. Here they are, in their senior year, finally getting to live together. The timing couldn't be more perfect.

Maddie walks to the car and starts helping Kaylee unload boxes and boxes of her stuff. Everyone knows that Kaylee doesn't travel light.

She hauls a bag through the sliding glass doors at the back and into her new room.

Everyone also knows which room is Maddie's — she's put the letters of her name in the window, and her signature pink cowboy boots sit on the sill. Maddie's vanity is just behind. When it's dark and her lights are on, anyone walking by can see her putting on her mascara.

Maddie took over the King Road lease from graduating Pi Phis, and she's pulled together a great group, her family away from family. Perfect for a year of transition, which is what it's going to be. Jake graduated and is back home in Boise, but their plan is to make it through this year together, long distance. They speak every night at eight. Maddie has been meticulous about keeping the appointment, a source of amusement for her new roommates, who are now all moved in.

Xana has taken a room on the main level. Of course Maddie invited Emily too, because Xana and Emily are almost as inseparable as Xana and Ethan, but Emily had already made plans to room with Josie, her childhood friend from Boise, next door at the Whites, the building where her boyfriend, Hunter Johnson, has also rented an apartment.

So 1122 King Road's other two rooms went to two blond Pi Phi sophomores who finagled a way to move out of the sorority house: Dylan Mortensen, who is Emily's Little, and Bethany Funke, Maddie's Little.

Maddie bangs on each of their doors. "Xana, Dylan, Bethany!" she yells. "Photo time."

They groan but accept their fate, and the five women in their skimpy, summery dresses gather on the King Road deck. Maddie hands Ethan the camera. They pose, squinting into the afternoon sun: Dylan, Xana, Bethany, Kaylee, Maddie.

Meet the Roommates, Maddie captions the photo, and she makes the post public, as she always does.

She doesn't think of any risks associated with that. Why would she? The more followers you have, the better for your career in marketing.

Maddie's life, in this moment, here and now, is pretty much perfect and going exactly where she wants it to.

Chapter 13

Moscow, Idaho

Emily's Dream

The following scene, a recurring nightmare, is what Emily later says—after she's lost her friends, before justice has brought closure—she imagines could have happened that summer. The details of the surroundings change from dream to dream, but the gist of what happens stays the same. It's the only explanation she can come up with, the only one that makes any sense. It haunts her day and night because the uncertainty of whether it's real or not real will never go away.

Maddie wipes down the table and turns to get fresh cutlery to seat the new customers.

As jobs go, waitressing at the Mad Greek is a pretty good gig. The forty-seat restaurant with a vegan-friendly menu isn't one of the more popular ones in Moscow, so servers—all college kids, friends—don't get run off their feet.

Maddie's grateful for the pay. She can make as much as eighty bucks per shift, which covers her gas and her Ulta card and the trendy clothes she likes so much. And there's the added bonus that the manager asked her to redo the restaurant's website.

Maddie continues laying the table.

Then she turns and notices him. Unusual-looking. Intense bulging eyes. Thin, almost emaciated. And pale, almost ghost white. He's raising his hand. He wants her attention.

She smooths her skirt and walks over with a smile.

He orders a vegan pizza to go. He's staring at her intently. Maddie is used to male attention, but this time it feels... uncomfortable.

"I'm Bryan," he says. "What's your name?"

Maddie hesitates, then tells him. Why wouldn't she? Everyone here knows it.

She hands him the check and, as he pays, he asks, "Would you like to go out sometime?"

This is an easy one, Maddie thinks. The idea of going out with this strange-looking guy is surreal. He doesn't know it took Jake, her boyfriend, a whole two years to become her boyfriend. Maddie is anything but easy, even for guys she likes. And she doesn't know or like this one.

She flicks back her hair. "Uh, no," she says. She smiles, laughs a bit. It's a nervous habit she has, especially with guys she turns down. She doesn't mean anything rude by it.

But this guy looks at her strangely, like he doesn't believe what he's hearing.

He gets up slowly, still staring at her, and walks out.

Maddie shakes her head and goes about her business. She doesn't give the guy another thought.

She doesn't see the guy walk to his car, a white Hyundai Elantra, sit in the driver's seat, and type her name into his phone.

Her Instagram, with the photos of her past and present, is there for all to see: Maddie in a bikini. Maddie with her roommates. Maddie and her friends posing in skimpy clothes for a fit check before a night out.

Maddie, Maddie, Maddie.

He looks. He presses Like once, twice, three times. And he looks and Likes some more.

Chapter 14

Coeur d'Alene, Idaho
September 2022

Kaylee stares at the guy on the couch incredulously.

Did he really just say that?

"Bitch, go make me a quesadilla."

Wow!

She wishes that she weren't at his house on this awful date.

She wishes that she hadn't broken up with sweet Jack.

Maybe she'd been too hasty. Kaylee has erased him from nearly all her social media posts—normal protocol when couples break up.

But now she's wondering if Jack might be the nicest guy on the planet. And if most other guys are assholes like this one in front of her.

Jack would never have used the B-word, she'll later tell her older sister, Alivea. Never.

He couldn't even be mean or distant after she broke up with him. If he felt any pain or animosity, he didn't show it. He's just kind. Sweet. Gentle. He still swings by the King Road house every few days to pick up Murphy, their goldendoodle.

She texts him about Murphy, telling him she's coming over with the dog or she needs him to come get their pet, but she's never sure if she's reaching out for Murphy or for herself.

The truth of it is, Kaylee still loves Jack. She didn't want to hurt him; she didn't even want to part from him—she just wanted a chance to discover herself, to break ties before leaving for a new town in a new state.

Kaylee's internship with Extreme Networks, the IT company in Austin, has turned into a full-time job that she now squeezes around her classes. In January, she's headed to Texas to work there on-site.

She's rightfully proud of her role as a channel manager, which means she comes in after the IT equipment has been sold to a business and explains to the customer how best to use it. She's particularly proud of a winning pitch she made to Coffee Box about where to install Wi-Fi in their stores so customers can easily order on their phones while standing in line.

She made a ten-minute video, and despite her lack of experience, the video was singled out by her bosses and sent companywide. "Kaylee keeps impressing me," Paul Semak, the head of sales for the Americas, emailed his executive team, and he included a link to the video presentation Kaylee had made—and worked her ass off to get right.

Every morning this summer, she's had a preparatory remote session with Alivea, a project manager who lives in LA and buys real estate with an eye to renting the properties out on Airbnb. Alivea is wicked smart and she's talented with tech. And after Kaylee goes back and forth with Alivea, she checks the lingo with her dad, Steve, whose entire career has been in IT support.

So now she looks at the jerk in front of her who just called her a bitch and told her to make him a quesadilla.

No one pushes Kaylee around like that.

Especially not a guy in a state she's leaving. Kaylee is an independent woman. She makes good money from Extreme Networks and from her tips at La Casa Lopez, a Mexican joint in Moscow. And she spends her own money, three hundred bucks a week, on the gym and meal plans. She knows she's looking her best right now.

Kaylee doesn't like this guy. She doesn't need any guy . . . except maybe Jack. Who she's gonna phone when she gets home. She's gonna phone Alivea too and tell her that.

She looks at this dude one more time. What a prick.

"You can make your own quesadillas."

She gets up. She grabs her purse. And she walks out.

On the drive home, she looks forward to the weekend back on campus and reenacting this scene for her new roomies. She can already see Xana roaring with laughter and Maddie wryly throwing her hands in the air.

Yes, she thinks, they will have *plenty* to say about it when she tells them. *Kaylee,* they'll cry, pretending to be exasperated, *why is there always so much drama around you?*

Chapter 15

Moscow, Idaho
September 1, 2022

Xana is waiting in her dark blue Honda for Karen, Emily's mom, at the little airstrip that is the Pullman-Moscow Regional Airport.

She's excited. She wants to show off her progress to the woman she considers the mom she never had.

It's just a ten-minute trip to Xana's new place. Xana shows Karen her room on the main level of 1122 King Road.

Karen admires the bedding, which now matches. Xana says she saved money this summer and opened a bank account, something Emily joked she'd never do. At Maddie's suggestion, she joined the staff at the Mad Greek and makes eighty bucks or so a shift. She shows Karen the wall mirror she bought with some of her earnings.

Karen is proud of Xana, who is beaming. She tells Karen she loves her new roomies.

But it's a bittersweet moment because, for the first time in three years, Emily is living separately from Xana—albeit not far away, just across the street from where Emily is rooming with Josie at the Whites. Xana still sees Emily every day, and Karen heads over there now.

Later that evening, Xana and Ethan drop by Emily's apartment, as they always do after a long day, to decompress and gossip. Karen is in her pj's.

She recalled: "Ethan sits down on the corner of Emily's sectional couch. And instead of sitting on the couch, Xana sits on top of him. She snuggles. She's happy...and she's telling us all about her day and what they did, and dah-dah-dah-dah-dah, who said this, everything."

Karen couldn't look away from the comic visual of the effervescent, gesticulating woman sitting on top of her patient boyfriend. It was like a sketch out of *Saturday Night Live*.

Karen said, "Finally he says, 'Jeez, woman, stop wiggling!'

"And she just throws her head back and laughs like she normally does, and just goes on, doesn't even miss the beat. It doesn't even faze her at all. She just keeps wiggling and talking.

"She laughs at him and he just laughs back and he just continues to let her sit there and wiggle all over him, even though he is so uncomfortable, obviously. But he is so patient with her and he adores her."

The bottom line was clear not just to Karen but to Emily, Hunter Johnson, Josie, and Linden — all of whom were assembled in the room that night:

"Ethan would rather have Xana wiggling on his lap than be sitting anywhere else."

Chapter 16

After the roommates have a rare dinner at home together, Kaylee brings them into the living room.

"It's time," says Kaylee, "to memorialize our group, in our house, on TikTok."

Their house on 1122 King Road has become, on their watch, a UI fixture. It might not surpass the Shark Tank's legendary reputation as a party house, but it's still a place where people want to come, relax, have a drink—usually a shot offered by Xana and Ethan—and kick back.

The view through the sliding doors is perfect for stargazing. You can stare at the trees and down the winding road for an ever-present reminder that there's another world, called reality, beyond the college bubble.

In just a few weeks, Kaylee will graduate and leave to begin her new journey in the real world. In anticipation of Thanksgiving, when Alivea will be back, she's spending most of her time in Rathdrum and taking many of her classes remotely.

They come up with a commemorative screenplay: "The roommates pretending to be each other." It's like charades, with clues drawn from invented scenes that highlight each friend's character.

"Ready, go!" says Kaylee.

First up is Maddie pretending to be Kaylee: She stomps up the stairs and complains of a "dank" smell. "Murphy, you've been a bad boy." She pretends to chastise the dog for pooping indoors.

Next is Xana pretending to be Dylan. She comes out of her room, backpack on, flustered. "Fuck. It's nine ten. Guys, can anyone drive me to class? I'm fucking late for my meeting. I was supposed to be there ten minutes ago."

Next, Kaylee pretends to be Xana. She anxiously grabs a broom and starts to sweep frantically. "Did anyone do their chores today?" She doesn't wait for an answer. "Ugh. I'm just gonna do it."

Next up is Bethany pretending to be Maddie. "Shit, you guys, it's eight. Gotta go, Jake's calling." She stands up from the couch where they're all sitting and heads for the door, repeating, "Jake's calling."

Next up is Josie (standing in for Dylan) pretending to be Bethany. She looks at a photo of herself on her phone and grimaces: "Oh my God, you look horrid!"

Xana is now Dylan; she cuddles up to Murphy before realizing the dog smells rank. "Oh my God, Murphy, you are so cute." And then, putting the dog down, she exclaims, "Oh my God, you've gotta get out of here, you've seriously got to get out of here."

Now Bethany is Kaylee. She reads a text in front of the group. "Hey, guys, I know I talk about myself a lot . . . but, seriously, what would you guys do in my situation?"

Now Maddie is Xana, headed downstairs: "I've gotta go do a test," she says. "I've failed two of them already." And now Maddie is Bethany: "Is anyone doing a wine night? Let's just do a wine night."

Dylan being Xana: "Dude, is it okay if I throw a party? Just three or four people . . . at most."

They do several takes and several edits before declaring themselves happy with the video that Kaylee then posts.

Whatever happens in the future, she'll always have this to hold on to, this picture of this house and the five of them in it.

Chapter 17

Moscow, Idaho
November 5, 2022

The week after the Chapin triplets celebrate their twentieth birthdays, it's family weekend at the University of Idaho.

Stacy and Jim Chapin are in Moscow buying their kids mimosas for breakfast. The three are still as close as they were growing up. Xana is excited for them to meet her dad, Jeff, who lives in Arizona but is putting in an appearance. Stacy can see how happy Ethan is with Xana. Stacy can also see the signs that their kids are becoming independent adults.

When the weekend is over, as Stacy and Jim drive away from campus, Stacy shares a realization with her husband. The Chapin triplets are maturing into giving, thoughtful people, and it's clear that they're almost ready to lead their own lives. For parents, this is a milestone. A bittersweet turning point that all parents hope and dread they'll face.

Our job is done, Stacy thinks. Then she says it aloud. "Our job is done!" She and Jim look at each other. They grin. They high-five in the car.

Our job is done.

Chapter 18

Moscow, Idaho
Friday, November 11, 2022

The residents of 1122 King Road start pregaming at around noon for the Pi Phi formal.

They have no intention of going to the official formal. That would entail a bus ride—and staying sober beforehand in the sorority house. The older girls, who officially left Pi Phi the year before, wouldn't even be allowed in. The youngest two, Dylan and Bethany, prematurely left the house to live off campus and are loyal to Maddie, Xana, and Emily, so they won't receive a warm welcome.

It's picture time. They use a white shower curtain as a high-contrast backdrop for their LBDs—little black dresses—though Xana, who likes to be different, has donned a little *red* dress.

Maddie poses for a photo with Dylan. Then Kaylee poses with Dylan. They post both photos on Instagram.

The usual gang comes over: Emily, Josie, the Chapin brothers, Peter, Linden. Maizie pops in but not Hunter Johnson; he is working over at the high school.

Drinks are poured. More pictures are taken.

6:00 p.m.

They're all feeling particularly festive because tomorrow is game day. The UI football team is playing UC Davis.

Out on the back deck, Maddie films a video of the Chapin brothers, Emily, and Xana shotgunning their drinks. She closes with a cameo of herself pretending to look ladylike and shocked. It's funny.

The group is well on their way to getting drunk.

Though the Vandals hardly ever win, game days in Moscow are local celebrations regardless of the score. Everyone flocks to the Kibbie Dome. Everyone. Chief Fry is always there. So is the mayor, Art Bettge. Parents with camper trailers host tailgating parties for the kids in the stadium parking lot. Tomorrow's weather forecast is bad, and the group has no access to a trailer tailgate, so the 1122 King Road roommates plan to party on campus instead of outside the stadium.

Nonetheless, it's going to be fun.

They take another swig of their drinks. Cheers to that.

Saturday, November 12, 2022
8:00 a.m.

Emily wakes up early and gets to the dome by eight thirty.

She works part-time assisting UI football recruiting, which means she helps set up the stadium so that coaches can meet with visiting parents and official and unofficial recruits.

She's annoyed to be separated from her friends. She keeps getting updates on their activities in group chats. Xana is rallying the troops on campus.

11:30 a.m.

Xana summons people urgently to King Road.

Get over here she texts Josie a dozen times.

Xana puts her hair in two braids because Emily's not there to help her style it and her roommates are busy getting ready.

Everyone at UI knows it's essential to look good on game day.

The 1122 King Road roommates take their time getting ready. They stick to tradition and drink champagne while they apply their makeup. *Sexy casual* is the unwritten dress code.

By noon, everyone's gathered at the King Road house: Kaylee, Maddie, Xana, Ethan, Dylan, Bethany, Hunter Chapin, Josie, Linden, Peter, and Hunter Johnson.

1:00 p.m.

They move the party over to the Whites, where Emily and Josie's rooms are and where the APhis have an apartment.

2:00 p.m.

Xana tugs at Ethan's hand and tells him to come outside.

Obviously—obviously!—the residents of 1122 King Road want a roommate photo. They ask Hunter Johnson to take it.

First, they arrange themselves for an all-girl photograph. Kaylee removes her Idaho sweatshirt for a sexier bare-midriff look; coquettishly, she kicks her left foot behind her. The members of the group look at her. Dylan, who has her back toward the wall of the Whites, is on one side. The others—Bethany, Maddie, Xana—hug sideways, lined up tightly.

Hunter clicks away fifteen times. "Higher? Lower?" he asks.

Kaylee checks, finds a decent one, and posts it to her Instagram.

Now they need Hunter to take a photo with Ethan in it. The girls joke that the picture is incomplete without their honorary roommate.

"Landscape or vertical?" Hunter Johnson asks.

The answer is easy: vertical. Kaylee, now in her sweatshirt, squats down so Maddie can climb onto her shoulders. They can fit better in the frame this way, next to gentle-giant Ethan.

Dylan is on the left, Bethany on the right. Between them: Kaylee, with Maddie hoisted high; and Ethan, who, as usual, has his arm around Xana.

Hunter takes fifteen shots on Kaylee's phone and hands it back to her.

She texts her favorite to the group. Emily smiles when she sees it. She misses her friends already. She and Xana have hardly spent a day apart in two years! Kaylee forwards the photo to her mom, Kristi, and to Karen Laramie, Maddie's mom.

3:00 p.m.

The group returns to the APhi apartment, where Hunter Johnson, Ethan, and Xana are watching Auburn versus Alabama, a college game they find considerably better than the one in the Kibbie Dome.

Hunter Johnson tells Xana and Ethan his sad news: He'll be leaving them at the end of the semester. As part of his graduate degree, he needs to intern in either Boise or Post Falls.

"But you'll come visit?" Xana asks.

"Bummer," says Ethan. He tells Hunter to think of it not as goodbye but as a temporary separation.

4:00 p.m.

Maybe because he's distracted, Hunter Johnson puts his phone down and forgets about it. Maddie and Dylan eye it and decide to have some fun.

They pose up a storm and take dozens of selfies, imagining Hunter's surprise when he discovers them an hour or two later.

4:30 p.m.

"You want to come with me to the game?" Hunter Johnson asks Ethan and Xana.

He's going to meet Emily and bring her home when the game is over.

Ethan pretends to be distressed. No one cares about the actual game, only the tailgating. "I can't," he says, fake-crying. "I've got my sister's formal in a couple hours."

"Asshole," says Hunter Johnson good-naturedly.

He walks out of the room, having no clue it's the last time he'll see Ethan alive.

7:00 p.m.

It's Theta's formal at the local brewery.

Maizie is taking Ethan; Hunter Chapin is going with Maizie's roommate.

Stacy, their mom, is so happy that the triplets are all together for Maizie's formal. She asks them to send lots of photos. She wants a full recounting of the evening.

9:00 p.m.

Once the formal is over, Maizie's brothers try to persuade her to keep partying with them. But Maizie's tired. She asks her brothers to drop her back at the sorority house.

Jim Chapin has told his sons that they always need to see Maizie home safely. The job comes with a perk: The Theta fridge normally has some pretty good sandwiches in it, and the boys get to help themselves before continuing their Saturday night.

9:30 p.m.

The Chapin brothers go to the Sigma Chi fraternity house on Nez Perce Drive, across a field from 1122 King Road.

Xana is there already.

10:00 p.m.

The fraternity party is in full swing. Ethan wants his friends to enjoy it with him.

Where are you? Ethan texts Hunter Johnson and Emily.

Emily is in bed asleep, exhausted after her day working at the football game. Hunter Johnson texts Ethan that he'll be over when she wakes up. He doesn't feel comfortable leaving her. Most unusually for a Saturday night, Josie and Linden are also home, asleep, at the Whites, in Josie's bedroom next to Emily's. It's been a hard twenty-four hours of partying.

11:00 p.m.
Ethan thinks about who else of his group is missing from the Sig Chi party.

His sister.

You are so lame! he texts her. He hates being separated from her.

Maizie doesn't see the text until the next day.

When it's too late.

Sunday, November 13, 2022
12:00 a.m.
In downtown Moscow, Kaylee and Maddie are together, jammed inside the Corner Club, a popular bar the size of a three-car garage.

The Corner Club is always packed, but on a game day, it's heaving. It might be a windowless box, but it's Moscow's windowless box. This is a small college town where people look out for one another.

Marc Trivelpiece, the club's owner, keeps a careful eye on the customers. He's been in business too long to make rookie mistakes. Underage students like Dylan and Bethany won't pass the Moscow cops' strict protocols about IDs.

A team of kids from Greek life work the bar, discreetly watching for anyone who's getting sloppy or might need help getting home. One of them is Adam Lauda, friend, fraternity brother, and roommate of Kaylee's ex Jack.

1:20 a.m.
The best friends have had enough. They're tired and hungry. And more than a little inebriated.

"I told Adam everything," Maddie says of Kaylee's quandary with Jack.

Kaylee throws up her hands, concerned that Maddie has overshared with Adam, the guy behind the bar.

The friends swerve as they make the eight-minute walk to the main street, where the Grub Truck is always parked.

Food. They need food.

1:30 a.m.

At the Grub Truck, Kaylee orders a carbonara mac and cheese for her and Maddie to share.

They know the guy in the hoodie who's standing behind them, Jack Showalter. He's an occasional visitor to King Road. He's a good guy, they think.

The girls flirt a little with him. Kaylee asks if he's interested in going to another party somewhere, but he's tired.

Speaking of . . . so are they.

It's been a long day. They need a ride home. Kaylee texts a designated sober driver.

1:50 a.m.

Hunter Johnson texts Ethan to ask if he's still at the Sig Chi party. Emily is still asleep.

1:56 a.m.

Kaylee and Maddie head back home to King Road.

They chat in the living room.

Dylan is in her room, wasted. Bethany is in her room, asleep.

2:00 a.m.

Ethan responds to Hunter Johnson that he and Xana are still at Sig Chi.

Approximately 2:15 a.m.

Xana and Ethan return home.

2:15 a.m.

Kaylee and Maddie chat on the couch a little longer and then go upstairs and collapse on Maddie's bed. Murphy, Kaylee's goldendoodle, is in Kaylee's room. Kaylee often leaves him there when she's out.

For the umpteenth time, Kaylee tells her friend she's unsure what to do about her ex, Jack DuCoeur. They start texting him. He lives only three doors down. Kaylee misses him. She wants him to come over.

2:26 a.m.

Kaylee phones Jack. He's asleep and doesn't hear her call.

She calls a second time.

She calls a third time.

A fourth time.

A fifth.

2:44 a.m.

Kaylee calls Jack a sixth time.

Then Maddie phones him three more times.

He sleeps through all of them, blissfully unaware of the imminent danger.

2:52 a.m.

Kaylee tries Jack one last time.

3:00 a.m.

Emily wakes up at the Whites. So, too, do Josie and Linden. Josie realizes she's left her phone in her car.

She goes to get it. *It's foggy out,* she thinks. *It's dark and quiet.*

When she comes back, Hunter Johnson gets up and locks the door to the apartment. He doesn't know why. He's never done that before.

He and Emily go to sleep. No one thinks to text Ethan or Xana. They assume everyone is asleep.

In fact, Xana is awake and scrolling on TikTok. She orders DoorDash from the Jack in the Box in Pullman, the only place open at that hour.

4:00 a.m.

Xana's food arrives. It ought to be the ordinary end of an ordinary game day.

Except for Maddie, Kaylee, Ethan, and Xana, it isn't.

4:17 a.m.

Dylan is in her bed, drifting in and out of a fitful post-game-day sleep. The walls of her bedroom are so paper-thin that earlier Dylan could hear almost everything Maddie and Kaylee and Ethan and Xana were saying as they chatted on the couch in the living room.

Next thing she hears is the familiar stomping as they go up the stairs. She can dimly hear music from one of their bedrooms.

But then everything turns surreal. Not sure whether she's dreaming or awake, she thinks she hears someone frantically say, "There's someone here."

Huh? That doesn't seem right. And yet it also does, because so many people come in and out of 1122 King Road.

She gets up and opens her door a crack. Nothing.

Dylan goes back to bed. But then she hears someone crying. Is it Xana?

She gets up again and opens her door a fraction of an inch. She hears a male voice say: "It's okay. I'm going to help you."

There's a thud. And Murphy starts to bark. Dylan shuts her door again. Is she going crazy? Now there's silence again.

She opens the door a third time.

That's when she sees the firefighter. Or at least, bleary-eyed, that's what she thinks she's seeing. He's got bushy eyebrows; he's wearing a mask. He's holding a firefighting object, a bit like a vacuum. They make eye contact for a split second.

She shuts her door and looks around for her Taser. The battery is dead.

Bethany? She tries calling her friend downstairs. Nothing. But then, thank God, Bethany phones her back.

Dylan tells her she thinks she saw someone. In black. Masked. Their call lasts less than a minute.

Dylan then calls Xana. No reply.

She calls Kaylee. Nothing.

She calls Bethany again. They speak for forty-one seconds. Dylan is breathing heavily. She's terrified. Has she gone crazy? Is she hallucinating?

Then Bethany phones Xana.

She also gets no answer.

Dylan tries Maddie. Nothing.

Bethany phones Ethan. Nothing.

At 4:22 a.m., Dylan texts Bethany the tragically obvious: **No one is answering** and then: **I'm rlly confused rn.**

She texts Kaylee *again:* **Kaylee**

What's going on?

There is still no reply.

On the lower level, Bethany switches to Snap and then back again to text message. She texts Dylan: **Ya dude wtf** then **Xana was wearing all black . . .** It's a question, not a statement.

Dylan replies to Bethany's texts. To the former: **I'm freaking out rn**

And to the latter: **No it's like ski mask almost**

Bethany writes back:

Stfu

Actually

Dylan's fingers trip on the keys as she types: **Like he had soemtbing over is for head and little nd mouth**

There's no time to fix typos. **Bethant I'm not kidding o am so freaked out**

Bethany: **So am I**

Dylan: **phone is going to die fuck**

Bethany tells her:

Come to my room

Run

Down here

* * *

It's 4:24 a.m.

Can Dylan run? Is it safe?

Dylan tries Ethan's cell once more. She and Bethany have another quick exchange.

At 4:27 a.m., she tries Kaylee again, then Xana.

Still nothing.

Dylan makes the decision to run. She sprints to Bethany's room.

The two friends cling to one another.

They keep trying to reach the roommates. Bethany tries Maddie twice, then Kaylee twice. Dylan texts Kaylee.

Bethany goes on snap and Instagram looking for clues.

Nothing. Nothing. Nothing.

It's 4:37 a.m. Exhausted and terrified, the two girls pass out.

Neither of them falls into a deep slumber. Bethany wakes at 7:30 a.m. and calls her parents, telling them both about the strange events of the night before. *Maybe,* she tells herself, *Dylan just had a very bad dream.*

Dylan comes to around 8 a.m. and also tells herself she had a very bad dream after drinking too much. She immerses herself on Instagram for a couple of hours. The house seems quiet. Calm.

She agrees with Bethany. She must have hallucinated the whole thing.

* * *

Around 10:23 a.m., when it should be time for the others to start waking, Dylan texts Maddie: **R u up?** There's no reply, but that's not abnormal.

Dylan dozes off again. Over an hour later, she rouses and also texts Kaylee: **R u up?** Nothing.

Now she's starting to panic again. Was it all *not* a dream?

At 11:49 a.m., Dylan calls her classmate and Pi Phi sister Jenna McClure and asks her to come over.

Then she phones her "Big," Emily, who is at her apartment having breakfast with Josie, Hunter Johnson, and Linden. "Can you come over?" Dylan asks. "Something weird happened last night. I don't really know if I was dreaming or not, but I think there was a man here, and I'm really scared. Can you come check out the house? I texted Xana and the others, but no one's answering. I'm in the basement with Bethany."

Emily laughs. Dylan can get really, really drunk. This is not the first time she's heard a story like this from her Little.

"Ha-ha. Should I bring my pepper spray?" she asks.

Emily gets up and goes looking for a sweatshirt, and when she comes back, she sees Hunter Johnson has already left the apartment.

Hunter makes his way up the steps into the house.

He heads up the stairs and sees Xana's bedroom door slightly ajar. Unusual. He opens it. He sees her lying inert, as if she's fallen backward on the floor face-up.

There is blood everywhere.

He takes in Ethan on the bed behind her facing toward the wall.

Hunter's heart is about to explode.

He doesn't go any farther into the house. He turns around, goes downstairs, and says as calmly as he can to Dylan and Bethany: "Call 911. And stay outside."

He takes a breath, goes back up the stairs, and heads to the kitchen, across the hall from Xana's room. He opens a drawer and takes out a kitchen knife. He's terrified.

He's about to reenter Xana's room when he hears someone coming up the stairs. It's Emily. He stops her. "Emily, I don't think Xana's going to wake up," he tells his girlfriend as softly as he can.

She doesn't understand. But something in his expression chills her and she stands still, rooted to the spot.

"I'm going in to take their pulses," he says, knowing already that he's too late.

But he goes in anyway. And after he's done that, he checks the closets for any sign of the murderer. There is none.

Emily has gone downstairs.

He follows and waits for the cops in the living room. Hunter says nothing to Emily or to the others who are outside. He's trying to protect these innocents from both the sight and the reality. But he already knows the horrific truth: Xana and Ethan are dead.

Hunter doesn't know if Kaylee and Maddie are even in the house, but he fears the worst.

The devil has been at 1122 King Road, and he has no idea why.

PART TWO

Inception

Chapter 19

Saylorsburg, Pennsylvania
2013

The three teenage boys are racing through the trees pretending they're Marines.

This is the Poconos. Racing around in the woods with knives or guns is normal here.

In these dense woods, the kids can play paintball all day. And Airsoft. And they can hunt critters. And they can lose one another for hours on end. Two of the boys don't notice exactly where the third boy, a tall kid with bulging eyes, positions himself. They don't see if he's close to the house or even inside it.

The house is invisible from the road. Its owner, Mark Baylis, a former Navy SEAL who is the father of one of the boys, bought it for precisely that reason.

He liked its remoteness, that it was surrounded by woods. Mark is a skilled hunter. Of animals but also of men.

But even though he's a Special Forces veteran with skills and experience, he cannot catch the person who is repeatedly stealing his knives, his coins, his prescription pills, his girlfriend's jewelry. It maddens him.

He keeps calling the cops, but they are worse than useless. They show up, file a report. Do nothing.

So Baylis stays frustrated. Could the thief be one of the veterans he houses nearby as part of the charity he founded? That's a bad feeling.

He doesn't put it together until years later that the thief must have been one of his son's friends.

He doesn't see it in the moment, but he's sure, later, how it happened: The first time, he believes, the tall, pale kid who weirded him out waited for the others to run off into the trees, then forced the lock and entered the garage where Mark kept his collection of army knives. And took one.

On the next visit, Mark thinks, he took another. One by one, they vanished. Next, it was Baylis's coin collection. Worth twenty-five thousand dollars.

Baylis talks to his son Jack and his nephew Brandon about the thefts. He says he's going to catch the thief if they try again. Shoot him.

Jack tells the third kid, whose name is Bryan, that his dad is pissed. Bryan tells Jack he reveres his father. That's what he says, or at least what he puts in a text.

But what he does—or what Mark thinks he does—smacks of something different than straight-up hero worship.

Someone starts to stalk Mark Baylis. The stalker hides in those trees, camouflaged, munching on Reese's Peanut Butter Cups, dropping the wrappers on the ground, waiting for Mark to leave on one of his orange motorbikes or in his pickup truck.

The stalker forces the door open with a knife and heads for the bathroom, where Baylis keeps old prescription drugs.

And the thief can guess where he'd keep jewelry: in the bedroom. One time the thief is up in the bedroom and hears wheels in the driveway. Baylis is back.

Later, much later, Baylis puts the scene together in his head.

He comes to believe that Bryan, knowing he has the element of surprise on his side, hides, waits for the veteran to walk toward the back of the house, then sprints out the front door and into the woods he knows will protect him.

Through the trees and onto the road.

Safe.

For now.

Chapter 20

Brodheadsville, Pennsylvania
Fall 2012

When the tall, thin man and the fat teenage boy enter his boxing gym, near Big Cheese Pizza off Route 209, Jesse Harris thinks, *This is a familiar sight: Anxious parent bringing in troubled child.*

The former pro boxer opened this gym here for precisely this reason. He thinks of himself as having a dual role: physical-fitness guru and mental-fitness guru.

Jesse set up the gym to offer local people who've given up—teens, mostly—hope. Purpose. Anyone who's failed in life can make it in Jesse's gym: Boys looking for brotherhood. Girls looking for sisterhood or to learn self-defense. Anyone who's prepared to work. To train.

Jesse is proud of his results. There are regular stories in the *Pocono Record* about the correlation between the work done in his gym and the reduction of crime in the area. Years after they've trained with him, people stop him in the street or wave him down in his car to express their appreciation. It makes Jesse feel great.

Today, the lumbering kid who barely makes eye contact lets his dad do the talking. The man introduces himself as Michael Kohberger and says with forced brightness, "This is my son, Bryan."

He says Bryan wants to lose weight. He's changing his habits, his life. He's going to start a vegan diet, but he needs to build muscle, speed up his metabolism.

The father's clearly a nice guy, Jesse notes, but a talker. Hardly pausing to breathe.

He tells Jesse he's got his own HVAC business. Works for the Pleasant Valley School District. He glances around the gym and tells Jesse he'd be happy to help with any maintenance issues for free—fix a refrigerator, that sort of thing.

Jesse says he can help Bryan—as long as Bryan is prepared to help himself.

He tells Bryan, whose eyes stay glued to the floor, that he can use the gym daily for as long as he wants.

The other guys in the gym look at the fat kid and roll their eyes. They've given up on him already. *He'll never fit in,* they are thinking.

Jesse wonders if they are right. He, too, isn't sure about this kid.

But the next day, right after school, the kid appears, swinging his backpack off his shoulders. The gym is in easy walking distance of the high school, but his dad drops him off.

Jesse's regulars ignore the kid as he gets to work. No one else in the room is anywhere near that size. He must be more than a hundred pounds overweight.

Jesse shows Bryan the gloves, and they do basic pad work. Jesse stands on one side of a face-size ring hanging from the ceiling and Bryan stands on the other. *Pow. Pow.* Left. Right.

Though his bulging eyes can't seem to stop moving, the kid looks focused. His considerable body weight goes into the punch. *Jab. Jab.* One, two. And then one, two, three.

Jesse can tell that the kid likes the rhythm of punching. *They all do,* Jesse thinks. *That's why boxing is better than therapy.*

The kid is surprising. He's back the next day. Jesse shows him the power pad. The kid stands on it and pulls the bands up to his sides. If he keeps at it, Jesse tells him, he'll be able to pull the bands over his head.

And the kid comes back. Again and again. Every day the dad drops him off, coming in to chat with Jesse if the coach has the time. He mentions that Bryan's had trouble in school. He's been bullied. Doesn't like their new house. His friend Jeremy was a bad influence, and they've had to separate them.

Jesse notices as the days pass that Bryan is getting leaner. And more focused. He spends two to three hours at a time in the gym.

It's almost as if he's got nothing else to do, Jesse thinks. *He probably doesn't.*

Now when the dad comes in, he tells Jesse he's proud of his kid. Jesse tells him he's proud of Bryan too.

The kid's no bother, not to Jesse or anyone else. Keeps to himself. Works out, then leaves.

The regulars start to acknowledge him. "Hey, Bryan!" He's one of them. For now.

Chapter 21

Effort, Pennsylvania
April 2013

Casey Arntz is playing a video game, the Sims, on a Friday night when she gets a text from Bryan Kohberger.

She smiles because she likes Bryan. That's a bit of a controversial stance in her friend group. Bryan has had his ups and downs with her younger brother Tom, who says Bryan likes to get physical for no reason. One of Tom's friends, Brandon Andreola, says Bryan has a temper. There's also the fact that Bryan hangs out with Jeremy Saba, who Casey thinks is a dick. And Saba is known to be a junkie these days.

But she likes Bryan.

He may not say much, but Bryan has always been sweet to her. He's solicitous in his texts. He always asks her how she is. Most recently he's been asking about her work at the glitter manufacturer in New Jersey, about her career plans. (She wants to go into interior design after college.) Casey knows Bryan's plans. He graduated high school early, in March, and wants to go to college, maybe East Stroudsburg University, in the fall to study criminal justice.

Tonight, he's texting Casey because he needs a favor.

He tells her his car broke down, and he has to get to his cousin's house near Luna Rossa, a restaurant in Brodheadsville that's a twenty-minute drive up Route 209. He doesn't say why.

Casey says fine. She's happy to help Bryan. She feels sorry for him that he's stuck all the way up in Indian Mountain Lake in that weird gated community. It's a full mile from his new home to the security guard's booth.

So she gets into her car and drives the three miles up the mountain to meet Bryan, who's waiting for her outside the security gate. She drives him to Luna Rossa. He pops in and out of the restaurant, then asks if she can swing by CVS quickly because he needs to buy needles for his aunt, who is a diabetic. Casey thinks that's a bit weird. Shady, actually. But it's hard to argue with such apparent compassion. She gives him the benefit of the doubt.

When he's inside CVS, she thinks fondly of the times they've joshed together, like when they used to play the Game of Things with Tom and Brandon, a party game where players guess who wrote which anonymous answer to prompts like "Things you shouldn't say to your mom." She misses those happy times.

A few days later, he remembers to text her happy birthday. She thanks him, as she always does.

But when she next sees Brandon, he tells her it's common knowledge that Bryan gets heroin at Luna Rossa. That's why he needed Casey to give him a ride there and back. And why he stopped to get needles at CVS.

Casey feels sick.

She realizes that most likely she was carrying heroin in her car. Had she been pulled over, she could have been arrested.

Now Casey is mad.

At 7:49 p.m. on May 21 she sends Bryan a Facebook message, a rare instance in which she is driving the exchange, not him:

> I would like to hand you a big congratulations for lying to
> me about driving you around. I should've added up before

hand but thought I was doing something nice for someone. So thank you, if you would've gotten caught, I would've gotten in trouble just for driving you around not even knowing why. Needles for your aunt? Wow. Real great story. Bye.

A full day later, at 8:33 p.m., he responds: **I'm in rehab.**

I know that, Casey writes back. She receives no reply.

But as the weeks turn into months, she forgives Bryan. How could she not? He's back from rehab and he's so patently lonely.

He texts her repeatedly to ask if her parents will let them hang out. And when she doesn't respond, his texts become sadder and less frequent.

In early 2014 Bryan tells her to be proud that she's making something of her life. **I'm NOT haha,** he writes.

Casey wishes that she could be nicer to him. That they all could be nicer to him. He seems to be struggling.

On March 27, 2014, nearly a year after the car ride to Luna Rossa, he sends a text:

> you know i love you guys
> always will even if we stop talking one day

What is Bryan talking about? What does it mean?

Chapter 22

Indian Mountain Lake, Pennsylvania
2014

Michael Kohberger doesn't want to make the call he's about to. But he has no choice. His own son is a threat to the family.

None of it has worked. Not the boxing. Not the diet. Not the trips to the gun range or the move away from Jeremy Saba, Bryan's childhood friend who has gotten into heroin, too. Not even a stint in rehab.

Bryan can't stop using.

Which means he can't stop stealing.

Now he's taken Melissa's cell phone and sold it. At a mall kiosk for two hundred dollars. Half what it's worth.

Actions have consequences. Children, whatever their age, need to understand that.

So he closes his eyes briefly, then dials 911.

The police arrive, read Bryan his rights, and cuff him. The kid is civil. Barely looks at his dad. He knows who called the cops and why.

There's a time to be calm, to talk to the police politely. Bryan knows that because he's only sixteen, there's a good chance this will be expunged from his record if he behaves.

He'll go — again — to rehab.

Outwardly he'll be the good, polite son everyone wants.

But inside?

Alone in the basement, Bryan lets his true feelings out on Tapatalk and SoundCloud, writing, recording, and posting an original rap song made for other sufferers of visual snow, a neurological condition that is the visual equivalent of TV static.

The rage, the loneliness, just pours out of him. The words are layered over a beat that is equally staccato and furious. A track no one in his family is likely to hear.

But this is the real him.

> *Always the same thing that disrupts my life.*
> *Wonder when I'll change, I guess when the time is right.*
> *Procrastinating my derange to change would be a fight.*
> *So I'm pacifist, like I'm afraid to get a bloody fist.*
> *Look at this, my mind is pissed, and I keep running.*
> *Why is this when I hit it always leaves them stunning?*
> *I stuck in the future, but I'm never lookin' at the fuckin'*
>   *present.*
> *Keep it up, act like you're all that.*
> *Leave your loved one's cryin' like some seagulls.*
> *You are not my equal, you are evil, but I'm*
>   *[unintelligible — people? Evil? Devil?]*
> *And now I'm goin' regal.*
> *Don't fuck with us.*
> *Hope you learned your lesson.*

Chapter 23

Indian Mountain Lake, Pennsylvania
August 2016

B ryan sits in the basement. He's out of drugs, of cash, of friends.
Now his mom is on him to go to Bible study with her. She thinks that will fix him. He's gone a couple of times.

A text beeps on his phone. Bryan reads it. Maybe there's something to the Bible stuff after all. This is divine timing.

Jeremy Saba has been arrested for a DUI and possession of drugs. He's in jail.

One man's misfortune is another's opportunity.

Bryan calls a familiar person. "Connie?" he says to the woman who picks up. She trusts him. Wrongly.

"Bryan," she says, and thanks him for what she assumes is a call of condolence and support.

Jeremy's mom tells him that she and Jeremy's dad will visit their son tomorrow at the jail by the courthouse in Brodheadsville.

As Bryan hopes, the trusting woman shares the time they're planning to go. Would Bryan come visit Jeremy right after?

Bryan says yes.

But as he ends the call, he might have been forming his *real* plan.

Connie later said that the Sabas' absence from their home gave him the perfect window to get what he needed. He used to live next door, so he knew the house, knew where Connie kept her jewelry and where she left her iPad, things he could sell to get his next fix. And he knew exactly how to break in: through the garage.

The next day he executes the plan perfectly.

As Connie and Jiries Saba leave the courthouse in Brodheadsville, Connie wonders where Bryan is. Why hasn't he shown up? He sounded so concerned and solicitous on the phone. Something Jeremy once said nags at her: "Bryan is manipulative."

When the Sabas pull up to their house in Effort, she sees at once why Bryan didn't come.

Someone has been in their home—the door from the garage has been forced open.

Her iPad is gone.

She doesn't need to wonder who the thief is.

She knows.

Will she call the police?

Her fingers hover over her phone. She thinks about Bryan's mom, Maryann, a teacher who, like Connie, works in the local school district. Maryann has in the past occasionally and uncharacteristically shared some of Bryan's struggles with her. There was his Asperger's syndrome diagnosis, and, later, the drugs.

She puts the phone away without calling anyone.

She doesn't know any of the specifics, but she intuits that the Kohberger family is in enough pain right now without Connie Saba adding to their problems.

Chapter 24

Effort, Pennsylvania
2018

S he hasn't seen him in months. Then she turns, and suddenly there he is. In her kitchen. Standing there, unannounced, startling her. Jeremy's mom, Connie, isn't even sure which door he came through.

He is just there. Tall—well over six feet. Towering over her. Eyes bugging out. And he's thin, she notices. Really, really thin.

"Bryan," she says. "What are you doing here?" Even as she asks the question, she knows the answer, because she knows what they teach in rehab.

He's come to atone. To make amends. He's come to say he's sorry for stealing from her. "I knew it was you," Connie tells him.

There's much more Bryan could say. That he's started working toward a psychology degree at Northampton Community College. That he's lonely. He misses Jeremy. But he doesn't say any of that. He doesn't get the chance.

After he's done apologizing, Connie thanks him. And then, with as much kindness as she can muster, Connie asks Bryan to leave and never come back to the Saba house.

She needs to protect her son from the tall, newly thin former neighbor.

Maybe, as he claims, he doesn't do drugs anymore.

But somehow, she senses that he is still a threat to their family.

Chapter 25

Center Valley, Pennsylvania
2018

Bryan's new classmates in the psychology program at DeSales University call him "the Ghost." There's something spooky about him.

Every day he enters class in the same uniform—a wrinkled, black long-sleeved button-down and a tan leather jacket. He's always carrying his silver laptop and a Starbucks coffee cup.

After class—*poof.* Bryan's back in his car and gone in a cloud of dust, starting the forty-five-minute drive along Routes 78 and 33 back to Effort for his nighttime security-guard job—and any other job he can get.

A lab partner, Josh Ferraro, likes how organized Bryan is with their biology project: testing how caffeine affects the heart rate of water fleas. But the guy's eyes seem unnaturally wide open, and they're constantly darting around while his face is completely still.

It's unnerving, Josh thinks.

Josh notices that Bryan becomes less aloof and more animated in Psychological Sleuthing, a class taught by Dr. Katherine Ramsland, a famous criminologist. But it's fair to say they all love this particular class. Because it's fun.

Dr. Ramsland takes her students into a building they call "the crime scene house." It's like a theater set. The students pretend they're detectives called in to investigate a crime.

They're given a scenario like this: "The gun was found here, there was brain spatter on the roof, two bullet holes there, and a rifle was in Johnny's hands." Then they're asked to theorize as to what happened.

Dr. Ramsland teaches her students that killers get tunnel vision when they are committing murder. That's why mistakes get made. Amid the high adrenaline and hyper-focus on the act itself, killers can forget things they otherwise would not.

Bryan takes careful notes. He will later write in an essay for his finals that he's learned "staging is common" among killers. And that investigators must wear "fiber-free" clothing to avoid having their DNA contaminate the crime scene.

The DeSales students also study criminal profiling; they learn what sort of person chooses what sort of murder weapon. Typically, Ramsland tells them, white men choose knives.

They are taught about digital forensics and learn that it's almost impossible to delete one's digital footprint.

And they learn about procedure and law — for example, how the legal process would likely play out if one of them was charged with murder.

Not that anyone thinks that would happen. Most of the students expect to go into law enforcement. Bryan is no exception. He texts his friend Jack that he wants to catch high-profile offenders.

Dr. Ramsland emphasizes to these future crime fighters how difficult it is to spot the killers in their midst before they strike.

She's an expert on serial killers like Jeffrey Dahmer, Ted Bundy, and Ed Kemper. She wrote a book based on her years of correspondence with Dennis Rader, the infamous BTK Killer, whose moniker stood for his grisly methods: bind, torture, kill.

Rader, she tells the class, did not kill for fifteen years while he was busy raising his own child.

How to differentiate between him and us?

Dr. Ramsland says there's a new theory arguing that psychopaths aren't the product of socioeconomics and environment alone. Biology has a larger role than people previously thought. The brains of psychopaths are structurally and functionally different from other people's. Which means the only way to cure a psychopath is to get him therapy at a very early stage, by around age four, and try to train his brain to change.

Bryan listens carefully to this and takes more notes.

His classmates can't see what he is writing.

Chapter 26

Center Valley, Pennsylvania
2018

The image on their screens is mesmerizing.

A dark-haired twenty-two-year-old man with movie-star looks sits behind the wheel of his black BMW, his head tilted to one side. His face is bathed in the reddish glare of a setting California sun. He talks slowly, thoughtfully, to the camera, as if to hypnotize his viewers with his words.

"Tomorrow," he says, "is the day of retribution. You forced me to suffer all my life. Now I'll make you all suffer."

His name is Elliot Rodger. He's from a wealthy family. He flies first-class. His dad is a well-known movie director. He appears to be blessed in many ways.

But he's still a virgin. And he's furious about it.

In the video, one of a series he recorded in May 2014, he delivers a message to all the girls who have rejected him since he hit puberty. Hours later, he embarks on a murderous rampage.

In his apartment, he stabs his two roommates, Cheng Yuan "James" Hong and George Chen, and a friend, Weihan "David" Wang.

Outside the Alpha Phi sorority house near the campus of UC Santa

Barbara, Rodger fatally shoots two women, Katherine Cooper and Veronika Weiss, and injures a third, Bianca de Kock.

At a local deli, he shoots and kills another young man, Christopher Michaels-Martinez. Then he drives his sleek black BMW through the crowded streets of nearby Isla Vista, shooting indiscriminately out the window; he injures thirteen more people before crashing his car and committing suicide with a single bullet to the head.

Not only did Rodger meticulously plan the mass murder and suicide; he also broadcast his scheme in a series of videos on his YouTube channel.

If you hit the mute button, you'd think you were gazing at the next Tom Cruise.

But if you unmute . . .

"To all the girls that I've desired so much, they've all rejected me and looked down upon me as an inferior man . . . I hate all of you. I can't wait to give you exactly what you deserve."

In fact, Katherine Ramsland explains to her forensic psychology class, Rodger *had* waited. His ultimate act of vengeance was carefully thought out, the result of years of pent-up anger about his lonely life. He kept a journal outlining his sexual and social frustrations and his various coping mechanisms: video games, late-night drives, trips to the gun range, buying lottery tickets, a new life in Santa Barbara. But none of it gave him sex or girls or the friends he so craved.

When he lost his only childhood male friend, he was triggered and began to plan the diabolical end. He intended his final act to be so performative that it would catapult him to global fame. The last words he wrote in his journal were "Finally, I can show the world my true worth."

Rodger titled the 137-page manifesto "My Twisted World" and emailed it to his therapist, who sent it to his mother, who received it minutes before her son began his killing spree.

At the time of Rodger's "day of retribution," he was seeing multiple therapists. The month before, his parents had reported his troubling mental state to authorities, and the police visited his home. But as Rodger was well aware, the law was narrow and precise about grounds for search warrants.

He wrote in his manifesto: "If the police would have searched my room, found all of my guns and weapons, I would have been thrown in jail, denied the chance to exact revenge on my enemies. That wasn't the case but it was so close."

Professor Ramsland explains that the police need better training to spot the telltale signs of a potential suicidal mass murderer. One key tool comes from the American Association of Suicidology. Each letter of the acronym IS PATH WARM represents a warning sign:

I — Ideation

S — Substance abuse

P — Purposelessness

A — Anxiety

T — Trapped

H — Hopelessness

W — Withdrawal

A — Anger

R — Recklessness

M — Mood changes

As they learn this, the students don't realize that one of them, Bryan, exhibits every single one of these symptoms. No one person has full visibility on all the parallels between Bryan's life and Rodger's.

No one knows about the complaints Bryan texts to Jack Baylis about life on "Broke Batchelor Mountain." He describes himself as "a good Catholic university student — full homo."

No one knows that, like Rodger, Bryan is a virgin who hates women.

No one knows that Bryan copes with loneliness by immersing himself in video games. Like Rodger, he goes for night drives. Like Rodger, he visits the gun range.

And, like Rodger, he goes to a local bar and tries to pick up women.

Chapter 27

Instead of heading back to Effort on the highway, Bryan takes the scenic route through the Lehigh Valley.

Fifteen minutes after leaving Center Valley, he's parking across the street from the Seven Sirens Brewing Company, which looks more like a vast Manhattan loft space than a college-town bar.

The students from nearby Lehigh University come here often. Bryan knows this. That's why he's here.

Elliot Rodger wrote that he kept trying to place himself in settings where he could pick up women. But no one noticed him.

Bryan must think that surely he'll be noticed. Women must spot his looks, his intelligence, and they must want him.

They don't.

So, typically, after a few drinks, Bryan pushes his way into unwanted conversations with both female bartenders and female patrons. He even asks for their addresses.

Women have started complaining to the brewery's owner, Jordan Serulneck, about the creepy guy with the bulging eyes. So he put the kid on his watch list.

Tonight, Serulneck isn't going to give Bryan the chance to have more than one beer.

"Hey," he says. "I need you to leave women alone. There've been some complaints."

Bryan feigns astonishment. He gives a heck of a performance, almost Broadway-level. Serulneck will remember and demonstrate it in the future.

"I don't know what you're talking about," Bryan says. "You have me totally confused."

Bryan takes another sip of his beer. And another.

It's like they are playing a game of chicken.

Bryan finishes his beer. Casually, he saunters out.

Serulneck doesn't know if his words have had any impact. But as the days tick by, he registers something that makes him happy.

The kid doesn't come back.

Chapter 28

Effort, Pennsylvania
2021

Bryan is immersed in studying for his master's degree. Even though he's been stuck at home, working remotely thanks to COVID, he's doing so well that one of his professors, Michelle Bolger, wants to recommend him for a PhD in criminal justice at Washington State University.

She's only ever recommended one other person.

Bryan is feeling elated.

But soon after March 16, his phone pings with the news that Jeremy Saba is dead.

The facts are tragically familiar: Saba was found upstairs in his bedroom. A lethal dose of fentanyl killed him. Extraordinary what a small pill can do.

Earlier, he had been tinkering with a car in the driveway, then drove off in it to go get some oil, he'd told his mother. Minutes later he was home. And then dead. The local police took his phone and computer, but they never found the dealer.

Bryan is away when Jeremy dies. His parents had wanted to keep the news from him until he returned because they knew how hard it would hit. All that's left for Bryan are memories. Memories of Jeremy, as high as a kite, making them all walk "the yellow brick road"—the dotted painted lines on the highway. Jeremy driving his Mazda; Jeremy playing video games; Jeremy working out.

The last time Bryan's parents saw Jeremy, he'd been doing well, apparently. Mr. and Mrs. Kohberger had run into Jeremy and his parents at the Texas Roadhouse, a steak house in Stroudsburg. It was a good meeting. Bryan's dad told Jeremy he was proud of him for getting clean.

Now Bryan pounds the table with his fist.

He doesn't phone Jeremy's parents. He won't even attend the memorial service for Jeremy or contribute to the memorial page online.

He knows that the tipping point for Elliot Rodger was the loss of his best friend, James Ellis.

"If only he were still my friend," Rodger had written of James.

Bryan gets it.

If only Jeremy were still alive.

Chapter 29

Pullman, Washington
April 2022

Chief Gary Jenkins, head of the Pullman Police Department, looks at his list of questions and then up at the intern candidate he's Zooming with.

The name of the guy staring back at him on the screen is Bryan Kohberger. Jenkins has no idea where he's from or where he's situated for their online meeting. He certainly has no idea that just last month Kohberger purchased a Ka-Bar knife, sheath, and sharpener on Amazon for unknown purposes.

What Chief Jenkins *does* know is that Kohberger is an incoming graduate student and teaching assistant in the well-regarded criminology department at Washington State University. WSU—or "Wazzu," as it's called—is in Pullman, so it's on Jenkins's beat.

Kohberger has applied for an internship with the Pullman PD.

Chief Jenkins can see the guy is hyper-focused. Not much else stands out about him, good or bad.

But there's something odd about him that makes Jenkins say later he didn't think this guy would be able to build trust in his department. There's something antisocial about him.

They chitchat for thirty minutes.

Chief Jenkins winds up giving the internship to someone else. And he doesn't think much about the guy after that. Barely remembers his name, even.

Bryan packs up his gear, his new knife included, and gets in his car for the long road trip to the other side of the country. WSU is in Pullman, Washington, on the border of Idaho. The Pacific Northwest.

Elliot Rodger gave himself one last chance before planning his day of retribution—he moved cities, went from LA to Santa Barbara for college.

"I realized that my miserable, lonely virgin life was going to continue and my only hope was to give Santa Barbara a try," Rodger wrote.

Bryan puts the key in the ignition.

One last try.

Chapter 30

Pullman, Washington
Late August 2022

It's the week before classes begin at Washington State University in the small town of Pullman. The little airstrip Pullman shares with nearby Moscow, Idaho, is just a seven-minute drive from the hilly campus.

WSU is a large school, much larger than UI, with over thirty thousand students. WSU territory is marked by the massive billboard bearing the logo of the Cougars, WSU's football team, who are competitive in their division, unlike Moscow's Vandals.

But football is not the school's only selling point.

This August, WSU's famed criminology and criminal justice graduate program has attracted an international elite bunch, a self-described "cohort" of eleven students, seven women and four men, who will be pursuing master's or PhD degrees. One student comes from South Korea. Another, Sah, is from Bangladesh. Leon is from Taiwan.

At a meet-and-greet with the twenty-odd faculty members, the students pile their paper plates high with mounds of Panda Express and size one another up.

They make small talk and learn about their differing areas of interest, ranging from cybercrime to human trafficking to police militarization and domestic terrorism to drug crimes and drug courts. One person says he studies maps, a subject the others can't quite fathom his interest in.

At forty-two, Ben Roberts is the second oldest in the group. He suspects he's the only one from the West Coast. He looks at the others' serious, scholarly demeanors and thinks he's probably the only one who has ever used a chain saw.

Ben notices one of the students in particular.

His name is Bryan Kohberger.

Bryan stands out because he's painfully thin. His eyes move too quickly, and the bags under them are dark and too prominent for someone his age.

Ben also notices that Bryan never takes off his jacket, even in the August heat. Ben assumes—wrongly—that he needs insulation on account of his willowy frame.

Ben does not know about Bryan's history with heroin. He doesn't know that Bryan might be keeping his forearms covered in public to hide the telltale track marks of his past addiction.

Ben is flattered when Bryan comes over to chat with him. Bryan is doing a PhD, which makes him senior to Ben, who is in the master's program.

Bryan asks a lot of questions about Ben's background. The conversation kicks into high gear when Ben tells Bryan that he worked for the TSA—he was head of security at a small airport.

Bryan lights up. "I've worked in security too," he says.

"Cool," says Ben. "Where?"

Bryan becomes vague. "Oh, back home..." He doesn't say where home is, exactly.

Ben shares some experiences he thinks Bryan might have had himself. He tells Bryan that there were times at the airport when he found it particularly "inelegant" to have to exercise "access control"—that is, having to tell people who believed they had clearance to enter a certain area that in fact they didn't and then barring their path.

"Did you have any of that?"

Bryan nods vigorously.

Ben continues. "And the worst, I found, is when people do have the clearance, but they haven't got the right paperwork on them. It's so embarrassing to have to stop them going through."

"I know exactly what you mean," says Bryan.

Ben wonders for a split second if that is, in fact, true. (It "felt like he might have been stretching," he later said, but at the time, Ben went with the flow.)

Bryan seems very articulate, Ben thinks. He spits words out with the fluency and confidence of someone who expects to be listened to.

Ben has no idea that Bryan is in fact giving a bravura performance, playing the role of someone he has never been—namely, someone who belongs in the room. The silent, awkward introvert has been replaced, for now, by a confident, articulate intellectual.

Bryan might be figuring that at WSU he can start fresh. Become the man he dreams of being.

No one needs to know about his troubled past.

Bryan turns from Ben and makes a beeline for the group of senior faculty members. Like a Wall Street CEO, one by one, he pumps their hands and works the room.

"I'm Bryan," he says, "and I'm excited to be here."

Chapter 31

Pullman, Washington
Early fall 2022

The cohort is sitting in a circle in a classroom in Wilson-Short Hall. It's the third class in the research methodology course taught by their toughest grader, a redheaded French professor named Amelie Pedneault, whose expertise is in sexually violent offenders.

Bryan is in the seat next to Dr. Pedneault, on her right. He takes this seat each time, because he knows it means he'll be called on to present his assignment first as the professor makes her way around the circle. Bryan appears to like going first. He appears to think it gives him an advantage over all the Beckys in the room.

Becky is a term used in the "manosphere" chat groups Bryan is familiar with. Bryan knows all about incels—that is, involuntary celibates.

Incels are members of a "movement" of frustrated men, all virgins, that sprang up on 4chan in 2014 just hours after Elliot Rodger committed mass murder and then suicide, the act that Bryan studied back in Professor Ramsland's class at DeSales. The idea of the movement, started in Rodger's honor, is that one day the incels will succeed in their "Beta Revolution" and overthrow the Beckys, Stacys, and Chads who have managed to make the Betas feel so small and rejected. The group is increasingly associated with violence.

Bryan looks around the class. These women could *all* be considered Beckys, defined by incels as feminists who dye their hair, post stupid opinions, and need to be the dominant ones in relationships. By contrast, Stacys are stereotypically nubile, used to male attention, prolific on social media, and date hunky, rich Chads.

According to incel lore, Beckys need to be put in their place.

After Bryan gives his presentation, the Becky next to him starts hers. He leans in closely, paying attention.

As soon as she's done, he begins his offensive. He peppers her with questions that, he appears to think, show how smart he is and how dumb she is.

Did she think about this theory? And what about that one? And had she read that book?

She's getting annoyed, he can see that.

Bryan looks over at Ben, as if seeking affirmation. But Ben looks away.

Some of the women are visibly pissed.

Bryan doesn't seem bothered by their discomfort.

Elliot Rodger would have been proud.

Chapter 32

Pullman, Washington
Fall 2022

It's been a long day. Bryan is tired. He's sitting in the back row in the class of Dr. Hillary Mellinger, a recent graduate herself, who teaches a course on the role of cultural issues like immigration and homelessness in criminal justice.

Bryan isn't particularly interested in Dr. Mellinger's course. Incels might consider her another Becky. She is an advocate for immigrant women and girls who are fleeing men perpetrating gender-based violence by knocking them around.

Incels are reportedly at the heart of rising gender-based violence. In 2018, a Canadian self-described incel, Alek Minassian, was motivated, he said, "by a hatred of women" to plow a van onto a crowded Toronto sidewalk, killing eleven people. He's been sentenced to prison for life — and he's become an icon in the movement.

Dr. Mellinger interrupts his reverie. "Bryan," she says suddenly. And she asks him a question about immigration that he hasn't prepared for. Did he even hear it correctly?

Shit. He doesn't know that one.

The Beckys have turned around and are staring at him.

So is Ben, who observed later, "You could kind of tell that he was trying to say something, but it just wouldn't come out. He couldn't find the words."

Dr. Mellinger looks shocked.

Ben said Bryan looked like a dog caught in a thunderstorm. "If his ears could have been pinned back, they would've been pinned back. He was just stiff as a board, didn't move, didn't speak, just kind of wide-eyed."

Fortunately for Bryan, this happens in the final few minutes of class.

He's the last to leave the room, so no one sees his face as he heads to his car.

No one can see if he's red-hot angry or red-hot ashamed.

Either way, the stuttering, awkward guy, the real self he'd tried to leave behind in Pennsylvania, just appeared like a jack-in-the-box.

He knows that you can put him back, but you can't erase the discomfort in what just happened.

Chapter 33

Pullman, Washington
Fall 2022

On page 118 of his manifesto, Elliot Rodger wrote:

> I had nothing left to live for but revenge... I lived in a college town full of young, attractive students who partied and had sex all the time and I didn't get to experience any of it. No one invited me to any parties, and in all the times i went out by myself to Isla Vista, none of the beautiful blonde girls showed any interest in having sex with me. Not one girl. These are crimes that cannot go unpunished. The more I thought about all these injustices that were dealt to me, the more eager I became for revenge. It's all I had left.

Months later, the people physically closest to Bryan — the members of his cohort — look for the smallest clue as to why it all went down. There will likely be a trial at which they hope to find answers, but this, or something like it, is what they speculate happened sometime that August:

Bryan goes for an evening drive.

He drives and drives in the dark.

He drives when he can't sleep. When he needs to clear his head. And when the nightmares and visual snow recur, which they are doing now.

Tap, tap, tap. He's back in the basement and on Tapatalk, the online message board, back when he was a teenager.

> I feel myself slipping away ... It is as if the ringing in my ears and the fuzz in my vision is simply all of the demons in my head mocking me. I fall asleep, but I wake up quickly to bloody screams. Is any of this here? Am I brain damaged? NO?! Then why am I like this?

Bryan has no one to share his hopelessness with, even if he could find the words to do it. The others don't seem to want to hang out. He knows the cohort gathers on weekends for a beer. No one has invited him to join them.

Just like Elliot Rodger, who swung between two college communities—one in Santa Barbara and the other eleven miles away in Isla Vista—Bryan has one other option to find a Stacy willing to date him: Moscow, Idaho. Across the state border.

He parks the car in town and heads to a place he's read about online: the Mad Greek. They serve vegan pizza.

As soon as he walks inside, he notices the blond waitress.

With her long hair and sphinxlike blue eyes, she would definitely be marked as a Stacy by the incels.

She's the epitome of the women who turned down Elliot Rodger. Her name is Maddie, like Elliot's childhood friend Maddy, who grew into someone who ignored Rodger.

Will she notice Bryan?

She comes over to ask what he'd like.

He knows what he'd like.

Her.

Chapter 34

It's pitch-black, but anyone can see Maddie sitting at her vanity, as clear as day, through the window. She has no idea who is out there in the parking lot, looking.

But neighbors, like Lexi Pattinson, see her nightly routine. They know that she always takes her time putting on her face: Foundation. Then blush. Eye shadow, mascara or fake lashes. Sometimes she uses a curling iron to style her long blond hair.

Anyone who didn't know Maddie's name would learn it in an instant, because the letters spelling it out are in the window. Anyone can see right into her room's pink interior and discover the minutiae of her life as a "cutesy" girl who likes order. Even her quilt is pink.

A passerby who stopped and stared would know she has a boyfriend, because on weekends, he sits on the bed when Maddie and the other girls model clothes for Instagram and TikTok. She tags the boyfriend on social media. His name is Jake. Recently, the boyfriend brought Maddie cookies and a bouquet of flowers that stands in a vase on her dresser.

Her mom, or at least a woman who looks exactly like Maddie, often pops in, and so does an older, graceful-looking woman (Maddie's grandmother, whom she calls Deedle).

Anyone can see just from watching that Maddie is close to all these family members. She's even making a little quilt for someone, a baby.

Kaylee, one of her friends, often pops in from next door. These two are obviously close; they pore over their phones, comparing social media posts, taking photos and videos of each other.

They're so immersed in their phones and their coziness that they never think to look farther than the sanctuary of their yard.

They don't see anyone out there, staring.

Corporal Brett Payne of the Moscow police later alleges, based on AT&T cell phone records and the pings Bryan's cell phone made off a Moscow cell tower, that that was what Bryan did. Payne alleges that he was there at least twelve times between August 21 and November 13—almost always late at night, cloaked in darkness.

The theory among Maddie's friends is that she rejected him. So he watched. Waiting.

Elliot Rodger wrote of reuniting with a childhood friend, named Maddy, in the months before the day of retribution:

> She was a popular, spoiled USC girl who partied with her hot, popular blonde-haired clique of friends...my hatred for them all grew from each picture I saw of her profile. They were the kind of beautiful, popular people who lived pleasurable lives and would look down on me as inferior scum, never accepting me as one of them. They were my enemies. They represented everything that was wrong with this world.

Corporal Payne alleges that on the night of August 21, Bryan was there at King Road between 10:34 p.m. and 11:35 p.m.

* * *

At 11:37 p.m., at the junction of Farm Road and Pullman Highway, on his way back to Pullman, Bryan is pulled over by Latah County sheriff's deputy Corporal Duke. His car doesn't have a front plate. It's registered in Pennsylvania, where front plates aren't required. He'll need to change that in Washington and Idaho, Duke tells him. Bryan says okay.

He's smooth with the officer. Natural.

The officer has no clue as to what Bryan is really doing in Moscow.

If Bryan is asked about it — which he will be — he'll deny that he was doing anything other than going out for a drive. Like he always does when under stress.

He often goes out stargazing, he'll say.

The police can't see into his mind. No one can.

Even though the people out here in the Pacific Northwest do try.

Boy, do they try.

Chapter 35

Pullman, Washington
Fall 2022

Cassie Handziak is a WSU freshman majoring in psychology and minoring in criminology. Her largest class is the undergraduate criminal justice course with Professor John Snyder. With white hair and a mustache, Dr. Snyder is one of the most popular professors in the department. He's the reason Cassie wanted to come to WSU. She's excited.

But as she sits attentively during Snyder's first class, Cassie encounters something off-putting. Rather, some*one* off-putting.

The professor talks and talks for forty long minutes, often calling on class members in his fun, benign way. A tall, thin guy with bulging eyes stands in front of the class facing them the entire time. He has a coffee in his hand. He fiddles with it.

Cassie wonders who the heck he is and why he's staring. The way he holds himself exudes—not confidence, exactly, but self-importance, perhaps.

Finally, Professor Snyder introduces him: "This is your new TA, Bryan Kohberger."

A couple of slides of a nice-looking family come onto the projector screen.

"Hi, I'm Bryan," he tells the class. "I'm here to continue my degree from Pennsylvania. I've got a master's in psychology. Here's my family."

They look normal, Cassie thinks.

Bryan tells them he'll be here with Professor Snyder regularly and he'll be grading their papers. Then he sits down.

Why didn't Bryan just sit at a desk in the front row until he was introduced? Cassie wonders.

Her neighbor whispers to her that this guy is weird. Cassie smirks.

Cassie sees Bryan twice a week, every time she has a class with Professor Snyder. There are two TAs, both guys. One often has his laptop in front of him. Bryan just sits there staring at the class, fiddling with his coffee cup. He doesn't say anything.

It's strange.

Where he's communicative, Cassie notices, is in his grading. She can tell he puts a lot of thought into marking her papers.

He gives her As. And writes a lot of commentary.

She assumes that's because she's good at writing essays. She doesn't think she's a standout student, though.

Until, that is, she hears from some of her female classmates that he's not so generous with their grades. And when he thinks they've gotten something wrong, he writes pages and pages explaining why. He is tough, they say.

They think it's because they're women.

Walking to class one time, a couple of classmates tell Cassie they've emailed Professor Snyder about it.

Wow, Cassie thinks. That's a step.

Chapter 36

Pullman, Washington
October 2022

The weather hovers between fall and winter. It's bitterly cold, but the first snow has yet to arrive.

After class at around five p.m., Ben Roberts is milling around in Wilson-Short Hall when he bumps into Bryan, who offers to give him a lift home.

Ben hesitates. He lives only a few minutes away, but he does need a ride. And he's curious. Ben wants to understand what underlies Bryan's antagonistic behavior toward the women in class.

So he makes a decision. He accepts.

Ben gets into Bryan's white Hyundai Elantra. Bryan keeps the car's interior clean and tidy, he notices.

The conversation begins straightforwardly enough, at least in Ben's mind; they talk about some of the negative impacts of social media. Ben says he believes that social media encourages people to stay within bubbles of like-minded people. Dating app searches, for example, Ben points out, are designed algorithmically to keep men and women in certain groups.

Bryan gets personal. "Are you seeing anyone?" he asks.

"No," says Ben. "And I'm fine with that."

Ben doesn't add something he doesn't think Bryan knows and that is none of his business anyway: He's not straight.

He wants to change the topic. But Bryan wants to talk about women. What he thinks of them.

He tells Ben that he believes in traditional gender roles, the implication being that their female colleagues are wasting their time in class and have no business pursuing master's degrees.

Essentially, Bryan believes that men should make money and women should be homemakers.

Ben thinks the sentiment is tasteless as well as anachronistic—and odd for someone who's chosen to attend WSU, a progressive academic community where women outnumber men on the faculty. The department's head is a woman! Dr. Melanie-Angela Neuilly, who is interested in feminist theories, no less, in researching comparative homicides, specifically violent homicides. She also has a wider interest in criminology theories, including feminist theorizations of crime.

But Ben is even more horrified by what Bryan says next: "I can walk into any social gathering and get any girl I want."

It's an extraordinary thing to say, and in Ben's mind, it puts Bryan at "creep level"—and not just because Ben doubts, given Bryan's weird physical appearance, that there's any truth to the boast.

Ben doesn't rate himself highly as a specimen of physical attractiveness, but *this* guy? *He looks more like Gollum than George Clooney,* Ben thinks.

He doesn't know that Bryan has in fact seen a girl he wants and cannot get: a beautiful girl with long blond hair and blue eyes.

Bryan continues talking, seemingly looking for a sign of agreement from Ben. When they arrive at Ben's place, he gets out of the car, hoping they're done.

They're not.

Bryan asks to use his bathroom.

He lingers in Ben's tiny, sardine-can studio apartment until 7:45 p.m.

Both men remain standing for the conversation, because Ben has only two chairs and one of them is piled high with stuff.

Ben does not consider these hours well spent.

As for Bryan? He probably realized Ben wasn't the kindred spirit he'd hoped he was.

Chapter 37

Pullman, Washington
September 23, 2022

The way the cohort hears it, this is what goes down in Professor Snyder's office.

Dr. Snyder calls Bryan in to talk about all the complaints. Women have emailed him saying the TA is grading the female students unfairly. And some of his cohort say his interruptions in class are misogynistic.

Professor Snyder informs Bryan of what's being said and suggests he change his ways.

"Stop interrupting the women," he tells the strange young man — or he says something along those lines. "They're complaining. Stop writing them essays on their essays. It's offensive. Be generous — and brief." A rumor goes around that Snyder makes the point that the undergraduates cannot be expected to have the same level of knowledge as Bryan.

Snyder is trying to be helpful.

But apparently (or so they hear later; none of them was in the room, obviously), Bryan's anger spills out of him.

Fuck it. No more point pretending . . .

Something sends him out of control.

"They deserve what they get," he says.

The professor sees that Bryan might be smart, but his Achilles' heel is a big ego and a high opinion of himself.

And there's something deeper that sets Bryan off. Something ugly.

Professor Snyder thinks he hears Bryan mutter, "They don't belong in the classroom," but he can't be sure. So in his report on the "altercation" to the higher-ups on the faculty, he focuses on what he cannot ignore: the young man's anger.

A week or so later, on October 3, department chair Melanie-Angela Neuilly and graduate director Dale Willits call Bryan in to discuss his lack of "norms of professional behavior."

Professor Willits is there as a witness so there's a record of what happens in the meeting—which, it turns out, will be needed.

Bryan listens, but he doesn't hear them. He's angry, defiant.

He says he wants to meet his critics head-on. Have a discussion in class. Explain his grading. He graded his students poorly because they didn't know the topic well.

After he leaves, the faculty members are concerned. There's no way Bryan's "discussion" with his students is likely to go the way he thinks it will.

Chapter 38

Pullman, Washington
November 2022

Ben Roberts is still in shock about the delusional self-regard Bryan expressed in the conversation that revealed his offensive, anachronistic view of gender roles. But increasingly, Bryan's appearance becomes even more startling.

Ben assumes that Bryan is as stressed as they all are with finals looming. The workload is almost intolerable, and none of the students appears to be in perfect health. In class, Bryan looks positively ill, like he's physically deteriorating.

"He looked like the walking dead," Ben said later. "I mean, we're talking, his eyes were just completely dark most of the time. He just looked gone." This wasn't just sleep deprivation. It was more serious, ongoing.

He heard the rumors that Bryan got reprimanded by Professor Snyder, but Bryan doesn't offer any information.

Ben goes to WSU's student-care network and fills out a form indicating his concern. He wants to send it to the administration. The school's website states that these reports can be made anonymously.

But before pressing submit, Ben looks for the anonymous-reporting function. He can't see that his anonymity will be protected for sure.

Ben wants to help his exhausted classmate, but he doesn't want Bryan searching out—and finding—the person who submitted the form. He doesn't want this coming back to him. There's something about this guy that is just too weird.

So Ben deletes what he's typed, never imagining that the act of pushing the backspace button on his keyboard will come to haunt him.

Chapter 39

Pullman, Washington
October 14, 2022

Bryan is driving his white 2015 Hyundai Elantra when he hears the siren.

Damn! Again!

He pulls over and sits there as WSU police officer Isobel Luengas gets out of her cruiser and approaches him.

Bryan rolls down his window, looking as calm as possible even though his heart is racing.

"Hello, Officer."

Officer Luengas politely greets Bryan. Wearing a body camera, she starts by telling him that the stop is being audio and video recorded. Then she says, "I think you know why I stopped you. You ran the red light."

"What actually happened was, I was stuck in the middle of the intersection," Bryan answers. "So I was forced to turn left."

"Yeah, I was behind you the whole time," Luengas says a little skeptically.

She explains that she watched Bryan enter the intersection illegally. She asks for his license, registration, insurance.

Bryan hands them over. He's cooperative. He apologizes profusely.

Luengas seems receptive, so Bryan plows on, getting in deep. All that practice being verbal in class is paying off.

He tells the cop that he's from a rural part of Pennsylvania, as his vehicle registration shows, and when it comes to pulling into an intersection like he just did, it "never even occurred to me that was actually something wrong." Back home you could drive like that with impunity.

His performance works. He gets away with it, just like he did back in August.

The officer lets him go with a warning.

For Bryan, it's likely an empowering moment.

Back at DeSales, in Professor Ramsland's class, he learned that a month before the day of retribution, Elliot Rodger was paid a visit by police officers—they left with no clue that he was planning a mass murder.

It's possible that Bryan, too, can get away with anything he wants.

Chapter 40

Pullman, Washington
Fall 2022

She asks Bryan, her neighbor, to install a home surveillance system. She's noticed that her home in the Steptoe Village Apartments has been broken into, and various items were moved around (but nothing was stolen).

Bryan is always floating around the place — it's where a lot of the graduate students live — and they've gotten friendly. And she knows he's into tech, because he's always talking about how good he is with computers. She can see him on his computer at his window late into the night.

So instead of going to the police, she goes to Bryan, who agrees to help place cameras around her home.

He could not be more helpful. And the new cameras work really well.

She's grateful. Until...she looks at the cameras and at what she can see from her phone. There's been a rumor that Bryan followed a woman student to her car. This technology is smart but so simple. Anyone with the password can log on and see inside her apartment.

Anyone...but there's only one person other than her who knows the password: Bryan.

Her mind races. He's seemed off lately. Strange. He asked her to go out for coffee and seemed mad when she said no.

Really mad.

She changes her password.

She has no idea that just two months after this, her brief encounters with Bryan will become a newspaper story that goes viral.

She has no idea that she will need to shield her identity, hide from the media and the public.

No idea that her experience will make her a potential witness in a murder trial.

That Chief Jenkins will say that investigators believe there was likely a connection between Bryan's "work" on her security and what happened at 1122 King Road.

She has no idea of who the weird guy with the bulging eyes really is or of what is about to happen.

Chapter 41

Pullman, Washington
November 2, 2022

Less than a month after their previous meeting with Bryan, so the cohort hears, graduate director Dale Willits and department chair Melanie-Angela Neuilly are once again confronting Bryan about his behavior. There are no friendly suggestions this time.

Drs. Willits and Neuilly tell Bryan what he already knows: Short of a miracle, he'll be fired.

The cohort hears that the discussion about grading had not gone well. Women had later complained to Dr. Snyder and said Bryan had stared at them, that he'd positioned himself by the door and they'd had to get uncomfortably close to him to exit the room. One suggested he followed her to her car.

As if. Bryan is so pissed. They'd be lucky to get close to him.

He has stopped showing up to teach.

So two weeks ago, John Snyder had formally notified Bryan he had failed to meet expectations as a TA.

The students assume that Professor Neuilly wants to give students the benefit of the doubt, and that is why she and Professor Willits are giving Bryan a chance. Today, Drs. Neuilly and Willits suggest an improvement plan for Bryan, a way for him to show them he can lose the misogyny and genuinely behave professionally at an institution that expects that of both students and teachers.

This improvement plan, they agree, will be emailed to Bryan, and they will meet again in a month to see how it's going.

Bryan listens. Bryan's career as a graduate student is over. In this room now, they're just going through the motions. His bubble is bursting. His dream of a new life, a new persona, is being cut short.

Professor Snyder emails the plan to him the next day. It contains words like *courtesy* and *respect*.

The kind of thing he considers politically correct bullshit.

So they want change . . .

On page 118 of his manifesto, Elliot Rodger wrote that he planned to carry out his day-of-retribution scheme in November. At first he'd planned to do it on Halloween, because, he said, it was the ultimate party night:

> There would literally be thousands of people crowded together who I could kill with ease and the goal was kill everyone in Isla Vista, to utterly destroy that wretched town.
>
> But then . . . I saw there were too many cops walking around . . . The Day of Retribution would have to be on a normal party weekend, so I set it for some time during November 2013.

In the early hours of November 13, 2022, police allege, Bryan leaves his home in Pullman. At 2:47 a.m., his phone shows he's moving southeast of his Pullman home. One minute later, his phone stops reporting to the network—or any network—and doesn't come online again until 4:47 a.m.

Between those times, Corporal Brett Payne alleges, a masked intruder fitting Kohberger's description enters 1122 King Road. As they are sleeping or relaxing in what they assume is the safety of their own home, Maddie Mogen, Kaylee Goncalves, Xana Kernodle, and Ethan Chapin are fatally stabbed.

What no one knows is why.

PART THREE
The First Six Weeks

Chapter 42

As soon as she wakes up and sees the half-light shining through the slit of a window in Bethany's bedroom, Dylan remembers him.

The firefighter. His bulging blue eyes that caught hers. His thick, dark eyebrows.

And the mask.

Her dreamlike memory of the night before begins coming back to her in hazy snippets.

She remembers falling into a half sleep, half stupor. At around two a.m., she'd heard everyone come home. Kaylee and Maddie had chatted on the couch in the living room.

Late last night, she heard the girls say the name of Kaylee's ex: Jack, Jack, Jack.

Dylan now thinks Maddie and Kaylee stayed up for a while. She heard them stomp up the stairs to the top floor. And then . . .

She thought she'd heard that cry. Was it Kaylee?

"There's someone here."

Given her soporific haze, Dylan can't be sure of the timing, but she thought it sounded like Kaylee had said those words just moments after going up the stairs.

Then Dylan had opened her door and peered out.

Nothing.

She thought she could hear Xana moving around, doubtless getting a food delivery like she always did after a big night out.

It wasn't unusual for people to pop in and out of King Road even at four a.m. It was a party house. And people knew to come in through the sliding doors by the kitchen. Everyone in their circle, even their parents, knew that the lock was broken. You just had to lift the mechanism up and the door released.

So Dylan went back to bed.

But as she lay down, she thought she heard Xana crying.

She opened her door again—and she thought she heard an unmistakably male voice say: "It's okay. I'm going to help you."

Then there was a thud. A whimper. And Murphy began barking and barking.

Murphy never did that in the middle of the night.

Dylan shut her door, freaked out.

Her heart thudding, she waited some more.

She opened the door a third time. And then she saw him. The firefighter.

Or that's what she thought he must be, since he wore a mask and was clad head to toe in black. He had something in his hands. A vacuum, maybe?

Was there a fire? Where was the smoke? She was confused.

He was walking toward the back sliding doors. Their gazes locked for a split second.

Dylan was momentarily frozen. But she quickly closed her door and locked it, heart pounding, waiting for further sounds. She remembered being scared. And looking around her room for her Taser. The battery was dead.

She listened and listened at the door. But after that…there was just silence.

Whoever he was, whatever he'd been doing, he was gone.

Dylan wondered in that moment if she'd gone crazy. How wasted *was* she?

That was when she reached out to Bethany. And the others. And, eventually—after getting no reply for ten minutes and seeing that her phone was dying—she'd gulped, opened her door again, and raced down to Bethany's room, where she'd locked the door and climbed into bed with her best friend.

Her other housemates must be sleeping, she told herself. And she fell into an uneasy slumber.

When she woke up around eight a.m., early for a Sunday, Bethany was already awake. She'd spoken to her parents and told them about Dylan's panic—paranoia most likely—the night before.

Dylan *has* had crazy thoughts before, when completely drunk. So at first she thinks it must've been a nightmare, which now has passed, just like the dark.

She and Bethany lie in bed, both on their phones. Dylan tools around on Instagram and then on Indeed. At 10:23 a.m. she texts Maddie to see if she's up.

No biggie, she thinks, when there's no answer.

But the clock ticks on and, as Dylan sends messages on Instagram and Snapchat, there's still no noise from upstairs. At 11:29 a.m. she texts Kaylee. Still nothing.

Now the panic from last night sets in again.

Dylan turns to Bethany: What if whatever Dylan saw . . . was real?

Bethany calls Jenna McClure, one of their besties. She says she'll come over.

And Dylan decides to phone Emily, her "Big," the person she trusts the most on campus.

Surely Emily will fix this. She has to.

Chapter 43

Moscow, Idaho
November 13, 2022

Emily Alandt is at her apartment in the building next door having breakfast with Hunter Johnson, Josie, and Linden when she answers Dylan's call.

"Can you come over?" Dylan asks her big sister. "I don't really know if I was dreaming or not, but I think there was a man here, and I'm really scared. Can you come check out the house?"

Emily is amused. It's not the first time Dylan has said crazy stuff after she's had a few drinks.

"Ha-ha. Should I bring my pepper spray?" she teases.

Emily takes the time to find a sweatshirt before trotting toward the King Road house.

But Hunter, driven perhaps by some sixth sense, is ahead of her.

He enters the house and passes Dylan and Bethany, who are barefoot, hands over their mouths, crying. They wait while he goes up the stairs and heads to the passage that will take him to Xana's room.

The first sign that something is very wrong is that Xana's door is cracked open a few inches.

Xana never sleeps with her door open.

But Hunter soon sees that Xana isn't in bed asleep.

She's lying on the floor as if she'd fallen backward into the room. Ethan is motionless in the bed behind her.

There are rivers of blood.

Adrenaline takes over. As does a strong protective instinct. He goes back down to Dylan and Bethany. "Call 911," he says. "And stay outside," he says as calmly as he can.

He turns and heads back upstairs, where he goes into the kitchen and gets a kitchen knife. Is the person who did this still here?

He heads across the hall back to Xana's bedroom. When he's at her doorway, he hears someone coming up the stairs.

He turns around and sees Emily coming toward him.

He stops her, putting a hand on her shoulders and talking as softly as he can: "You cannot go in there," he tells her.

Emily doesn't understand.

He tries again. "Emily, I don't think Xana's going to wake up," he says firmly.

And Emily stops moving; she stops speaking; she's rooted in shock.

"I'm going in to take their pulses," he says.

Eventually she turns and heads back down the stairs.

Hunter goes into Xana's bedroom.

He takes Xana's pulse, knowing that he won't feel a beat.

He doesn't.

And then Hunter goes over to the bed, to his best friend, Ethan, lying there, facing the wall, peacefully but lifelessly. Again, there's no pulse.

He now walks around the room, checking the closets. There's no one there. In a trance, he walks out of the bedroom, knife in hand, and stands in the living room.

Meanwhile, the others are outside on the phone with the emergency responder. The operator is asking them to stop passing the phone around but in their panic that's all they can think to do.

Bethany and Dylan are too upset to be intelligible so Josie tries to give the address as clearly as she can, explaining that one of the roommates is unconscious. "One of the roommates is passed out and she was drunk last night and she's not waking up . . . oh and they saw a man in their house last night."

Dylan takes the phone back and tries to start in about what she saw at four a.m., but the operator cuts her off.

She wants to know what is happening right now. Is someone passed out *right now*?

There's a pause as they call for Hunter inside the house, who hollers back to them.

"She's not waking up," Dylan tells the operator.

Hunter comes out and takes the phone from Dylan.

"Is she breathing?" the operator asks.

"No," Hunter says, with all the calm he can muster. Then he hands the phone back to Dylan and goes to wait inside.

The operator tells Dylan that she's summoned help, and to stay on the line. She asks Dylan if she can find a defibrillator.

Dylan asks the others. None of them knows where a defibrillator is.

None of them, other than Hunter, knows anything.

But wordlessly they are each screaming the same questions:

Why is Xana not waking up?

Where is Ethan?

Why is Hunter Johnson telling them to say outside?

And what about Kaylee and Maddie?

Huddled on the sidewalk, dressed in their nightwear, the friends have no idea whether Kaylee and Maddie are inside the house. They do know from their location-sharing apps that the girls' phones are there.

But they also know that neither is answering.

Chapter 44

Moscow, Idaho
November 13, 2022

They are still on the phone with the 911 operator when the first patrol car arrives.

The man who gets out, patrol officer Mitch Nunes, is twenty-two. The same age as Hunter Johnson.

Nunes joined the Moscow PD only a year ago.

The kids look at him, slightly stunned to see someone their age in an officer's uniform. Nunes is expecting a routine situation. He asks Hunter Johnson, who is standing just inside, still holding the kitchen knife, to come with him to show him the unconscious person. He's ready to administer CPR.

But right from the get-go something tells him this isn't the usual case of a student who has over-imbibed.

Hunter Johnson doesn't let go of the knife.

He takes Nunes up to Xana's room. He shows him Xana and Ethan. Nunes takes their pulses.

They are dead, clearly the victims of a brutal stabbing.

Nunes can see that in addition to other wounds, Xana's fingers are almost severed. It looks like she put up a fight against someone advancing into the room.

Ethan looks as if he died while sleeping. He's on his side in the bed, facing the wall, stabbed in the buttocks and the neck.

Nunes takes out his gun.

He might be the department baby, but he knows how to follow protocols from his time in the army and his police training. He knows that while he waits for backup, he needs to look around for a perpetrator. His first priority is to clear the residence of any threat. His second is to get medical aid to anyone who needs it.

Nunes casts his eyes around. There's no sign of a perpetrator.

And it's clear that Xana and Ethan are beyond requiring medical assistance.

He calls for backup. He takes Hunter down to the living room. Then he makes his way up to the top of the house, his body cam recording every second of his movements and the horrific visual of what he sees.

Upstairs, on the top floor, Nunes finds a dog, a goldendoodle, in the room on the left. He enters the room on the right, Maddie's room, and sees two young women, Kaylee and Maddie, lying in Maddie's bed.

Also stabbed to death.

Even before he takes their pulses, he knows they are dead.

Nunes hasn't seen anything as horrific as this in his short time at the Moscow PD. The last murder in town happened long before he joined the force.

Two other patrol officers, Corbin Smith and Eric Warner, are on their way, but Nunes knows he needs to go up the chain of command fast. This is way serious.

Chapter 45

Moscow, Idaho
November 13, 2022

It's 12:30 p.m. on what ought to be a lazy Sunday, but someone is shaking Hunter Chapin awake.

"Cooper?" he says groggily to the guy who climbed up the ladder to his sleeping loft and is prodding him.

Cooper Atkinson, an older Sig Chi brother who recruited him and Ethan, is standing there, visibly agitated.

"Hunter, wake up. There are cops on King Road."

Huh?

Hunter doesn't see what the big deal is. The King Road house is a notorious party house because of the deck in the back. The cops are always being called by a neighbor angered by the noise.

Hunter sees that the university has sent out a campus-wide alert about an unconscious person. But he still isn't worried. Maybe Xana or one of the other roommates over-imbibed on game day. It wouldn't be the first time someone passed out from drinking.

But Cooper drags Hunter out of bed, and the two make the short walk across the lower field to the house.

As they get near, Hunter can see their usual gang sitting on the sidewalk: Emily, Hunter Johnson, Josie, Linden, Dylan, Bethany.

Where's Ethan? he wonders.

Oh. He answers his own question: Ethan is probably helping the cops inside. He'll be helping whoever is in difficulty. That would be typical of Ethan. Xana's not on the sidewalk either, so maybe the person who needs help is Ethan's own girlfriend.

Hunter scarcely notices that Cooper leaves his side once he catches up to his group of friends on the sidewalk.

Because there's something in his friends' faces that tells him that the world has just ended.

They don't speak. They just hug him.

Hunter is afraid to say anything, but then Hunter Johnson gently motions for him to follow him to a nearby dumpster. When they are alone, Hunter Chapin plucks up the courage to ask, "What's going on? Like, where's Ethan? Is he helping whoever's inside?"

Hunter Johnson speaks softly: "Ethan's not here anymore."

Hunter Chapin doesn't comprehend the words.

"What do you mean, 'Ethan's not here anymore'? Like, where did he go?"

"Your brother's dead."

Dead?

Hunter Chapin can't feel anything. How can this be happening?

How on earth can Ethan, whom he last saw in the early hours of this morning, be dead?

Hunter Johnson continues: "I think—I don't know—we think Xana, Ethan, Kaylee, and Maddie were all murdered last night."

Murdered? Ethan? Xana? Kaylee and Maddie?

Hunter Chapin is so dizzy he has to sit down.

Ordinarily, he'd tell the other Hunter he's out of his mind. To stop with such a cruel joke.

But ordinarily, there isn't yellow police tape around the house and a swarm of cops moving in and out and not speaking to the little circle of sobbing kids.

For maybe fifteen minutes, Hunter Chapin is mute. They all are. No one knows what to say.

He can't process this. He can't deal. He has spent almost every minute of his entire life with his triplet brother. Ethan has been his leader, his role model. His brother has entered every room, every game, every contest, one step ahead of him but also with his hand stretched out toward him. Ethan is Hunter's entire world.

Now he's gone? Murdered?

He has no idea what to do. What to say to his sister, his mom, his dad. He doesn't want to speak to the cops—and it seems they don't want to speak to the kids. The police avert their gaze as they go in and out of the house.

Eventually Hunter speaks.

For the first time in his life, he has to dig deep and find Ethan's spirit within him.

Chapter 46

Moscow, Idaho
November 13, 2022

I need a phone," Hunter Chapin says. "Mine isn't working."

Hunter Johnson hands him his.

He calls his sister. No answer.

It will emerge that Maizie is showering. And when she comes out and sees a missed call from Hunter Johnson, she doesn't assume that it's anything urgent. Why should she?

But then he calls again. Weird.

She answers. "What do you want, Hunter?"

But it isn't the Hunter she was expecting. It's her brother, and he sounds strange.

"Maizie, you need to come to Xana's."

Maizie thinks this is also weird. "Why?"

"You just need to come."

Maizie is kind of pissed. "I don't have a car."

"Find one."

Maizie wakes up Reagan, one of her roommates, and asks her to drive her to Xana's.

But they can get only as far as the bottom of the hilly slope on which 1122 King Road sits. The whole block is cordoned off; police are everywhere.

Maizie gets out and walks toward her brother Hunter and the usual friend group.

They are all crying. Her brother appears to be on the phone.

Maizie thinks her stomach might fall out of her.

"What the hell happened? Someone? Anyone?"

Silence.

Maizie is filled with rage, with good reason. Why are they all just shaking their heads and not speaking?

"Someone tell me. Jesus Christ!" she yells.

Her brother hangs up the phone and approaches her.

"Ethan and Xana didn't wake up."

Maizie snorts. "What do you mean, they didn't wake up?" Did someone drug them? Poison them? It doesn't make sense.

Maizie still doesn't think it sounds that bad.

But her friends' reactions nag at her. Bethany is crying so loudly that it feels like her life depends on it. Dylan is positively screaming. And shouting something like "I can't believe someone would do this!" Maizie has never much liked Dylan. She's histrionic, in Maizie's view, and Maizie is irritated by it.

"Shut the fuck up," Maizie says to Dylan. "It's really annoying."

Why do they all want to hug her?

Maizie sits down with them. She sees Ava Wood, a blond APhi who lives in an apartment building next to the house, putting a blanket over Emily's shoulders. And comforting her.

Jack DuCoeur, who Maizie knows is Kaylee's ex-boyfriend, is also with them. He seems confused. Dazed. When he says he's Kaylee's ex, the cops seem to want to talk to him. They stick him in the cop car, but only for a few minutes.

Maizie hasn't thought about Kaylee and Maddie, Xana's roommates. She doesn't know them, really. She's focused on Ethan and Xana.

What's happened to them?

The group just sits there, watching the cops, waiting, hoping for an answer that is better than the one they fear.

Suddenly it's 1:04 p.m. All their phones ping.

It's another campus-wide alert.

Much worse than the first.

MOSCOW PD INVESTIGATING A HOMICIDE ON KING RD. NEAR CAMPUS. SUSPECT IS NOT KNOWN AT THIS TIME. STAY AWAY FROM THE AREA AND SHELTER IN PLACE.

Oh my God.

The group collectively bursts into fresh tears.

Maizie is struggling to grasp the reality of the words on the screen.

But Emily loses it. The young cop has come out of the house and she lets him have it: "How dare you send out a Vandal Alert before we know where our friends are!" she screams at him.

The officer replies with a stony calm that he does not feel as he delivers the grim, official, life-changing news.

"All four of your friends are inside the house. And they're all dead."

Chapter 47

S tacy Chapin is filling her cart in the produce aisle at Haggen when she sees her friend Barb.

It's a lazy Sunday. Her husband, Jim, is on his way back to the tiny condo in nearby La Conner they bought after they sold their big house in Mount Vernon. He's been at his workshop at a sawmill outside of Coeur d'Alene, a mammoth six-hour-plus drive away. Jim left at eight a.m., so Stacy has plenty of time for a catch-up.

She puts her basket down to exchange news with Barb. When her phone rings and she sees it's Maizie calling, she figures no big deal, she'll call her back when she's finished talking.

Although, as she thinks about it, it *is* unusual for Maizie to call. Normally she texts her mother and they arrange a time to talk.

Of all her kids, the quickest to communicate is Ethan, from whom she's yet to hear this morning.

Which is odd. She texted Ethan a few hours ago asking him for photos from Maizie's formal last night, but he hasn't responded. Ordinarily, he's the first of her kids to reach out in the mornings, no matter how heavy the night before. And usually when she texts him, he answers right away, no matter the hour. It's like there's a psychic bond between them.

Anyhow, no big deal. Stacy carries on talking.

When she's finished, she sees that Maizie has called her multiple times. Now she's trying her again.

This time Stacy picks up. "Maizie?" she says.

But it isn't Maizie. It's Hunter calling from his sister's phone. He's on speaker. Stacy can hear wailing in the background.

"Ethan's not here anymore," Hunter says.

Stacy doesn't understand. "Well, go get him."

Hunter tries again. "No, you don't understand. He and Xana aren't here."

Stacy is growing impatient. Like Maizie, she doesn't suffer fools. "So get in the car and go find them."

What is that—crying?

Hunter says, "Mom, you don't understand. They're not on this earth anymore."

Stacy doesn't believe what her son is telling her.

She abandons her cart in the aisle, walks out of the store, and calls Jim from her car. He's just dropping into the Skagit Valley. He's almost home.

"I think something's happened to Ethan and he's been killed," she says.

Jim doesn't understand; he can't process. But he knows one thing and so does his wife: Whatever's happened, they have to get to Hunter and Maizie.

Right now. They have to get to their kids.

Chapter 48

La Conner, Washington
November 13, 2022

S tacy and Jim Chapin meet at their condo in La Conner, Washington, and get into Jim's black Chevy Tahoe. They have a six-hour drive ahead of them, and the Sunday-afternoon traffic sucks.

Hunter and Maizie call and tell them they're being asked to go to the police station and that they'll be handing over their phones to the cops.

Which means that for most of that drive, Stacy and Jim cannot reach their kids.

Stacy feels as if she'll burst.

Why aren't they hearing anything from the police? From the university? From anyone?

She phones the emergency cell number for the university that parents of incoming students are given. She chews out the person who answers, asking why no one from the school is communicating with her about her son.

The voice on the other end says that's because there's a protocol with emergencies, and the police are the ones in charge of situations like this.

In perhaps the only time in the aftermath of her son's death, Stacy momentarily loses her cool. "That's not good enough!" she yells.

She has no idea to whom she's talking; in that moment she's not interested. But being Stacy Chapin, soon she wants to find him and apologize.

For now she just wants the snarled traffic to move. All she wants is to get to Hunter and Maizie and tell them that no matter what has happened to Ethan, they are still a family. And they are going to be fine.

Stacy, the mother hen, is going to make sure of this. She is going to be there for Maizie and Hunter. She is going to be there for Ethan, whatever has happened. She is going to be there for Jim.

She doesn't have a clue as to how they are going to get through this, but she is going to do her damnedest to protect her brood. Family first.

All the plans she and Jim had of traveling, retiring—those belong to the past. They are quite, quite gone.

Hunter and Maizie need to hear one message from her: Whatever happened to Ethan, they are alive, and they are going to be fine. She will make sure of it.

It's what Ethan would want.

Chapter 49

Clarkson, Idaho
November 13, 2022

W hat a beautiful Sunday!

Blaine Eckles, the UI dean of students, is nearing the Costco in Clarkson, near Lewiston, a forty-minute drive from Moscow. He's admiring the morning. He and his wife, Shelley, are doing the grocery run they normally do every six weeks.

He's seen a Vandal Alert about an unconscious person, and he hopes whoever needed first aid received it and is okay. More than likely an alcohol-related mishap after game day. Not unusual.

But as they are about to pull into the Costco parking lot, his phone rings.

It's Tyson Berrett.

"Blaine," says the police captain, "we've got four dead bodies and we think they may be students."

"What?" Eckles gestures to his wife to go on into Costco; he sits in the car and speaks to the captain.

"We don't have it confirmed yet. But given the proximity of where they are to campus, at King Road, and their ages, it's a good chance they are."

"Call me back as soon as you know anything," says Eckles.

Just like the police, Eckles has a checklist of what to do and whom to call.

His first call is to University of Idaho president Scott Green. His line is busy, so Eckles suspects someone else—Tyson, probably—is giving him the news.

Then he calls the provost, Torrey Lawrence, and informs him.

Jake Nichols, the director of campus safety, is temporarily unreachable because, it will emerge, he is on a boat on a river.

Eckles leaves a voicemail asking Greg Lambeth, the director of the counseling center, to phone him as soon as possible. (Lambeth, it turns out, is hiking in the woods.)

But the small group of people he *can* reach have an impromptu conference call, then decide to convene ASAP on campus.

Eckles goes into Costco and retrieves Shelley. He asks her to drive so he can set about putting things in order.

Eckles is trying to stay one step ahead of what to do, what to set in motion.

Berrett mentioned that the manner of the deaths was suspicious, but Eckles has no clue as to how the four students, if indeed they are students, died.

He wonders if it's drug-related; more likely, he thinks, they were shot.

So when a bewildered, irate Stacy Chapin reaches him, he genuinely has nothing new to tell her. He doesn't know what happened. But even if he did, he explains, it's up to the police, not him, to talk to her.

He notes that she doesn't ask his name, that in her panic, she may not be aware that it's him. Eckles does not know Stacy Chapin, but he knows who she is. When you're the dean, you notice when triplets enroll. Doesn't happen every day.

Nor does a mass murder.

Eckles started at UI in 2015, so he wasn't here for the previous horrific campus tragedy, in 2011, when Katy Benoit was murdered by her professor, who then holed up in the Best Western and, when the cops tried to bash down the door, turned the gun on himself.

Now, as the administrators huddle in a conference room, they have a whole host of questions to think about. Like security, and how to beef that up. Whether to cancel classes and, if so, for how long.

For Eckles, the priority is student care. He needs to find out where the kids lived, whether they were members of a Greek house, so he can reach out.

Tyson Berrett continues phoning him intermittently, and Eckles tells the captain that he will cooperate as best he can with any investigation.

But what no one in that room of university leaders considers is something that will become a problem for Chief Fry and his officers: By deciding to cancel classes, they are effectively sending home thousands of possible witnesses. Key people the police need to speak to.

Fry later shakes his head in exasperation at this, wishing the school had asked him first. But part of being a cop is knowing that you can control only so much. The university is not answerable to him and they need to make their decisions for their reasons, not his.

Fortunately, there is another law enforcement agency that has branches all over the country and can get to out-of-towners easily.

Fry knows he'll be calling it soon.

The Federal Bureau of Investigation.

Chapter 50

It's lunchtime and Evan Ellis, the news director of Pullman Radio, has just finished up in the studio. He's prepping for his Monday-morning show when local photographer Geoff Crimmins calls him.

"You listening to the scanner?" Crimmins is at his in-laws' house, and they keep their scanners set to the police frequency.

"Stopped when I left the studio," Ellis replies. "Why?"

"You're not going to believe this. We got four bodies over in Moscow. Eleven twenty-two King. I'm listening to it right now. The cops just walked in. The volunteers, fire and EMT, are saying there's blood everywhere."

"Meet you there," says Ellis.

With decades of experience between them, there's no need to have a conversation about the seriousness of the situation.

Ellis and Crimmins get to the King Road residence within fifteen minutes. A patrol car is barricading the entrance to the block and tape is around the perimeter.

Ellis can see a group of four or five kids sitting on the sidewalk in a circle, all sobbing uncontrollably. He's never heard wailing like this. There is terror and tragedy in those cries.

Ellis has been to and reported from every major crime scene in the area over the past twenty years. In 2007, he even arrived at an active shooting in Moscow. Outside the sheriff's office, Lee Newbill, a police officer, was killed, and two others, including sheriff's deputy Sergeant Brannon Jordan, were injured.

As a journalist, Ellis practices old-style reporting; he has values that, in the coming days and weeks, prove vanishingly rare. He believes that *off the record* means *off the record* and that sources are to be protected. He also believes that some people have a right to privacy, to not have cameras shoved in their faces—and these kids, in this moment, should not be interviewed.

He deliberately turns his phone away from them and even tries to block the noise of the bawling as he begins live streaming from the scene on Facebook.

"All right, I'm going to go fast here, we've got a sketchy signal where I'm at. Homicide investigation in Moscow." He tells his listeners where he is. "Moscow police on scene. University of Idaho has issued a Vandal Alert saying that the Moscow PD has a homicide investigation here at one of these apartments. Suspect is not known at this time. University of Idaho alert states that people need to stay away from this area and shelter in place. That is the alert from the University of Idaho, is to shelter in place, that's what the Vandal Alert said, with this homicide investigation here near campus. Suspect not known at this time. This is Evan Ellis—"

He stops streaming when he sees a cop come out of 1122 King Road. He recognizes the officer: Captain Tyson Berrett. Unlike the kids, Berrett is *not* off-limits, so Ellis approaches.

Berrett lets him. Because he knows that Ellis knows the Moscow cops. They trust him. He's never betrayed their confidence, and when they've told him stuff that is for background only, it's stayed that way.

So Berrett is happy to answer Ellis honestly when the journalist asks: "Is there a shooter at large?"

Berrett shakes his head. "No threat to the public," the captain says. "We're going to put that out there."

But Ellis is skeptical. Sure, he doesn't see anyone walking around looking like they want to attack anyone, but still... "Really, Tyson? Are you sure?"

Berrett says he is.

Ellis points at the house. "So is everybody in there?" His question is implicit: Is the murderer in there, dead too?

But at that, Berrett shuts down. "I'm not going to say anything else."

After years of dealing with these guys, Ellis knows better than to push. But questions race through his mind. *Are we talking murder? Are we talking guns? What are we talking about?*

Holy hell, he thinks as he walks away. He calls Chief Fry.

"Chief, Tyson's going with 'No threat to the public.' Are you sure? The university is saying shelter in place."

Fry is quick to answer. "We are going with 'no threat.' That's what we've got right now."

There's a pause.

"Hey, Evan," Fry says, speaking to his friend as much as to a journalist. "Tamp this down."

Fry doesn't want chaos on the campus. That isn't helpful to anyone. The police are going to need calm and order so they can get to witnesses and proceed with their investigation.

Fry knows that people *are* just as safe now as they were twenty-four hours before the murders. Common sense, not just his years of training and experience, tells him that when someone comes for you in your bed with a knife in the middle of the night... it's personal. Whoever did this is not likely to strike again randomly.

What Fry can't explain right now is why *four* victims were knifed and why two other roommates were not. But he knows that there will be an answer. And they will find it.

They always do.

He hasn't had an unsolved case once in his years of being a cop.

Ellis knows that Fry and Berrett are as good at their jobs as any cops you'll find anywhere. Better, probably, because there's a pride and sense of ownership that comes with policing a small town, something that likely doesn't happen in the big cities.

But Ellis also knows that the police are going to have another problem while they're hunting for whoever stabbed four students to death in their bedrooms.

And he's worried that these cops, as good as they are, aren't prepared for this aspect. Namely: publicity.

Everything about this crime—the age of the victims, the proximity of the house to the school, the fact of there being four of them, the fact that they were in the safety of their own beds, the fact that there appear to be survivors in the house, the fact that this is Moscow, safe little Moscow—all of this means that this story is going to be *big*.

Way bigger than the town's mass homicide in 2015, when John Lee, the troubled son of a beloved local couple, shot and killed his adoptive mother, his landlord, and a restaurant manager and injured one other person.

Way bigger than the sordid saga of Katy Benoit and her professor.

Bigger than the two Wells brothers gunning down a member of the Vandals football team. And bigger than Charles Capone strangling his wife and dumping her body in the river.

The Moscow cops are going to face questions from journalists who don't know them. Journalists who will ask, not unreasonably, how the police can be certain the public is safe if they don't have a suspect in custody.

That's why he's pushing here.

But in all his years of reporting, he's never gotten in the way of an investigation. And he's not going to start now.

So he taps the live-stream button again on his phone.

"All right, Evan Ellis with you, back again at the scene of a homicide investigation in Moscow. We're near campus; you can see the unit here where the investigation is taking place, eleven twenty-two King Road. And we've got the police tape here around the scene." He tells his audience that Captain Tyson Berrett of the Moscow Police Department specifically said that there was no threat to the public right now, although the University of Idaho had sent out a campus-wide alert telling people to stay away from the area and shelter in place. "The key here," he goes on, "is it's Moscow Police Department investigating, they do not believe this case represents a threat to the public at this time, and again that's different from what we've heard from the University of Idaho on their alert." It's possible, he says, that the university is being overly cautious, and he re-iterates that the police are saying there is no threat to the public at this time. "What exactly that means, you can speculate," he says. "We're not going to necessarily do that. Homicide investigation here again in Moscow, King Road. Here is new Greek Row, right back here. University of Idaho campus here."

Ellis's hand is shaking. So is his voice.

In this moment, he and Geoff Crimmins are the only members of the media there.

But he knows that within hours, that will change, and he worries that the police narrative he has repeated several times—that there is no threat to the public—will change as well.

Chapter 51

Moscow, Idaho
November 13, 2022

Jeff Kernodle is headed on the long journey back to his home in Arizona after family weekend. He's feeling justifiably elated.

It hasn't been a straightforward path, parenting his two daughters, Jazzmin and Xana. Their mom, Cara, has been in and out of jail for years. When Jazzmin and Xana were little, Jeff got full custody. It was not easy being a single dad, juggling children and a job. And, more recently, a move from Post Falls, Idaho, to Arizona.

But he and his daughters are as tight as can be. And his daughters are tight with each other.

He smiles when he thinks about the fact that they are just fifteen miles apart, Jazzmin at WSU, Xana at UI. Two beautiful young women, full of life, laughter, hope. And love for each other.

Jazzmin is a rising senior, studying business marketing and digital technology. Xana has mentioned wanting a career in digital marketing, or maybe sales, but she's always been the more carefree of the two. The one who laughingly has always said she has no plans for the future.

But Jeff noticed this past weekend that she's changing.

She wanted him to meet her boyfriend's parents, Jim and Stacy. Nice people.

She's never had a serious boyfriend before, and Jeff can tell she's nuts about Ethan. So nuts she's thinking about a future with him.

Why, though, did she not phone earlier? He'd thought they might have brunch today, but he didn't hear from her, so he hit the road.

His phone rings.

It's Jazzmin. She's crying.

"Dad, you need to turn around."

His heart drops.

"Meet me at Xana's house" is all she says.

When he gets there, it's cordoned off and swarming with police officers.

Jeff tells them he's Xana's dad, and an officer asks if he and Jazzmin can please follow him to the station.

When they get there, they are ushered into a room where an officer gently tells them there have been four victims of a homicide—and that Xana is one.

Jeff is speechless. What can you say to such a thing?

There aren't words.

Just tears and agony.

Chapter 52

Rathdrum, Idaho
November 13, 2022

It's lunchtime and Steve Goncalves is exactly where he likes to be on football Sundays: In his living room in front of the TV watching the Seahawks game, surrounded by his noisy family.

He moved to Rathdrum, Idaho, because he wanted to make life easier for his wife, Kristi. The cost of living was cheaper; the state was safer than California.

He wanted her to quit her job as an accountant at Chevron and be a full-time mom if she wanted to. She didn't—because that's Kristi for you. Independent, strong, a great role model. She'd decided to become a teacher.

Steve's a proud girl dad. Four of his five kids are daughters. But they all love football. Their cousin Bryce is hoping to get recruited by a college team.

An extra bonus today is that his eldest daughter, Alivea, will soon be home for Thanksgiving. She lives in LA, where her husband, Robbie Stevenson, works in postproduction on the series *Ted Lasso*.

But that morning there was a scare. Steve just discovered he has Ramsay Hunt syndrome, an inflammation of the facial nerve caused by the chicken pox virus. Alivea is twenty-two weeks pregnant with her third child, and Steve is worried about possibly being contagious, so he and Kristi are on and off the phone to Alivea, figuring out if it's safe for her to visit.

So when they call Alivea yet again, she doesn't sound surprised to hear from them. But then Kristi says, "I think something's happened to Kaylee."

They were not expecting Kaylee back from Moscow until Tuesday; she had gone to show Maddie her new Range Rover and hang out with her friends. But Kaylee's younger sisters, Autumn and Aubrie, have been getting strange calls from Kaylee's friends about police being at King Road. Something weird is happening there. An unconscious person. Then there's a Vandal Alert about a homicide. They try Kaylee. It goes to voicemail. They try Maddie. It rings but no answer. They try Jack. No answer. But they start to see photographs of the King Road house coming online. It's surrounded by police tape.

The Goncalveses are flummoxed. Where are the police? Why hasn't anyone said anything to them? Alivea phones Maddie's mom, Karen Laramie, to ask if she's heard anything. Karen says she's already on her way to Moscow. She, too, has received alarming messages, but nothing from the police. She promises she's going to bring both girls home.

But Karen doesn't get to the King Road house. The police reach her when she's almost to Moscow and tell her to go to the police station.

The Goncalveses, meanwhile, are sitting, waiting, hoping, praying that Kaylee and Maddie are okay. It's another few hours—between four and five p.m.—before the police show up on their doorstep to deliver the shocking news that Kaylee is dead and so are Maddie and two others. When Steve and Kristi ask how and why, the officers have no answer.

After they leave, Steve heads upstairs to the bedroom he shares with Kristi. He shuts the door and weeps. Tears of shame as well as grief. He's the family protector. He moved here to Idaho to keep his family safe. And he couldn't protect Kaylee and Maddie.

* * *

When Kristi tells her the news, Alivea goes numb. And then she takes control of the things she can.

She tells Robbie they need to get into the car with their two kids and drive through the night—twenty hours—to get to Rathdrum and her parents.

She doesn't want to fly because she doesn't want to be trapped with strangers in an airport. She wants to work while Robbie drives. She wants to talk to whoever Kaylee talked to in her last hours alive.

In the passenger seat, she goes into detective mode. Kaylee is on their mother's cell phone plan, and Alivea knows how to pull up her sister's phone log online to see who Kaylee called and who called Kaylee. She phones the people her sister spoke to. And she follows every lead she can find.

By the time she and Robbie pull up in Rathdrum, late afternoon the next day, Alivea already knows a few things:

Kaylee was at the Corner Club just after one in the morning.

Kaylee called a rideshare driver from the Grub Truck at 1:50 a.m. and she got into the car with a friend. Alivea knows this because she reached the rideshare driver via text message.

She knows that the friend was Maddie, because she was told by the driver that the Grub Truck had a camera on the roof and was live streaming, so she pulled up the video on Twitch and saw Maddie and Kaylee waiting in line.

She knows the two arrived home safely at 1:57 a.m. because she tracked down a neighbor's Ring camera footage.

And she knows that Kaylee's last call that night was to Jack.

Alivea tells her parents she's certain that Kaylee's murderer wasn't someone known to her. Alivea never met Xana and Ethan, but from Kaylee, she knew enough about them, their life, and their friends. She is certain that no one in their group would have done this.

She tells her father that she feels in her gut that whoever did this was a stranger.

The mystery is why.

When he looks back on Alivea's quick thinking, Steve can't help but be impressed by his eldest daughter. He's always been sad that, with her smarts, she didn't go to law school after college; she'd chosen instead to go to Los Angeles with Robbie so he could pursue a career in film and entertainment.

Alivea is fiercely intelligent—she scored 1300 on the SAT—and, like her parents, she never takes no for an answer. Not from anyone. Kaylee was the same way.

Here she is, pregnant, having driven with her husband through the night, two little ones in the back seat, on a mission to find answers.

Steve makes himself a promise: He will not rest until whoever did this is brought to justice. That is what Kaylee would want. That is what Kaylee would expect.

And Steve will not let the Goncalves women down.

Chapter 53

Moscow, Idaho
November 13, 2022

This is the worst crime scene yet.

Latah County prosecutor Bill Thompson pulls up close to the King Road house and makes his way toward the police tape.

He braces himself, knowing what lies within its perimeter.

He's never had to deal with a crime this violent and of this magnitude—and Thompson has led the county prosecutorial office for three decades. The previous week was his thirty-year anniversary.

Some anniversary gift! Four students stabbed to death in their beds.

He ducks under the police tape and tells the officer outside he's going to do a tour of the interior of the house.

The officers are deferential, making way for him, trying to be helpful. They revere Thompson. He might look like Santa Claus, with his long white beard and spectacles, but appearances can be deceptive. To the cops, Thompson is the epitome of the adage "iron fist, velvet glove."

At this point, he's a legend.

If, in thirty years of being Latah County's lead prosecutor, an elected position, Thompson has lost a case, no one can remember it.

He has no intention of letting this one blot his record.

Whoever did this will pay for it.

Thompson makes his way up to the main level, where he sees Xana and Ethan, and then to the upper level, where he sees Maddie and Kaylee.

He also sees the knife sheath beside the bed that Corporal Payne and the others had noticed earlier.

That's going to be a critical piece of evidence, if there is DNA on it.

Whoever did this made a mistake.

Thanks to the popularity of public genealogical websites like Ancestry and 23andMe, forensics can now take the smallest piece of DNA and construct an entire family tree around it in a method called investigative genetic genealogy—IGG for short. It's a game-changing scientific development for investigators.

Leaving the knife sheath might be the murderer's only mistake. Time will tell. There's no sign right now of a murder weapon, of prints. But they are just starting.

Thompson is confident they *will* find the perpetrator. They *will* find a motive. What he doesn't know is how long it will take.

But Thompson is patient. He prides himself on his patience.

His most famous case was that of Moscow automotive repairman Charles Capone. In April 2010 Capone's estranged wife, Rachael Anderson, vanished. Her body was never found, but Thompson was nonetheless able to convict Capone of her murder. Because he waited. And waited. For two years—until an accomplice who'd helped Capone strangle his wife and throw her body, wrapped in a tarpaulin, into the Snake River started talking. Ultimately, he became Thompson's star witness and testified as to exactly what had happened.

Capone was sentenced to life in prison.

Another famous case was the murder of UI football player Eric McMillan, who was gunned down on campus by two brothers from Seattle, James and Matthew Wells. There was no obvious connection between McMillan and the Wells brothers, but again, Thompson was patient. He wound up indicting not just the two brothers but multiple family members who'd committed perjury to cover up what had happened.

So no one who has worked closely with Bill Thompson—and that includes all thirty-six members of the Moscow PD—considers him soft.

True, he votes Democrat. Which makes him unusual in a Republican state.

True, he has advocated for the community to create more resources to treat mental illness, saying that this would prevent crime. He'd pushed publicly for this in 2007 after a local janitor, Jason Hamilton, who was known to be mentally unstable, went out drinking, then shot his wife, Crystal, in the head and went on a shooting spree at the sheriff's office, killing a total of four people, including beloved Moscow police officer Lee Newbill, and wounding another deputy, Brannon Jordan, before turning the gun on himself.

And true, he didn't press for a trial in the case of John Lee, a schizophrenic kid who was known to many, many people in Moscow. In 2015, Lee shot his adoptive mother, Terri Grzebielski, a popular nurse practitioner; his landlord; and two more people at the local Arby's. He'd then sped off to Pullman, where cops had made the arrest.

Everyone in Moscow knew and loved Terri. Everyone had watched John Lee grow up. They'd witnessed his mental struggle. So, yes, Thompson had accepted a plea agreement whereby Lee was sentenced to life in prison without the possibility of parole.

You could argue that that was soft, or you could argue that it was pragmatic. No one believed John Lee was in his right mind when he went on his killing spree.

But this case?

Four bodies? In a student house?

Stab wounds? Rivers of blood? Murders committed in the middle of the night in a densely populated area? With two survivors who, for whatever reason, waited eight hours to call 911?

Thompson knows that the chief will likely agree that the attack was targeted. The two meet every morning at eight. They know each other's thought patterns inside out.

It may take weeks to go through all the stuff on these kids' phones to find the link they need.

But they will find it.

There's always a clue. He and Fry know that from experience.

Back in 2009 a local man, Silas Parks, claimed his pregnant wife, Sarah, had died in a tragic house fire. In fact, he'd strangled her first, then set the fire himself.

James Fry had been the lead investigator on that case, Bill Thompson the prosecutor, and in the end, it was the autopsy of the mother and fetus that gave Silas away: Sarah did not have any smoke in her lungs. And the fetus had petechial hemorrhage in her eyes, an indication of trauma.

Thompson had told Sarah's family to hang tough and let justice unfold, as it surely would.

Now, he watches as the state police forensics team arrives with a trailer full of equipment. When they've gathered all the evidence they need—fingernails, skin scrapings, everything and anything—the police will call the county coroner, Cathy Mabbutt. She's probably already been told to cancel her dinner plans.

Thompson considers if he might go down to the police station where the roommates and immediate circle of friends are being questioned. He needs to learn what happened in the hours before and after the murders. The timeline is essential.

He also wants to ensure that whatever he learns is kept secret. Leaks can kill investigations; they can literally obstruct justice. He never talks publicly about a case until the very end—until sentencing—and even then, he's brief.

Beyond the evidence truck, a crowd is gathering with microphones and cameras.

This one is going to attract more press attention than usual.

Oh, well. They can gather. But they are all going to have to wait.

It's business as usual.

Chapter 54

1122 King Road
Moscow, Idaho
November 13, 2022

It's cold.

Even with the blanket Ava has placed over her shoulders, Emily is cold. She's in shorts. So are Dylan and Bethany. None of them is wearing shoes.

They've been sitting out here for hours now. Crying, freezing, numb.

Captain Berrett gently asks them to go to the police station for interviews.

Emily feels for the captain. She can tell how sad Berrett is to see her and Ava crying like this. They are like daughters to him.

Emily just wants to *do* something.

She's just lost her best friend. She has no idea how or why or who did this.

Her world is in free fall.

She wants to be able to control *something*.

She looks around. She *can* look after Dylan, her Little, and Bethany, who has lost her Big, Maddie. She can give them clothes, protect them as best she can, like a mother hen.

So before driving to the police station, Emily pops into her apartment to get clothes for all of them. And bottles of water, and snacks.

When they get to the station, it feels as if the officer on duty isn't sure what to do. It dawns on Emily that it isn't just her world that's been rocked.

None of them, not even the police, are ready for a tornado like this.

The friends sit together, mostly in silence. Random people enter and leave. John Hennrich, the director of student care and case management, appears, along with a woman counselor who asks if they want to talk about their feelings.

The group says no. They aren't ready to talk about anything with anyone. They just want to be left alone.

Hennrich assures them before he leaves that the last thing they need to worry about is classes. He'll be in touch with all their professors.

Emily peers downstairs at one point and, with a pang, sees Jeff and Jazzmin Kernodle being led into a room on the first floor.

She intuits that the story is overtaking them. That the news of what's happened is likely to reach their nearest and dearest before they can get to them, thanks to social media.

So she phones her mom, Karen.

"Mom, I'm at the police station, I'm safe, I don't really wanna talk about it, but I'm not gonna have my phone for a while."

Karen is in disbelief. She hasn't seen or heard anything. And Emily wants to protect her from the details for as long as possible.

"All you need to know is that . . . they're just all gone. And we can talk about it later."

One by one, the friends are peeled off and taken to interview rooms like you see on crime dramas. A room where the tape recorder is going and the window is a one-way mirror.

They never learn who is watching their interviews. They just know they are being watched. They don't know if the prosecutor, Bill Thompson, is there or not. They later wonder if he might have been. He's going to need the answers to the questions they are asked.

Like why, the police want to know, were Emily, Hunter, Josie, and Linden awake so late the night before?

Why would Emily have texted Xana at that hour?

Who exactly did Dylan see?

Why did she think he was a firefighter?

Did he see her when she saw him?

Was he in the house already when everyone got home?

Why does she think the masked man in black walked away from her?

(*Thank God,* Emily thinks, *the man in black did walk away from her.*)

Is this person now coming for *them*?

After their interviews, the friends determine they are not going to separate. No one wants to go home; for Bethany and Dylan, that's not even possible.

They swear to look out for one another. To protect one another at all costs from whoever attacked their friends.

It's the only positive step they can take when everything else has gone irretrievably backward.

Chapter 55

Moscow, Idaho
November 13, 2022

Daniel Ramirez, a journalist for the *Argonaut,* the University of Idaho's student newspaper, is getting coffee at the drive-through with the *Argonaut*'s editor, Haadiya Tariq, when their phones ping simultaneously with a Vandal Alert warning students to shelter in place.

Ordinarily, this sort of Vandal Alert is issued when there is a moose on campus.

This time it says there's been a homicide.

The alert also tells them to stay away from the King Road area.

So they do what every good journalist would: They head straight for 1122 King Road.

They see the multitude of police cars and the tape. Standing in front of the house, directing the others, is Tyson Berrett, whom they recognize because he's the campus-police commandant.

They ask Berrett for a statement, but he only repeats the Vandal Alert with no further details.

So Haadiya and Daniel head to the *Argonaut* newsroom on the top floor of the Bruce M. Pitman Center to see what they can learn online. The students are conversing on the college-chat app Yik Yak, a kind of anonymous, closed version of Twitter, and there is huge confusion because at three p.m., another Vandal Alert is posted, this one saying that there is no threat to the community.

What does this mean? Daniel and Haadiya can see that the students are confused and scared. Can they really walk around safely?

The student journalists want to be able to report on this, but what can they say that is accurate?

Conspiracy theories are already flying on Yik Yak. So too are the names Xana, Ethan, Maddie, and Kaylee, but not in such a way that Daniel and Haadiya feel they're reportable.

They are student journalists, yes, but they consider themselves journalists first, students second. They take their job seriously.

On Yik Yak, the consensus seems to be that 1122 King Road is a party house, so a lot of students are suggesting that fentanyl must have been involved.

Maybe, it's even posited, the homicide has something to do with Emma Bailey, who was seen in the Whites, the apartment building next to the house, the weekend before. (The following spring, Emma will be charged with the delivery of a controlled substance in connection with the death of another UI student. Prosecutors will dismiss the case.) Could she have been at the King Road house last night?

At around five p.m., a friend of Daniel's in a Catholic students' group forwards something that Daniel deems the most reliable source so far as to the victims' identities—the students have been urged to pray for the four victims, whose names are given.

Even so, Daniel and Haadiya wait to publish anything until they get confirmation from the police. And they know from bitter experience that it's going to be tough to get much from the Moscow PD.

Haadiya is *still* waiting for the public information officer, or PIO, to get back to her about someone she refers to as "knife guy." A man dressed in black riding a bicycle and holding a knife had harassed a couple of people on Paradise Street back in September. Haadiya had written that up and done a follow-up piece, because the police had issued a report saying he was no longer a threat to anyone but didn't explain why.

Just like she's waiting for answers about the two other campus deaths that have occurred while she's been at the *Argonaut*.

One student died of an overdose, a suspected suicide, in the spring. The *Argonaut* never wrote about it because the police never got back to Haadiya about it.

Another student, Hudson Lindow, was found dead in the creek in May; sources said it was a direct result of hazing. He'd been made to drink out of a five-gallon bucket and was then abandoned by the people who'd made him do it. Haadiya wanted to report what her sources told her, but with no confirmation from the police, she couldn't. She felt that would be irresponsible.

So now she and Daniel have nothing official to go on regarding what happened at King Road.

Yik Yak, meanwhile, is exploding with all sorts of speculative storylines.

One is that a group of men dressed in black entered the house.

Another is that they were killed by members of a Colombian drug cartel who had known Xana's mother in prison and wanted payback.

Another is that one of the four victims had been about to expose the Greek houses for sex trafficking (the idea being that new sorority members were coerced into dating fraternity members).

Yet another is that they were killed to cover up some kind of hazing sexual assault.

Another is about a love triangle involving Ethan, Xana, and either Maddie or Kaylee.

Every minute, there's a new invented plotline. This is like no story the duo has covered before. They aren't sure of protocol.

Surely it isn't right to start reaching out to the victims' families so soon? Haadiya feels that would not be respectful. She assumes—incorrectly, as it turns out—that other journalists will feel the same way.

That evening, Daniel sees that PBS appears to have a lead no one else does.

A segment on the four homicides in Moscow comes on the news. According to the PBS report, the students were shot.

Daniel and Haadiya look at each other. How on earth can PBS know that? Did the police tell PBS something they are not telling other news organizations? Surely PBS can't have gotten it wrong. Can they?

The two are confused but also beginning to feel an emotion that will become all too familiar in the coming weeks as members of the national media descend on their town and report a barrage of nonsense in the absence of facts.

What they feel is disappointment.

Chapter 56

Troy, Idaho
November 13, 2022

It's dark by the time the police chief gets close to the crime scene.

First, Fry goes home, showers, dresses in his uniform, and puts on his gun, a SIG Sauer P320. A murderer is out there, after all. Then he drives to 1122 King Road, Moscow.

He doesn't imagine for a second that any of these actions will come back to haunt him.

He doesn't yet realize that every move he makes will be fodder for criticism from a press skeptical that a little police department in a little town can find whoever killed Xana, Ethan, Maddie, and Kaylee.

He doesn't yet grasp the snobbery of the coastal elites, who consider Moscow the middle of nowhere and assume the police chief must therefore be inexperienced and inept.

He doesn't yet comprehend that the media is going to hound him so much, he will have to cover his office windows with butcher paper.

He doesn't yet realize that the job of a police chief in the modern era has little to do with the training and experience he's gotten in thirty years on the job, including ten weeks spent at the FBI National Academy in Quantico, Virginia, a program for which only the country's very best police officers are selected.

He doesn't yet understand that what he will need over the next six weeks is a PhD in communications. And that is something he is not equipped with.

Fry is thinking about process, the well-being of his team, and protecting the investigation the way he knows how and the way Bill Thompson wants it.

With silence.

The good thing about having a small department is that Fry trusts his men implicitly. He knows there will be no leaks, whatever they find.

What he doesn't yet know is that in the absence of a real story, people invent fictitious ones.

And that is where the real harm lies.

Chapter 57

Moscow, Idaho
November 13, 2022

At around seven p.m., the Sigma Chi fraternity house gets a visit from Blaine Eckles, the dean of students.

Sixty-one young men gather in the lodge, their ashen faces tearstained. If ever they needed to feel the comfort of leadership, it's now.

Dean Eckles rises to the occasion. He has no children of his own, and these young men right here—they are his family.

First things first, the dean tells them. He's aware they are the only Greek house on campus that doesn't have a chef, and he knows today most of them will not have thought about buying groceries, so he's got them covered—food, water, milk, are on the way.

Second, he's opened the counseling center 24/7 so its team is available for anyone who needs it.

Third, the Idaho State Police is going to provide round-the-clock security for the house.

And fourth, everyone can just get the hell out of town.

No need to email professors. No need to turn in assignments. "Go," he tells them. "Be with the people you love."

Fifth, he's going to let the fraternity president, Reed Ofsthun, deal with the press however he wants. He advises the group to stay off social media, chiefly to be sensitive to the victims' families.

The release of tension is palpable.

Some of the fraternity members cry openly. These are tough young athletes, but they have never experienced anything like this.

Ethan's frat brothers feel his loss. But they also feel like participants in whatever terrible trauma he suffered.

The back of the frat house has a view of 1122 King Road. So, after waking to what most had assumed would be a lazy Sunday and learning the news, one by one the whole chapter had gathered there, staring grimly across the Lower 40 at the mass of police cars and emergency vehicles, listening to the wailing sirens, fearing the worst as their phones blew up with surreal texts about their frat brother Ethan and about Xana, whom they loved like a sister.

Only last night they'd all been joshing together at the postgame party.

And now? Their worlds were upended.

Most of them watched Hunter Chapin leave the house that morning with Cooper Atkinson. They watched Jayden Shepherd receive a call, after which he turned to them and said, simply, "Ethan's dead."

They received texts about a gruesome killing, blood everywhere.

They watched as, hours later, against the backdrop of a swarm of police officers, the forlorn figures of Hunter Chapin and Hunter Johnson walked back to the fraternity house, packed up some stuff, and headed to the police station.

The fraternity brothers had hugged Hunter Chapin. Told him they loved him. They weren't sure he could even hear, he was so grief-stricken.

Once Dean Eckles leaves, they head to their rooms. Many of them phone their parents and ask them to come get them right now. Others start to load up their cars.

None of them knows what exactly happened to Ethan, their brother.

One of them, David Berriochoa, walked across the Lower 40 at 3:59 a.m. and felt a strange chill as he did so.

It's a chill they all feel now.

Their instinct tells them to run. Get the hell out of Moscow, get as far away as possible.

Run. Run.

Chapter 58

I t's nine thirty p.m. when Jim and Stacy Chapin pull into Moscow.

When she sees Maizie and Hunter, Stacy hugs them tightly. Then Jim does. Stacy has one message for her two surviving children: "I don't know what the hell just happened, but this won't sink us as a family. We'll figure it out. Together."

They head to the police station for a so-called debrief, but the police don't have any information for them that they don't already know. Chief Fry is now on the premises, back from King Road. He and Tyson Berrett sit with the family in a conference room.

The chief is instantly struck by the strength and grace of both Stacy, a statuesque woman with long blond hair, and Jim, her quieter, kind-eyed husband who is dependably by her side, not in front, not behind, but right there next to her.

The worst part of this job is having to deliver news like this to families, and yet Fry is often impressed by the dignity and resilience of the parents and siblings he's gotten to know, some of whom he has forged close relationships with.

Stacy Chapin is special. He can see that. Even now, she's expressing concern about his team, about what they are going through, and offering her support.

He tells her that they will find whoever did this.

He's appointed Captain Tyson Berrett to be the Chapins' point person. They should call him whenever they want, and he will call them every day.

But now?

Strangely, there's nothing for the Chapins to do except go home. And wait.

But they aren't going to drive back home tonight. Jim has already been at the wheel for almost twenty hours straight. So the family heads to the Best Western hotel, where the university has booked a block of rooms.

In the lobby they encounter Emily, Hunter Johnson, Dylan, Bethany, Josie, Linden, and Ava, all huddled together, exhausted.

Stacy hugs all of them, noticing immediately that Hunter Johnson and Emily are clearly in shock. Hunter Johnson can scarcely speak.

"Are you guys all right?" she asks, knowing they are not.

She asks if she can bring them food, water, blankets.

She knows Emily and Hunter Johnson well, and in the absence of their own parents, she steps in. Her years as a school principal have taught her a thing or two about mental health, and she can see that Hunter has been especially traumatized and will need counseling.

She's going to make sure that he gets it; she offers up there and then the same team in Moscow that the police have provided to help Maizie and her own son Hunter, a gesture that strikes everyone as remarkable, given what she herself must be going through.

In the coming days, weeks, and months, many people will marvel at Stacy Chapin's bandwidth and compassion for others in the face of personal tragedy.

Stacy herself will later say that of course she checked on the kids and their families. What else could she have done?

Deep inside, she's lost. But she knows that now, more than ever, she's needed as a mom.

She's always been everyone's backbone. And she's not going to stop now.

*   *   *

In Emily's hotel room, the friends huddle together. They are terrified but also reassured when they hear sirens going on and off all through the night, the police cars circling.

Bethany is withdrawn and quiet, but the rest of them take turns talking.

Dylan, especially, is in full flow, reliving what she thinks she saw the night before.

She realizes that the man she thought was a firefighter must have been the murderer. So why did he walk away from her? They'd made eye contact.

If he was after Maddie or Kaylee, why did he kill Xana and Ethan?

Had he been upstairs all along?

Dylan thinks maybe he was. But how did he get in?

The lock on the back sliding door is broken. Until now, that was quite useful, because their parents and friends knew how to get into the house if they didn't have the code to the front door.

But how did *he* know that?

Emily asks what Dylan did after she saw the killer.

Dylan explains that she raced into Bethany's room and slept there. She says she was scared, yes, but she hadn't wanted to trust her own instincts.

Emily doesn't blame Dylan for telling herself at the time that she was drunk, tired, crazy, hallucinating. But she can see that Dylan—Bethany too—is likely headed into a shitstorm of pointed fingers for not calling the cops sooner.

Emily doesn't blame her Little for bolting herself in with Bethany and falling asleep. She, too, would likely have second-guessed herself in the same situation.

Her maternal, protective instincts kicking in yet again, she decides she's going to do her best to defend Dylan in the coming days.

People come and go at all hours at 1122 King Road, she later explains. "Your first reaction if you see someone at four a.m. just isn't going to be

Oh, here's a guy who has come to murder us. Common sense tells you, *Oh, it's just someone visiting."*

But common sense is an approach this group has now dispensed with.

Over the next days and months, all they will feel at night, in the dark, is fear bordering on terror, wondering who is out there—and if he is coming for them next.

Chapter 59

It's around four or five a.m., pitch-black outside, but the Chapin parents don't even try to sleep. They just lie on the bed and watch as Hunter and Maizie finally pass out from exhaustion. Eventually, Stacy gets up.

She wants to go for a walk. She needs to do something.

Jim immediately says he'll come with her. He wouldn't dream of leaving his wife alone in this moment.

It's freezing, and they are bundled up. For once this couple doesn't speak. There's no need. They simply stride.

They exit their hotel and head north, toward the water tower and the Kibbie Dome. Past the golf course that Ethan so loved and the arboretum where he went for runs.

They go to the Sig Chi house, like they often do, expecting to be able to turn the doorknob, go in, walk through the house, and go back across the Lower 40.

But the door is now locked. So they walk around the place.

And somehow, Stacy doesn't remember how, they wind up standing outside the King Road house.

All the cars and law enforcement officers—they are gone.

There's just one cop standing in front. It's eerily silent.

Were it not for the yellow tape, one wouldn't know anything had happened here.

"My son is still inside the house," Stacy says to the officer, who isn't sure how to react. In fact, the bodies are no longer there. They've been taken to Spokane to be autopsied. But Stacy doesn't know this. "I just wanted to see it. I don't know."

There, with the first light streaking the sky, as Stacy holds Jim's hand, she realizes this is it.

This is goodbye to her beloved elder boy, a prince of a young man.

Chapter 60

Rathdrum, Idaho
November 14, 2022

It's completely dark when Jack DuCoeur arrives at the Goncalves ranch house at around nine p.m.

Jack knocks on the door, crying, and when Steve opens it, he is business first.

"Jack, I gotta ask you to roll up your sleeves. I hate to do this, but I've got to do it."

The kid shows him his arms, wrists, and hands. Nothing. No scratches. Nothing that would indicate that twenty-four hours earlier, he was wielding the huge knife that killed Kaylee.

They hug.

Jack walks the family through everything he knows at this point. He shows them his phone and all the missed phone calls in the early hours of Sunday morning.

He thinks he might burst.

He was asleep. Asleep! If only he'd woken up, if only he'd answered, Kaylee and Maddie might still be . . . he breaks down.

Steve tells him not to go there. There was nothing anyone could have done.

Kaylee and Maddie had done everything right. They'd gotten a sober person to drive them home, then they'd gone upstairs to sleep.

No one could have done a damn thing against someone with a knife in the bedroom.

Steve doesn't want to think about what terror his daughter, or Maddie, might have experienced.

He will later say that the pain is like a splinter that's wedged deep beneath the surface of the skin. It hurts all the more because he feels as if someone should help remove it.

But so far there's no one out there helping him or his family. At least no one official.

What option does that leave him other than taking matters into his own hands?

Chapter 61

Moscow, Idaho
November 14, 2022

J im and Stacy Chapin continue their walk in the new, cold dawn.
They pass by the Sig Chi house again. At the gate on Nez Perce
Drive, they stop, shocked by what they see in the parking lot.

The brothers are leaving the house en masse, flocking like birds
caught in the winter snow rushing to head south. When they spot the
Chapins, they put down the belongings they're clutching. One by one,
the brothers hug them as if their lives depend on it.

Everyone here knows Stacy and Jim, because Ethan and Hunter were
the lifeblood of the house. Even when Ethan was barred from living on the
premises, he'd made a point of showing up to help with recruitment during
Rush Week, working harder, putting in longer hours, than any of them.

For the worst of reasons, the dean has cleared campus. Though Thanksgiving break, to which they have all been looking forward, is coming early,
none of them has any idea what the future holds—or if they'll ever return
to this house, to this school.

"Their moms had called them home," Stacy later said. "They were broken, all of them."

This moment of togetherness, of solidarity in the face of fear and shock, is a foreshadowing of the way Stacy Chapin will handle the loss of her son in the weeks and months to come.

She will fight to unite the living when she cannot bring back the dead.

That morning, early, it isn't just the Sig Chi brothers who are packing up. There is a mass exodus out of Moscow despite the snowstorm that is descending.

The kids who were hunkered down in the Best Western all go home. Classes are canceled. Anyone who can leave, does.

Stacy and Jim go back to the hotel.

They, Maizie, and Hunter pile into the Chevy Tahoe and begin the winding two-and-a-half-hour drive up the hills to their second home in Priest Lake. Thanksgiving is always their last visit of the year to this house. The weather makes it too dangerous to get here in the freezing months.

Even now, it's hairy. Snow is blanketing the roads, and it's not clear what's streaming more, the white flakes outside or the tears rolling down the faces of the car's passengers.

Jim later can only remember that his mind was anywhere but on the road.

Just outside of Coeur d'Alene, before the steep climb up into the mountains, they hear sirens. Of all things, they are being pulled over.

Jim rolls down the window when the state patrolman approaches.

"It was our son that was one of the kids who was killed," he says.

The officer blinks. "I'm so sorry," he says. There's no mention of whatever driving infraction Jim might have committed. "Just get there safely," he tells Jim.

Stacy is taken aback.

("It was a profound moment for all of us," she later said. A reminder that there was good in the world and that they needed to focus on the living.)

Jim grips the steering wheel. And starts the engine.

They head on up, up into the mountains, to be alone with their grief.

Chapter 62

Moscow, Idaho
November 14, 2022

Canceling classes for the rest of that week doesn't prove to be straightforward.

Provost Torrey Lawrence canvasses his senior administrators, including dean of students Blaine Eckles and the head of the faculty senate, Kelly Quinnett, before making the decision that classes will be offered remotely—but also optionally—all the way through Thanksgiving.

Quinnett is the outspoken head of the drama department, and her husband, Brian, has already started a new routine of walking her down the ten-foot garden path from her office to her car. Quinnett doesn't hesitate before rendering her opinion: *Of course* students shouldn't have to show up to class in the wake of a trauma like this. A number of the parents agree. They want the school to cancel classes all the way to Christmas.

But Eckles is worried that a large number of students, who have already paid for their housing, don't have the ability to go anywhere else. He's concerned that those students, especially the ones who never met Xana, Ethan, Maddie, and Kaylee, might blame the university for depriving them of the education they have already paid for.

One of these unlucky students is Alex Salvador, a recruited tennis star from Spain.

When not attending classes, Alex divides his time between practicing on the UI courts and traveling to intercollegiate matches. The serious athletes at UI don't have the time or desire to join Greek life, effectively separating their campus experiences from that of the party kids.

But now, Alex and three tennis teammates—all on scholarships, all from Europe—are holed up in their shared apartment just three minutes from the King Road house. They'd once or twice fleetingly dropped in at parties there, but now they can think of little else but the gruesome fate of the four victims.

"Then it really hit me," Alex said.

As the town empties of the students who can easily drive home, Alex and his roommates find themselves confined indoors once the sun goes down, at around four p.m. They each buy handguns. Lock their door. And spend sleepless nights mostly peering out of their windows into the darkness, seeing just the blue lights of police cars endlessly circling the streets.

No one wants to venture onto streets where a murderer might be lurking.

"We were not safe there," Alex said, then refined his words: "We *thought* we were not safe."

Fear isn't the only emotion they feel. They are confused by seemingly conflicting directions from the administration: They can take their classes remotely, but in some cases, people don't have to take them at all.

As Alex reflected, "It was a mess."

A stone's throw from Alex and his roommates, Ben DeWitt, who had been in Xana's high-school class, is also staying put. As a features writer for the *Argonaut,* DeWitt has work to do.

Like many University of Idaho kids his age, he packs heat. He knows that it's legal to conceal and carry in Idaho—just not on campus. Even though he has a gun, DeWitt pushes his couch against his apartment door at night. An extra precaution.

Over in Pullman, Evan Ellis is in his studio by himself during a commercial break from his broadcasting. A hard-bitten journalist, he still locks the studio door.

"I've never done that before," he said. "That's how uneasy it was. I had this weird gut feeling, and I came to this realization: What if this animal is still here?"

Doug Wilson, the gray-bearded pastor of Christ Church, a conservative evangelical congregation of around three thousand, goes to get his car keys fixed and learns the local locksmith is overwhelmed.

"The guy told me that people who never locked their doors were coming in and ordering locks installed," he said.

Wilson is used to being treated with some hostility by his neighbors, but even he has never experienced a mass panic like this.

Dr. Rand Walker, a trusted local therapist whom Chief Fry has put on standby to treat his traumatized officers and their families, is observing rare and frightening instances of the six-degrees-of-separation connections among the town's residents. The fact that everyone in Moscow knows everyone else has morphed overnight from a source of comfort to something deeply unsettling. Neighbor suddenly mistrusts neighbor. Friend mistrusts friend. Customer mistrusts vendor. People are shutting themselves in. Hiding from one another.

Walker is hearing from his patients, from townspeople, from members of his own family, that suddenly the connectivity between them all feels toxic. Walker's son Kristian, a former UI student, knew the victims. His girlfriend is the daughter of the owner of the Mad Greek, where Xana and Maddie worked. Now the restaurant is closed, and a handwritten placard is in the window:

We are closed temporarily to mourn the loss of two staff members. We will update FB on status of store soon. Please keep all the family and friends of yesterday's victims in your thoughts. —MG Family

It's all too close to feel comfortable. Because who knows who among them is the murderer?

For Jeff "Smitty" Smith, the owner of Moscow Bagel and Deli, the sudden emptiness has an immediate economic consequence. His customer base is almost entirely wiped out days earlier than he budgeted for.

His girlfriend, Sarah Wicks, the owner of Vine wine bar, has a slightly different problem, one she shares with Marc Trivelpiece, her close friend and the owner of the Corner Club: They don't think it's fair to ask employees to work alone behind a bar at night. Who knows who might show up or approach them outside in the dark while they walk to their cars?

Trivelpiece solves this by taking on all the shifts himself. He tells his remaining student workers—a dozen or so have already gone home—to stay away. He's got their backs.

* * *

Local lawyer Mike Pattinson's chief concern is his twenty-two-year-old daughter, Lexi, who lives in an apartment at the Bricks, barely fifty yards from 1122 King Road. She lives so close that some of her neighbors reported to police that at around four a.m. on November 13, they heard a scream. They were interviewed down at the police station.

Lexi had been in APhi and found Kaylee to be a generous, thoughtful sister—a "bright personality" Lexi liked so much that the two roomed together during their second semester. They wound up becoming neighbors in their senior year.

Whenever Murphy the pooch wandered into Lexi's apartment, she returned the goldendoodle to Kaylee. Most evenings Lexi walked past the back of the King Road home to get to her car in the parking lot and saw Maddie through her window, putting on her makeup at her vanity. And just a few days before the murders, Lexi played beer pong with Xana, who, dressed in a yellow jumpsuit, was dancing and hugging every person who walked into the room.

So Lexi is badly shaken.

Her boyfriend puts his hunting rifle under the bed.

Her father tells her to get out of that apartment and come home immediately.

Pattinson has faith in Chief Fry's ability to catch whoever did this. He bets that when the cops get the perpetrator, they'll find a fraternity rivalry or some equally simple motive behind the murders.

But he's worried that the timing of this—right before Thanksgiving—and the brutality of the murders are going to take the cops into a media storm they've never seen before. He's not at all sure that the chief is trained for *that* part. And he's worried about Bill Thompson, who is in the twilight of his career and doesn't get a homicide every day. Certainly not a mass homicide. *He may have to trim that beard a bit for prime time,* Pattinson thinks cynically.

Meanwhile, though, he's genuinely scared of who is out there, just like everyone else.

For the first time in his twenty-plus years of marriage, he does not tease his wife, Marcela, when she bolts the door at night. He's always told her to relax, that she's not living in her native Colombia. "Honey, this is not South America, it's Moscow," he's often said.

He doesn't say it anymore.

Whoever did this is the sick person who skinned the dog.

Claire Qualls, a twenty-year-old student and first responder, was driving back to Moscow from Spokane when she got the alert. *No big deal,* she thought about the 911 alert that all the EMT volunteers get.

Until the news started ricocheting around about the four murders.

Today, she's haunted by them.

Her cousin was close friends with Ethan. And 1122 King Road is just two blocks from her basement apartment, which is at the bottom of a dark set of covered stairs, in what is generally considered the shittiest neighborhood in all of Moscow.

Every time Claire comes home, her thoughts turn dark.

She'll walk down those steps, and he'll attack her, and she'll hit her head on the concrete, and no one will see her lying there, dying...

Claire has never wanted a gun. She doesn't know how to use one, and as a trained first responder, she knows the statistics: The majority of firearm deaths are caused by accidents in the home.

Now, though, she's going to go buy a handgun and she'll ask Katie, her roommate, to teach her how to use it. And her dad is going to come and replace her cheap window that can easily be opened from the outside with a better one.

He and her mom want her to move home. But Claire doesn't want to.

She's not sure their home is any safer.

She's certain that whoever committed the murders is the same sick fuck who skinned her parents' neighbors' dog.

Two nights before the murders, the animal, a pet of close family friends, had been running around in the backyard as usual, but then it had not appeared indoors to eat. Unusual.

The next morning it was found—skinned. In a hunting community, skinning wild beasts is not uncommon. But a pet dog?

Claire shivers.

She's going to get a personal safety alarm and clip it on her backpack and keep it next to her at night. To activate it, you don't need to press a button. You simply pull it apart and it goes off, and its piercing sound rings out until it's put back together.

That way, Claire figures she'll have a fighting chance if someone attacks her on the stairs or in her bed.

Without an alarm, she thinks, poor Maddie, Kaylee, Xana, and Ethan didn't stand a chance.

Chapter 63

Moscow, Idaho
November 14, 2022

It's eight o'clock on Monday morning, not quite twenty-four hours since that first ominous 911 call. The police chief is sitting in his corner office at the station on Southview Avenue talking to Tyson Berrett, getting up to speed on where things stand.

Berrett says he's spoken to Blaine Eckles and asked him to pass on anything that could be useful.

Thus begins a pattern: Twice a day, Eckles passes on details about the four victims — their clubs, classes, professors — to the university general counsel, who passes them on to Berrett. There has to be a wall between them for all sorts of reasons, including protecting students' privacy.

Both Chief Fry and Captain Berrett know they must not tell Eckles — or anyone who doesn't need to know — how the victims died. It's imperative that no one has any inkling of that until after the knife sheath has been properly photographed, analyzed, and sent off to the labs to check for trace DNA.

Privately, the chief grouses when he hears that the university has released the kids to go home. Inadvertently, they've made the cops' lives so much harder.

Officer Dani Vargas is known to be one heck of an interviewer, and yesterday she, Lawrence Mowery, Mitch Nunes, and John Lawrence got the best they could out of those poor, shocked kids, the friends of the victims, before they checked out of the Best Western. But there's not much point in having a great interviewer in Moscow if the students you need to question are en route to, say, Florida or Texas.

Fry and his team are still trying to get their arms around what they've got at the crime scene.

The Idaho State Police has a crack team of forensic lab rats, and they're headed over now from Meridian, a five-hour drive away. Their mandate is to go over all the evidence for a second time before it's scooped up and shipped off for processing. No one wants any fuckups.

It will take serious manpower and a vast network to sift through it all.

People assume that technology makes a cop's life easier. In some ways, it does. But it might take a whole day just to download the contents of the kids' phones; simply deciphering the data is going to take hours, days, maybe weeks.

Fry looks down at his laptop and sees the sticky-note reminder from the receptionist.

Call back the FBI.

Fry knows he needs to call the feds in. In fact, he'll be screwed if he doesn't, given the mass exodus from Moscow already underway. He'll need the FBI's extra manpower and nationwide reach—and who knows what else.

The nearest Bureau field office is up in Coeur d'Alene, near the homes of Maddie's and Kaylee's families. Fry prides himself on having built up great relationships with both the ISP—the Idaho State Police—and the local federal agents. That doesn't always happen, especially not in big cities like LA and Chicago, where, infamously, pride and testosterone can cause unhelpful friction between the local and federal arms of law enforcement.

One of Fry's federal contacts, Lance Hart out of ATF (Bureau of Alcohol, Tobacco, Firearms, and Explosives), had found him an accelerant-detection dog to help solve the Silas Parks case. Five years later, in the immediate aftermath of the John Lee shootings, Hart was ready to help. "I hear the water down there is tainted again," the guy joshed. "What do you need?" What Fry needed was a ballistics analysis. "Send us the stuff," Hart said. And up it went so the deadly bullets could be analyzed and submitted into evidence. It's a pity, the chief thinks, that Hart is now retired.

Yesterday, Fry saw a guy in an FBI jacket at the King Road crime scene, probably there at the invitation of the ISP, he assumed. It wasn't one of the guys he knew well.

As it happens, that same agent is now standing in the briefing room at the police station with the lead from State, ready for the eight a.m. meeting.

"We've been trying to get ahold of you," the agent says.

"I know," says Fry. "I've been a little busy."

"Need us to come in?"

Both men understand the protocol. The FBI cannot officially assist on a case unless the local police chief explicitly asks them to.

"Yes," says Fry. "And fast."

And with that, the FBI special agent in charge calls his boss, the regional special agent in charge, and the government machinery clicks into gear. The scale and speed of it deserves respect.

In Salt Lake City, Utah, and elsewhere around the country, an operation begins to unfold. Fry imagines dozens of agents leaping onto planes that will bring them to Moscow, Idaho.

In the station briefing room, Fry and Bill Thompson are technically the bosses, but right now they're staying out of the way as three law enforcement representatives—one from the Moscow PD, one from the ISP, one from the FBI—stand at a whiteboard.

With the FBI, the task force is now composed of approximately forty-five law enforcement officers from local, state, and federal agencies. It's a tight squeeze, with a few folks standing at the back, but all eyes are forward as the leads divide them into teams:

Victimology. The officers on this team will assemble a profile of each victim by reaching out to family, friends, boyfriends, girlfriends, teachers—anyone who can tell them who Xana, Kaylee, Maddie, and Ethan were over the past two years. As the adage goes, "In order to know how a person died, you first need to know how they lived."

Interviewers. Detectives Vargas, Lawrence, Mowery, Payne, and others on this team will reach out and interview anyone who was near the scene of the crime, any possible witness.

Forensics. Fry still doesn't know *how* the guys on this team do what they do, but he knows *what* they are capable of doing: sifting through cell phone data, putting together DNA profiles, analyzing prints and blood.

Videos and local CCTV. Some camera somewhere must have caught something. The analysts on this team know what they're looking for.

Tip management. This team will handle the calls that are starting to come in on the phone number listed in yesterday's press release, all of which need to be answered and documented.

Note-taking. This team will keep a record of assignments, progress, and to-do lists.

No one complains about where they are assigned, setting a tenor that Fry will later point to with pride. The absence of agency infighting is extraordinary in an investigation of this complexity and significance.

Brett Payne is the Moscow PD leader in front of the whiteboard; he scribbles down names from his department. Payne, whose hair is tightly cropped, reminding the room of his former military career, is short, just over five feet, wiry, and tattooed. Payne may be young, but he's whip-smart. Fry hired him in 2020 because he has the talent to be an extraordinary investigator. He's good with details. And *very* good at getting information out of people. Every good detective possesses "the gift of the gab," as Fry refers to this key skill. But more than that, a good detective needs to be wily like a fox.

Payne will do very well, the chief thinks as he watches him dole out responsibilities.

Even so, this job is going to be the challenge of his career. Of all their careers.

Braggadocio is not Fry's style, but there's no disputing that the chief himself is a damned good investigator. One time he got a written confession out of a pedophile because he suggested, convincingly, that the guy might feel better if he wrote an apology letter to his teenage victims.

Before the first full meeting wraps up, Payne lays out the structure of the investigation. At eight a.m. daily, assignments will be made. Then at around five or six p.m., they'll regroup. The team leaders want to hear status reports from everyone in the room. No detail is to be held back.

After the briefing ends and they all head off, Fry calls in one of his captains. Anthony Dahlinger is an experienced officer and the likeliest to succeed Fry as chief. When Fry double-checks on whether Dahlinger is comfortable taking on the role of public information officer, the captain says of course, even though this is not an area he's had training in.

As busy as he's been, Fry would have to have been blind not to notice the hordes of press assembling in Moscow. They cram into the area around the King Road house like bees around a hive. His inbox is blowing up with media requests.

Fry ignores them all for now.

He is well aware that anything the police put out in the media, they are putting out to the suspect as well—and to a potential jury pool. The biggest mistake a police chief or sheriff can make, Fry believes, is to overshare.

Yet it happens all the time.

In 2017, the state police superintendent spoke during his press conferences directly to whoever had killed two teenage girls in Delphi, Indiana. Fry found this tactic inappropriate and possibly damaging to the case and vows to do things differently.

Fry shakes his head and goes back to work. He'll get to the press when he's ready. They want a story, but they will have to wait.

He's got an investigation to run.

Chapter 64

Moscow, Idaho
November 14, 2022

"Someone in a uniform needs to get in front of a mic, now!"

Art Bettge, Moscow's mayor of just eleven months and two weeks, can scarcely believe he's having this conversation — this *fight* — with the city supervisors. And with Bill Thompson, who was his neighbor for twenty years. And with James Fry.

How the heck has a former USDA biochemist with expertise in local agriculture found himself arguing about the need for law enforcement to handle the swarm of press in Moscow? He has never thought much about the business of the Moscow Police Department beyond looking at its budgets.

This is *not* what he's trained for or what he anticipated when he ran for mayor. He was elected on two main civic concerns: repairing Moscow's roads and infrastructure in the face of state legislative budget cuts and locating a new water source for the town before its aquifer runs dry. "I can talk your ear off about wheat," Bettge later said. "But I'm not good at standing up in front of the press."

But now he's found himself in the middle of complete public chaos. There are helicopters hovering overhead, sniffer dogs on the college campus. Even a biochemist can see this situation could be ruinous to his beloved town.

"We look ridiculous," he says to Thompson. He points out that all the police have said publicly is that there is no threat—yet the place appears to be overrun with "cartoon security."

The public is getting impatient, as are some of the victims' families. And the press is taking notice. "The lack of information" about the case, wrote reporter Katie Kloppenburg for Boise State Public Radio on November 15, "has frustrated people who say the community needs more specific answers."

The mayor doesn't doubt that the chief and county prosecutor will bring whoever did this to justice. He knows how good they are at their jobs.

But right now, Moscow has a public-perception problem. And a safety problem. Crazy rumors—including one about a Colombian drug cartel being involved in the murders—are running rampant. As Moscow's number one public official, Bettge cannot just ignore this. It's a great irony that last week he signed off on the wording for a recruitment ad for a crisis communications adviser. But it hasn't yet been posted.

So he keeps phoning, pestering people, barging into meetings of the city supervisors and yelling. And he keeps demanding the same thing.

He wants a guy in uniform to say something that sounds clarifying or at least slightly reassuring into a mic.

But Bill Thompson and Chief Fry won't budge. Thompson even warns: "Don't say anything, Art. You'll misspeak and mess everything up. You aren't trained for this."

The city supervisors are telling Bettge the same thing. Ordering him, even, not to speak.

And yet everyone, including the *New York Times*, is reaching out to him for comment. And Bettge is the mayor.

He needs to make a call. He needs to say *something*. He needs to assure people they can walk around safely, albeit cautiously, which is what Fry and Thompson seem to think. But they want to take their time saying it.

Time is what they don't have.

The *New York Times,* he thinks, is surely a safe place to give an interview. And so he does it. He's careful. He gives context.

But in the article, the context has disappeared, and there's just one startling takeaway:

> MOSCOW, Idaho — Four students at the University of Idaho were found dead near campus in what a local official described on Monday as a "crime of passion."
>
> Art Bettge, the mayor of Moscow, Idaho, said in an interview that the authorities were still investigating what had transpired but that the case was being treated as a homicide. He said the authorities did not believe that there was a "perceivable danger to the broader public," but he declined to say how the victims had been killed or whether a suspect was at large.
>
> "With a crime of this magnitude, it's very difficult to work through," Mr. Bettge said, adding that the police needed time to piece together what had transpired. "The overall assessment is that it's a crime of passion," he said.

Oh God, Bettge thinks when he reads it.

A crime of passion? He knows immediately that, far from soothing people, this could fan the flames of the rumor bonfire. He's achieved the exact opposite of his objective.

"I developed a great dislike for national media very rapidly," he said of that experience. "I tend to talk in paragraphs and they lift bits out of the middle of paragraphs, those sons of bitches."

Art Bettge correctly guesses what the reaction of Bill Thompson and James Fry will be.

The police chief calls up the city supervisor and tells him, "Could you please tell the mayor not to talk? Or I will—and it would be better coming from you."

Chapter 65

Pullman, Washington
November 14, 2022

T*hey've got to say something… They've got to say something… They're looking incompetent…*

Evan Ellis isn't just working his sources; he's watching the coverage of them.

It's not good.

A TV segment on the evening of November 14 from reporter Rania Kaur on Spokane–Coeur d'Alene KXLY Channel 4 is typical:

"At the home where the students were killed, a bouquet of flowers rests on a rock right at the front. Joanna Perez was among the students who dropped off a bouquet and teddy bear at one of the memorials," Kaur said.

Perez said that Ethan was in the same college program as she was. "He was kind of, like, in some of my classes. And some of my friends knew him so it just kind of hit close," she said.

"As Moscow police continue their investigation," Kaur said, "Perez is grappling with what happened."

"It's just, like, scary and frustrating," the student said, "because we want, like, answers to what happened, but they're holding back a lot of information from us."

Ellis dials Thompson for the umpteenth time.

For once, the prosecutor picks up.

"Bill, you've got to get ahead of this. You've got to say something. You've got to give a press conference. It's coming down hard."

Thompson is calm. "I know. We're working on it."

That in itself is shocking to the reporter. In thirty years, Bill Thompson has never made any public remarks about an investigation until it was over.

Ellis pushes on, asking the pertinent question that *everyone* is asking.

"Can you explain to me how we're supposed to say there's no threat to the public when obviously you haven't arrested anyone?"

Thompson is still calm. "I can't explain that right now. But there isn't." The prosecutor pauses. "You just have to trust me."

The reporter is frustrated. "Bill, you can understand how this doesn't seem to make sense."

"I understand. I understand your frustration, but I can't explain it to you either off the record or on the record."

Ellis knows the prosecutor well enough not to push this any further. He understands that Thompson has his reasons for everything he does.

But all the other journalists racing into Moscow from New York and everywhere else, spilling out of the Best Western, the Monarch, and the Hattabaugh hotels—they don't know these people the way Ellis does.

They don't know a damn thing about this place.

It would be easy for an outsider to underestimate Bill Thompson just by his appearance. At first glance, he has the look of an old-fashioned gold prospector.

Ellis is worrying about more than simply getting this story. He starts to wonder about whether the story has the potential to destroy the very people who ought to be driving it.

If the prosecutor or the police chief doesn't speak quickly, other people—people who know nothing—will create an alternative narrative. What happens if the public starts to *believe* the wrong narrative? If they start to feel the prosecutor and the chief don't know what they are doing?

Ellis shakes his head.

That would be a very bad outcome indeed.

Chapter 66

Rathdrum, Idaho
November 15, 2022

Alivea Goncalves is sitting in the home office the family calls the "yellow room" at her parents' ranch house in Rathdrum, Idaho, hunched over her laptop. The shelves are piled higgledy-piggledy with boxes.

She keeps looking impatiently at the clock.

What's the holdup?

It's now the afternoon after she got to her parents' house, and two days after the police knocked on their door and delivered the chilling news of Kaylee's murder but absolutely no details. She had walked in feeling like she was already behind.

Jack DuCoeur is sitting with her parents, clearly in shock. She feels terrible for him and not just because of the shock. She knows he'd never hurt Kaylee, but there's nasty speculation about him flying around on social media. Some people are suggesting that drugs were involved and that Kaylee and her friends deserved to be murdered. Alivea wants to do whatever she can to put an end to this narrative. She wants to tell the world that they were good kids, that they'd done everything right, and that she can feel in her gut that whoever did this was unknown to them.

Her parents still don't have a contact at the Moscow Police Department, so at around noon Alivea had gotten hold of a detective, Lawrence Mowery; he'd asked her to put all her findings from Kaylee's call log into a secure electronic file and send it, which she did.

Alivea expected the police to take a little time to verify it all, but she can't understand why it's now hours later and not only are the police saying nothing about the information she gave them, but they are still putting out the wrong time that Kaylee and Maddie returned to the King Road house. "It diminished us," she later said.

Time, Alivea knows, is of the essence in murder investigations. It'd be good for the public to know the details of Kaylee's last hours so they can start phoning in tips. It would also be good if the police shared anything they knew about what happened to Kaylee with the family, but the Goncalveses are just as much in the dark now as they were two days ago. It's beginning to feel as if the family is being iced out. And it's also starting to feel like the only person bringing in information is Alivea.

Alivea particularly hoped that the police would publish the video she'd found on Twitch of Kaylee and Maddie ordering food at the Grub Truck.

The video shows her sister standing on the sidewalk at around 1:30 a.m., Maddie beside her. Speaking slowly and haltingly, Kaylee orders: "I think I would like the...um...the...carbonara."

On the video, Alivea noticed a group of guys standing behind the girls, chatting, and another group off to the side. Maddie recognizes one of the latter, wanders over, and embraces him affectionately.

But in the group behind them, one of the guys, whose face is obscured by the light gray hoodie he's wearing, seems to be watching the two girls quietly.

And when Kaylee and Maddie walk off to get in their rideshare, he breaks away from his friends and goes after them. It's not clear from the video footage why.

Alivea has already discovered who "Hoodie Guy" is. He's called Jack Showalter, and he is in the same fraternity as Jack DuCoeur.

She's told the police this and she's hoping they will post it to get answers from anyone who saw the girls and the group they were with that night.

So again she looks at the time. Afternoon is turning into evening.

Why isn't the video up on the Moscow PD Facebook page yet?

She hits refresh again. Still nothing.

She knows that the police need to protect the investigation. Of course she does.

She understands how police investigations are run and how the media works. But the more people out there looking for this murderer, the quicker he — she feels it's a he — can be found and brought to justice. So she's frustrated.

And then someone — it takes her a while to learn it's the mayor of Moscow — gives an interview calling what happened a crime of passion.

For Alivea, this is a tipping point. It presents a completely misleading picture of Kaylee and her friends.

She is not going to sit idly by while all this misinformation gets out there and while the police continue to tell her family nothing.

By early evening, Alivea makes a decision. It's time to take control of the narrative. It's time to tell the public who Kaylee really was, and it's time to spur the public into action to help find the killer.

She's going to start talking to the press.

The first interview she does is with Hayley Guenthner, a local TV reporter for an NBC affiliate station in Spokane. Seated in her parents' living room on their black leather sofa, her face white with tiredness, Robbie by her side, Alivea makes a direct plea for the public's help.

"I would say if you know anything, if you think anything, if you heard anything, if you saw anything, just call it in," she says. "I know it's important to protect family. It's important to protect friends. And I know that those ties of loyalty are strong, but you should be scared. And this isn't someone that should be protected. So if you noticed odd behavior, if you noticed something in the shared bathroom trash can, if you noticed a weird smudge on the fridge after your roommate came home late, call it in. Any injuries, anything at all. Because, worst-case scenario, the police talk to them and they get to go home. If they have nothing to hide, then you just did your job. Call it in anonymously."

She feels better afterward. She's doing her part; she's upset that the police don't seem to be doing theirs. It feels too slow, too little, too late. "If I can't sleep at night, how can you, Chief Fry?" she asks herself rhetorically. She wants people to know how frustrated she and her family are.

So she speaks to Steven Fabian of *Inside Edition,* airing her vexation with the police. "We're not getting any answers, and we're *not* going to settle for that."

Chapter 67

Priest Lake, Idaho
November 15, 2022

Everywhere Stacy looks in the house at Priest Lake, she sees memories of her beloved dead son.

From the deck behind the kitchen at the back of the house, she can see the twelfth hole of the golf course. To the front, headed down a slope to the pond, is the thirteenth. How many times have she, Jim, and the kids roared with laughter coming over that hill, a few drinks worse for wear, mindful to aim their balls to the left side of the slope?

It's a tight-knit community out here, and everyone knew Ethan.

One of the neighbors affixed a cross to the front door, one of the many acts of kindness that will flood the Chapins in the next few days and weeks, none of which Stacy will forget.

In the afternoon, she and Jim head out into the snow for a walk, partly to catch their breath, but partly also to talk about how best to support Hunter and Maizie.

They are in the woods when their phones start to ring and ring with unknown callers.

Weird, Stacy thinks. She wouldn't have expected cell reception out here. But also, who, outside of family and law enforcement, wants them so badly?

It turns out that almost every news organization in the world wants them.

In the next hours and days, all four Chapins are besieged with voicemails, texts, DMs, and emails from journalists of every stripe.

Stacy later said: "It would be easier to list who did not contact us. Literally everybody. Everybody. Every news organization. CNN, Anderson Cooper, the *Today* show, *Good Morning America*...All of the Idaho stations...It was crazy."

They make a family decision: They won't talk to anyone.

It's a plus, they discover, that they bought the Priest Lake house relatively recently, because no one can find them in Idaho databases.

That night, Stacy and Jim lay awake again. One a.m.; two a.m.; three a.m. They check in with each other every hour, on the hour, and rise early to put on a pot of coffee and walk again.

The phones start ringing early, and not just with media. They get a call from the funeral home back in La Conner. Their friend Kirk Duffy runs it. He has a relationship with Cathy Mabbutt, the Latah County coroner.

He's on his way to Spokane, which is where Ethan's body has been taken for the autopsy.

He tells them they need to pick a date for Ethan's funeral service. Stacy and Jim choose the following Monday because that gives them enough time to be ready but also enough time for the students who come to get back to their families for Thanksgiving.

Maizie and Hunter still have their social media on, and Tuesday morning is when Stacy becomes aware of the rumors on TikTok in the wake of a new police press statement with information that an "edged weapon such as a knife" was used to kill her son and the other victims and that the weapon has not been located.

Social media is also rife with rumors that Ethan was part of a love triangle. Maybe drugs were involved. Maizie is so upset, she uninstalls TikTok from her phone.

It's in this moment that Stacy temporarily forgets her grief.

Instead, she feels a blazing anger. "I don't mind telling you, I went out of my fucking mind."

Nobody gets to defame Ethan. *Nobody* gets to speculate like this about her son. She doesn't know where this is coming from, but she's going to stop it.

Fortuitously, Priest Lake friends and neighbors Evelyn Allison, Ethan's ex-girlfriend, and her mother, Kim, who worked in broadcasting in Spokane, knock at the door.

Stacy asks Kim for help. She wants to call up one media organization and do one press interview, preferably with a local journalist whom they can trust.

A young woman named Conner Board at King Five, Seattle, is the journalist she selects.

Kim acts as director. She sets Stacy and Jim up in chairs in front of bookshelves in the living room and positions Stacy's laptop so that they all fit in the frame.

And the interview begins. It lasts around ten minutes. Stacy and Jim look alternately shell-shocked and tearful throughout as Board gently questions them about Ethan's love of sports and of people.

Through her grief Stacy is articulate and deliberate.

"It's important for us to get Ethan's story out," she says. "We don't really want anybody else representing him and it's hard to have people speaking on his behalf, so we think it's best for us to do this."

She continues, "I mean, the reason we've agreed to do this is there's some misinformation out there. And that's been hard for us and that's why we as a family talked about it and agreed to do this because the things that are being said are a hundred percent not true. There's not drugs involved. There's not some weird love triangle...All of the kids were just really good, great kids."

Not long after they are done, Stacy hears tires crunch on the driveway. It's Emily and Hunter Johnson. They've driven up from Post Falls, having spent the night with Hunter's mom.

They are clearly still in shock. Emily whispers that Hunter Johnson has not spoken for twenty-four hours.

Stacy phones Karen Alandt, Emily's mom, who is at the Alandt family condo in Mexico. "I just want you to know they are here and they are safe," she tells her.

But are they okay? Clearly not, Stacy thinks.

The young couple's plan is to fly to Mexico to join Emily's parents. Stacy is worried that isolation will worsen their trauma, not ease it.

This is a moment they all need the comfort of one another. That afternoon and evening, the group huddles in the living room, talking, remembering Ethan.

Hunter Johnson relaxes and, to Emily's relief, speaks. He and Hunter Chapin go down memory lane, at one point getting out their phones and comparing their text messages with Ethan on that last awful night.

Early that evening, the group drives down to Hill's Resort to find food. The team there has heard the news and welcomes them with open arms and group hugs. Stacy captures the moment on her iPhone.

She'll take all the comfort she can get.

She knows the coroner will call at any moment with details she doesn't really want to hear. Details as to how her son died.

She knows from Kirk that the autopsy is taking longer than expected.

It's possible that Ethan could be transported tomorrow, not today, from Spokane to Mount Vernon for his funeral service.

Her son will be on I-90, the same road that the family has to drive.

As she lies in bed that night, Stacy shudders, already worrying about tomorrow.

Pray to God, she thinks, *we don't wind up overtaking Kirk's white Suburban.* Other drivers won't know it, but she will:

It's Ethan's hearse.

Chapter 68

Moscow, Idaho
November 16, 2022

Chief Fry reads through his script one more time before heading to the podium in the police conference room.

He and Thompson have gone through the boundaries of what he *can* say again and again.

The key thing he is *not* going to tell the media (and, indirectly, the perpetrator) is that they've got the knife sheath found next to Maddie and that it has been booked into evidence and gone to a laboratory for analysis.

His job is to keep the mob happy.

So he puts his game face on and pats Bill Thompson on the back, and together they head into the room of panting press.

Chief Fry has never done a live press conference before, much less one in front of the national media. He makes sure the rest of the "PR team" is flanking him before he begins introductions. Beside him and Thompson are UI president Scott Green, provost and vice president Torrey Lawrence, Dean Blaine Eckles, Latah County sheriff Richie Skiles, Latah County chief deputy Tim Besst, and head of the ISP, Colonel Kedrick Wills.

Each one of them has been advised either by counsel or communications teams or both as to what to say and what not to say if questioned.

Eckles's wife, Shelley, begged him not to say something aggressive like *We are gonna get whoever did this.*

The assumption they are all going on is that the guy is watching.

Is it possible he's even in the room?

Evan Ellis is shocked to see Thompson up there. Bill Thompson *never* attends press conferences. Does the rest of the media realize the gravity of the situation that this implies? Ellis looks around at the stony faces. Probably not.

Fry begins the substance of his spiel, mangling the pronunciation of *Chapin* and *Goncalves.*

His news nugget is not really anything new. And he knows it. It's simply that the four victims were stabbed and that law enforcement hasn't found the weapon. There also appeared to be no forced entry into the home.

Fry confirms what everyone already knows. The ISP, FBI, and Latah County Sheriff's Office are all helping with the investigation.

Then he drops the powder keg in the room.

"We believe this was an isolated targeted attack on our victims. We do not have a suspect at this time, and that individual is still out there. We cannot say that there's no threat to the community, and as we have stated, please stay vigilant, report any suspicious activity, and be aware of your surroundings at all times."

He knows that come the Q and A session, there will be pandemonium.

And there is.

He gets the same question put four different ways from four different reporters.

"You guys have said repeatedly that there's no threat to the public," one of them says. "Why did you say that and why are you changing your mind?"

Fry rewords his answer four different ways, knowing as he does so that each one sounds worse than the one before.

The first: "In these cases, we take the totality of the things that we see and they're very dynamic, right? And they're very big and there's a lot of information and we try to take that information and some of what we can't share with you, correct. But we try to take that information, we try to make the best educated decision we can . . . so we at that time believed that there was not a threat."

The second: "Like I said, we took the information that we had at the time, but we do need to be aware the individual is still out there. We need to be vigilant."

The third: "Like I said, we take the totality of the situation. We try to make the best bit of information we can with everything that comes in, and then we make our decision off of that. So at this time, I'm not going to expand upon that."

The fourth: "We still believe it's a targeted attack, but the reality is, is there's still a person out there who committed four horrible, horrible crimes. So I think we got to go back to there is a threat out there still, possibly, we don't know."

It's brutal. He knows this is not going well. Understatement.

Over in Pullman, Mayor Glenn Johnson, who has a PhD in communications from WSU, watches and shakes his head. He says, "James is a nice guy; he got overwhelmed, I think."

When he hears about that, Fry thinks that the criticism is both fair and unfair.

Fry is just trying to do his job. And his job, until now, has been to catch the bad guys, not to feed stories to the press. But he's learning the hard way that, apparently, feeding stories to the press is now a major part of his job.

Irritatingly, there's the inevitable question about Art Bettge's statement.

"The mayor has called it a crime of passion. Is there any indication that that's true?"

"We're looking into every aspect of this. I'm not going to speculate whether it's one thing or another . . . "

His audience can see how uncomfortable he is. Worse, his audience isn't confined to this room. This is being beamed to TV screens around the country. His own mother is watching.

Someone brings up the Twitch video, mentioning that the Goncalves family has verified Maddie and Kaylee are in it.

Fry tries to sound a lot more patient than he feels.

"We are aware of that video and it has helped. It gives us a time and space where we know that two of our victims were, and that helps us a ton and we'll continue to follow up all leads that we can and continue to gather those."

And, inevitably, the questions about the two surviving roommates come thick and fast.

Why was there such a long delay before they called? Are they suspects? Then one reporter refers to them as witnesses.

They are now in dangerous territory, Fry knows. Bill Thompson will be bristling.

Protect the investigation. Protect the investigation.

"I don't think I ever said that they were witnesses. I said they were there."

When he gets the question about whether he's interviewing boyfriends, it almost comes as a relief. For once, he's got a strong answer.

"I will tell you, we are looking at everyone. Every tip we get, every lead we get, there's no one that we're not going to talk to. There's no one we're not going to interview. There's no one that we're not going to look into and we're going to do our due diligence. We're going to make sure that nothing goes unturned and that we do everything we can with the assistance of all the resources we have to get a final answer."

What Fry doesn't realize is that the country's true-crime internet mob will now take it upon themselves to "look into" anyone and everyone connected to each of the four victims, and those people will now have to deal with not only shock and grief but also an online onslaught of hate mail, trolling, and worse.

They will begin to fear not just the darkness of night but daylight and social media too. Some nutters will even accuse *Fry* of being the murderer. He's highly visible.

By the next afternoon, Chief Fry sees at least ten FBI agents scurrying around.

"Do I know you?" he asks when one of the female agents introduces herself.

"No, sir," she replies. "But I've seen you on TV."

Chapter 69

Puerto Aventuras, Mexico
November 18, 2022

Emily ought to feel relaxed by the azure water and the hot sun, but instead she's wired. She's glued to her phone.

Someone has texted her a link to a YouTube video on 4chan showing old TikToks of her and Hunter Johnson. The self-described internet sleuths are suggesting that Emily and Hunter committed the murders after some sort of drug deal went bad and then left the country.

She wonders how the heck anyone knows she's out of the country.

Then she realizes.

It must be someone who saw her Snapchat.

The night they got to Mexico, it was Hunter's birthday. They'd gone out for tall, strong margaritas. Emily had taken a selfie of the two of them, exhausted, hugging, their green drinks visible on the table. Without any context, it might have looked like a regular vacation pic. She'd posted it to Snapchat because she wanted Hunter to feel appreciated.

It backfired.

Immediately Emily makes her social media accounts private, something she never imagined she'd want to do. She'd never understood why people even bothered to have private accounts.

But now the dark corners of the internet are full of fingers pointed at the small group of friends who sat on the curb outside 1122 King Road on that Sunday. Commentators are guessing which of them committed the murders.

There's speculation about Emily and Hunter, Dylan, Bethany, Jack DuCoeur, *and* Jake Schriger, Maddie's boyfriend. And after the release of the Grub Truck video, there's speculation about the young man in the hooded sweatshirt who appeared to follow Maddie and Kaylee to their rideshare. Hoodie Guy is Jack Showalter. Emily learns that he's a Delt whom the older Pi Phis know.

Even Emily finds herself sucked into the grim guessing game about which of them might be the murderer.

She goes through the list:

Jake? Emily finds that super-hard to believe because he'd been texting them frantically, sounding panicked, when the friends were sitting outside the King Road house. She feels horrible that none of them responded.

Jack DuCoeur? No way. When he arrived at the King Road house, he was clearly as shocked as they were.

Hoodie Guy, Jack Showalter? Emily is hesitant to write him off because she doesn't really know him and some of the older Pi Phis have said that occasionally, when drunk, he can seem belligerent. And at least for now, there's no other strong potential suspect.

It's not Dylan or Bethany. So who?

Emily considers herself thick-skinned. She's never been the type of person to care what others say about her. But here in Mexico, thirty-seven hundred miles from Moscow, she's scared.

Truly terrified. Maybe the killer followed them here to her parents' house?

At night, in the dark, she clings to Hunter Johnson and keeps the bedroom light on. Neither of them walks anywhere alone after sundown.

"The one night of my college life that I wasn't with Xana, someone murdered her," she said.

Was that person trying to hurt *her?*

Is that person now stalking *her?*

Emily's mom, Karen, feels helpless watching the two young adults walk around like zombies, shells of the people they were just a week ago.

She can see that Hunter, mute for much of the trip, is still in the early stages of intense shock, while Emily is trying to mother Hunter, Dylan, Josie, Bethany, and Linden. That's her way of coping.

Karen regularly speaks to Jessica, Hunter's mom, wondering what they can do to put an end to the online bombardment. The advice they receive from Bill Thompson's office is simply not to engage.

But as every day passes, the speculation gets more lurid.

There are posts everywhere of old footage of Hunter wearing zip ties answering the door at 1122 King Road to police who'd been called about a noise complaint. This raises questions online as to whether he was into bondage.

Emily rolls her eyes at this. The truth is so prosaic if one isn't looking for anything salacious. Hunter answered the door to the cops at 1122 King Road because they were in the middle of a game of champagne shackles, and Hunter and Kaylee were the only members of the group of legal drinking age.

Another internet sleuth, Jonathan Lee Riches, makes a YouTube video suggesting that Xana's dad had put a lock on the King Road house's front door the week before the murders because he was worried that Emily threw wild parties there. Emily, it's suggested, is someone the police are looking at as the possible murderer.

In fact, Xana's dad never put a lock on the door of the King Road house.

At her wit's end, Hunter's mom, Jessica, phones Chief Fry.

"Please," she says, "can you do something to stop this? Can you say publicly they aren't suspects?"

The next day, Fry gives a press conference. He states that the surviving roommates, all the others at the house that morning, the rideshare driver, and the man in the hooded sweatshirt seen outside the food truck are not being treated as suspects.

For twenty-four hours, there is a reprieve online.

But then it explodes again, even worse than before.

Emily and Karen think this is partly because the Goncalves family sat for a TV interview in which Kristi said that the police might have cleared people too quickly, and Steve appeared to agree. Karen and Emily understand that Steve and Kristi want to find the murderer, but they wish that hadn't been articulated.

It's the first time that the families affected most by the murders disagree as to what the right plan of action is to bring whoever did this to justice.

But it won't be the last.

Chapter 70

Chief Fry is looking at the TV in bewilderment.

He's watching Moscow's coroner, Cathy Mabbutt, his longtime friend and colleague, appearing via Zoom on yet another news program to discuss the autopsy findings.

Cathy, seventy-two, is a local wonder. On top of being the county coroner, she's a public defender *and* a nurse who has worked in the ER for sixteen years.

In 2015, when John Lee shot his mother and two others at an Arby's, she acted simultaneously as a nurse for the wounded and as a coroner. In 2005, when the Wells brothers murdered UI football player Eric McMillan, the judge asked (tongue in cheek) if she could be both their defense lawyer *and* their health-care provider.

She started as coroner back in 2006, and the job had a steep learning curve for the first six months—there were *seven* homicides in the county. On her very first call, she and Chief Fry examined a body that hadn't been found for three days. Fry smeared Vicks in and under his nose, an old cop trick to avoid the smell. But Cathy was a rookie; she didn't know the trick. Eventually, Cathy could bear it no longer and told him she couldn't focus because he had extremely large boogers hanging out of his nose.

So Cathy and Fry go way back. He knows that she knows what she's doing. She understands procedure.

And yet...here she is on national TV.

Fry said later that this was the moment he realized how truly big this story was, how impossible it was for everyone around him to avoid getting caught up in it. "They say when people riot, they don't even know sometimes what they're rioting for. They just get caught up in the frenzy."

On TV, Cathy is telling interviewers that when she got to the scene at 1122 King Road at around 5:30 p.m. on Sunday, November 13, she determined that the victims had died from multiple stabbings. She knocks down suggestions of a murder-suicide.

"Most of them just had one [wound] that was the lethal one," she tells NewsNation's Ashleigh Banfield, adding that in each case, the lethal cut was to the chest area or above. Banfield asks if the victims were slashed, and her answer echoes the mayor's comments earlier in the week: "It was a pretty large knife, so it's really hard to call them puncture wounds... it was a stabbing...it has to be somebody who was pretty angry to stab four people to death."

What Mabbutt doesn't say on TV but does say in private, which perhaps explains why she felt moved to speak out, is that in all her years on the job, the scene she found when she got to King Road was "right up there" among the worst. She'd dealt with multiple homicides, but she'd never come across a scene like that, where all the bodies were "right there" together. "And then, just their ages too."

You'd have to be inhuman not to be affected.

But there's plenty about the autopsy results that she shares with law enforcement and the victims' families only. Telling the families the autopsy details—that's the worst part of her job.

For instance, she doesn't say on air that Ethan was stabbed once in the buttocks and once in the carotid artery, but that's what she tells Stacy. (Stacy doesn't want to know anything other than that Ethan died fast and without suffering. She never even reads the autopsy report.)

Cathy doesn't tell reporters that Xana's fingers were almost severed, a sign she fought back hard before dropping to the floor. But that's what she tells Jeffrey Kernodle.

She doesn't tell anyone that Kaylee's wounds suggest that she woke up and struggled. But that's what she tells Alivea Goncalves on the phone—when, that is, Alivea reaches her, *after* she's seen Cathy on a local news channel. It's the first time Alivea gleans that the killer was likely angry.

Cathy Mabbutt's reports of a frenzied stabbing trouble many locals, too. This is a hunting community. Most people have large hunting knives.

Rand Walker, the local psychologist whom Fry asks to counsel PD members, notices that his friends and neighbors start staring at his arms—and he starts staring back. Who among them has knife wounds? The problem is that many people do. It's common to nick yourself when skinning an elk. Most people return on Sunday nights after weekend hunting trips looking somewhat worse for wear. Until now, no one had thought twice about it.

Blaine Eckles, the UI dean, can't keep this question out of his mind: Was it one of his students who wielded the knife? He's worried because he needs to plan a vigil for some time after Thanksgiving, when the students are back. But by then, he naively assumes, police will have caught the suspect.

But when, a few days into his planning, he asks Moscow Police Captain Roger Lanier how he's doing, Lanier answers: "Each morning I wake up excited and each afternoon I go [home] dejected, because it doesn't feel like they're getting anywhere."

Chapter 71

Moscow, Idaho
November 20, 2022

It's been barely a week since the murders, and the chief has received maybe five hundred emails from strangers about the case. Some good, some bad.

Some are very bad.

One guy, who says he lives in California, writes that he's going to appear in the police station parking lot and take him out.

Then the same guy sends him dick pics.

At night, the chief keeps his twelve-gauge shotgun in the bedroom. He's grateful that two of his daughters are married and have different last names and that the third lives a five-hour drive away.

Another person, who says he's in Florida, starts emailing the chief weekly telling him he will fail and that this is going to be the next Jon-Benét Ramsey case.

A woman emails and tells Fry that she knows the truth: *He's* the murderer—and he's going to frame someone else in order to look good.

Many people claiming to be in law enforcement write and tell him that he's screwing everything up.

Fry is used to hate mail, although not this much all at once. But that's not his primary aggravation right now.

It's the image building across the country of Moscow being a Podunk little town where nothing ever happens, with a police department that looks like the Keystone Cops. One reporter criticizes Fry for going home to change into his uniform and get his gun before heading to the crime scene. His longtime ride-along partner, Paul Kwiatkowski, tells him Paul's own brother called from Cincinnati and asked: "What is this rinky-dink cop operation?"

Plus, Fry's now got to deal with all the conspiracy theories out there.

There's one floating around about the victims having been gagged and bound. Another says the police failed to look in the garbage at 1122 King Road. Another suggests Kaylee had talked about a stalker who must be the killer. The murder-suicide story is still making the rounds. Then there are all the accusations being hurled at the surviving roommates and the victims' close friends.

Fry knows that it was a mistake not to come out sooner than he did and say *something*. He inadvertently created an information vacuum, and that's why he now has to spend time he can't spare rebutting some of the crank stuff flying around on social media and Reddit. (Truth be told, he'd never looked at Reddit, didn't even know what it was, until his son told him he was now famous on it.)

This is a learning curve, but Fry's not too proud to admit after that first disastrous press conference that he needs help.

State brings in a public information officer from outside Boise, a guy named Aaron Snell, to act as his coach. From now on, the chief isn't going to utter a word in public without rehearsing with Snell and his colleagues first.

"They would literally drill me for about an hour," he said later. "They worked with me on the fluctuations of my voice...they would act like they were the national press, and they would come at me to see how I would answer each question."

In his head, he's clear on what information needs to stay privileged for the investigation.

The key is not to give any of it away. Which is proving harder than he imagined.

Fry has huge respect for the press. But he doesn't like that the national media, unlike Evan Ellis and the locals he trusts, seem to think they are *owed* a narrative from him, justice be damned: "They think they can have it right now. They want it right now."

Fry doesn't believe that either the press or the community should know everything. That isn't their right. One news organization even called the police station and said they required protection for their crew. "It's in our contract," the guy apparently said. Fry exploded when this was relayed to him. "Well, it's not in *my* contract," he said.

Whenever Fry walks anywhere, he is followed, photographed, and peppered with questions by the press.

He discovers that the media can see through the police station blinds to his computer screen, so he buys butcher paper and plasters it over the station windows.

Why? he asks himself periodically. *Why did I ever sign up for this?*

Fry's mom once asked him that question, and his answer wasn't too profound: "Because somebody's gotta do it, Mom."

But the truth is he believes in public service just like he believes in God.

He and his wife, Julie, share an unshakable faith that gets them through the day. Back in May 2007, when police officer Lee Newbill was killed, Fry was called in to the live shooting, and as he was running out the door, Julie said, "Hey, just one last thing: Come home to me." He got home over twenty-four hours later and asked if she'd slept okay. "I've never slept better," she replied.

He was puzzled. Why hadn't she been worried? "Do you love me?" he'd asked her.

"I do love you," Julie replied. "You've trained your whole life for this day. You have God in control of your life, and either He's going to take you or He is not. I have no control over that. I trust Him and I trust you."

So, yes, now, in his darkest moments, Fry does believe that the Lord has his back. And he trusts his instincts. They are good.

Blaine Eckles asks him if he could maybe throw a bone to the *Argonaut,* the college newspaper, at a press conference. Fry is happy to oblige; he takes questions from the students before he gets to anyone else. They, at least, know how to conduct themselves.

His second press conference, on November 20, focuses on the autopsy results and victims' last movements, and it goes much better than the first. From there, the trajectory climbs steeply upward.

Snell is happy with Fry's progress. He reminds Fry how much responsibility he bears, justly or not. He tells him, "Because you're the chief, if this [investigation] fails, you'll be a failure. If this *happens*"—if the case is successful—"you'll be a hero."

In other words, Fry is the face of the investigation. Literally.

Fry is usually clean-shaven and even instituted a department policy against facial hair. But this month, he and some officers have been doing a no-shave November to raise money for cancer patients at Gritman Medical Center. Fry planned to shave his beard at the end of the month, but Snell tells him he absolutely cannot do that until there's a suspect in custody. "The nation knows you with a beard," he says, and so the whiskers stay.

The days are so long and busy, Fry's mind almost becomes blank.

He fills eight pages of a notebook with details he might want to remember, even talk about, if one day this nightmare is fully behind him. At night, when he gets home, which is often at around eleven p.m., he pours himself a whiskey—until he starts to worry about the size of the drink he's pouring and wonders if he's headed in a direction he's warned his younger officers and their families about. After that, Fry asks Julie to pour it for him.

At least, Fry thinks, he's gotten the rookies and their families the therapists and support they'll need, something he didn't have when he was their age. The spouses have been educated about the signs of PTSD, what to look for and what help to get.

There's also mundane stuff to do, like filling out purchase orders, buying an extra computer server, having food delivered, carefully monitoring the morning and evening meetings, and signing off on whatever resources are needed to follow leads.

The investigators are spending a lot of time looking at video from CCTV cameras positioned around 1122 King Road, what's commonly called a video canvass.

Footage from a local gas station shows a white car leaving the area in the right time frame, but the face of the driver isn't clear and neither is the model of the car, which seems not to be displaying a front license plate. At first, the investigators believe it's a Nissan Sentra.

The police have issued a map showing the victims' last movements to the public, asking for anyone who saw anything suspicious to call the tip line; an FBI agent is monitoring all the calls.

It's not unlike the map Fry made for Michelle Wiederrick, the mother of poor Joseph Wiederrick, the student who, in 2013, wandered for eight miles after a fraternity party and wound up freezing to death by the river.

As if Michelle could read his thoughts, Fry receives an unexpected email of support from her. "We are praying for you," she wrote. "I know you are going through a tough time."

Emails like this—from the families of victims in prior cases with whom he has a bond and with whom he has stayed in close touch—are what keep him going.

Chrissy Dove, the sister of Sarah Parks, the young pregnant woman who was strangled to death and then burned in a house fire by her husband, Silas, in 2009, texts Fry a screenshot of him and Bill Thompson on TV: **I'm so sorry y'all having to deal with this; prayers for y'all and the families,** she wrote.

Fry had found the body of poor Sarah and her unborn baby after Silas claimed she'd died in the fire, but it had taken some time for him to be able to prove the case and for Bill Thompson to pressure Silas into taking a plea deal.

A few days later Chrissy texts Fry again with another photo: **You're on Good Morning America...I hate that y'all have to go through this because I'm sure it brings up many more things in your mind.**

The chief replies: **Yes, the demons have come to life again, but we do it for the victims and their families. That is our reward.**

That is the reward. He believes it. Fry wants to get whoever did this for the four victims' families.

But all the garbage out there in the press is not helping.

He can see on TV that the Goncalveses are using the media to flush out anything they can. Kristi is on NBC begging whoever did this to come forward. She says openly that she's frustrated with the little news they are getting from the cops. That's because on their nightly calls from Tyson Berrett, he's got nothing to report. And because, as Alivea will later put it: "We had no one to help us not put our foot in our mouth."

Fry sighs. Each of the families gets the same information, but he's noticing they deal with it differently.

Maddie's mom and stepfather, Karen and Scott Laramie, are quiet, shell-shocked; they let the Goncalves family talk for them. Maddie's dad, Ben Mogen, also stays out of the fray.

The Kernodles stay quiet as well. It's possible they don't want anyone focusing on them right now. On November 19, Kootenai police arrested Xana's mom, Cara Northington, on two charges of drug possession. She'd been clean, working as a waitress, but relapsed following Xana's death.

Stacy Chapin heard about this with a certain amount of shock as well as sympathy for Jeff and Jazzmin. Stacy didn't know that Xana's mom had been in and out of jail her whole life. Ethan never told her.

Stacy assures Berrett and Fry that they have her family's support, no matter how long the investigation takes. "We don't care if this takes you thirty years, we will still believe in what you're doing," she tells Fry. "We'll believe that you guys are doing it right and we're going to support you."

People like her are what make the chief's world go round.

On November 23, Chrissy Dove sends him a note: "I wish I could let the world know how hard y'all really work on cases... knowing all the heart and love that y'all show."

Fry replies: "They will know when we make an arrest. I have lost all respect for the national news and media.... All it does is hurt the families... and gives people false information."

Chapter 72

Mount Vernon, Washington
November 21, 2022

More than a thousand kids, friends, and family pile into Skagit Valley College's McIntyre Hall. There are too many to fit in the auditorium. Stacy had no idea there'd be this many. She and her family rolled in the night before and congregated at the Bertelsen Winery.

She's so grateful to her cousin Stuart and his wife, Kathleen. They swept into town and booked a hotel and a vast house to hold everyone and they'd taken care of all the logistics. Kathleen introduced Stacy to a friend who was a PR executive in Boston and who stepped in to act as the gatekeeper between the Chapins and the swarm of media people seeking their attention.

It's been a whirlwind few days for Stacy, and the kindness of people has been as overwhelming as her grief.

She was dreading putting Maizie and Hunter in sleeping bags on the living-room floor of the condo. She longed to be able to tuck her two surviving children in at night in a proper bed, to reassure them in the way only a mother knows how.

Her best friend, Susie DeVries, had intuited this ahead of time. The

Chapins arrived to find Susie had bought out the linen department at Bed Bath and Beyond and purchased a pair of inflatable mattresses as well.

That wasn't all. Also intuiting that in the window between now and Ethan's memorial, the Chapins would not have the bandwidth for chats with random people, Susie banned visitors. She also brought a carload of food and organized a meal train.

Kirk Duffy, the director of Hawthorne Funeral Home and Memorial Park, had brought Ethan's body back from Spokane, as he promised.

He'd also persuaded Stacy and the others to view Ethan in the casket.

The Chapins had been reluctant. Stacy knew from the coroner that the stab wounds that had killed Ethan were below his collar line. But even so...she was afraid of what she'd see.

Duffy had been firm, however. He told Stacy: "I've done this for a very long time and you need to see him."

In hindsight, Stacy knows the funeral director was right. She's grateful.

Stacy tucked a dry sock and, out of habit, a Taco Bell card into Ethan's coffin. "God forbid the guy would go hungry," she later said. She watched, surprised and touched, as Jim added a golf tee.

In front of the massive crowd of mourners at the memorial service, she says that, during the viewing, while she was gazing at her son and the mustache he'd grown and that she hadn't been such a fan of, Hunter had nudged her and said, "You guys know the real reason he has the mustache, right? He watched the new *Top Gun* movie and he wanted to look just like those guys on the sand volleyball court."

Stacy had *not* known that!

She and Jim spent hours working on their respective eulogies.

Jim was adamant that they tell the college kids that they *must* get on with their lives, that they cannot be derailed by this.

Jim has always been a glass-half-full kind of person. He's viewed his life as a blessing, with Stacy and the triplets being the greatest blessings of all. He'd gotten a second chance in the wake of an unhappy first marriage, and he wants to make the most of every moment.

He's the husband and dad who keeps them all going. "It's all good," he tells them whenever they are tired or cross.

If he's ever had a mean thought, Stacy doesn't know about it. She can *feel* how proud he is of her almost every hour. It has always buoyed her.

So when it's Jim's turn to speak, he puts on his Vandals cap and gives the young people in the audience a directive to follow, for Ethan's sake.

His son, he says, "would love for all you kids to get back to school as safely and quickly as you can, to carry on what he was carrying on there. It's very important . . . that you kids get back after you've healed . . . We all have a lot of that going on, but I want you to go back."

When Stacy speaks, she says that it's essential that, in addition to celebrating Ethan's personality and life, she needs to clarify how he died and debunk the nefarious rumors swirling around, not just for her own family but to ease the suffering of everyone in the room.

"So we want to speak about what has happened to our son, not about the investigation, but we want you to know a couple of things that make us feel better about what happened that day," she says. "There were no drugs involved; the autopsy cleared that. There were no love—weird love triangles.

"Ethan Chapin was where he wanted to be," she continues. "He'd had a wonderful day and in the end he was staying at his girlfriend's house. I mean, what a great thing, right? . . . So I mean, that's supposed to make you feel better. I mean, none of us could have changed the outcome of that day. Ethan was asleep when this really tragic event occurred, and we want you to know that no phone call would've saved him. He did not suffer. It went very quickly."

And when Stacy gets to the subject of Ethan's mustache, she uses the levity it causes to make a serious point to the parents in the room.

"I do want to remind you that in the end, those battles don't matter. Hair, mustache—those aren't the battles you pick with your kids. It just doesn't matter. Pick the hard ones."

Stacy mentions that Ethan's and Xana's best friends, Hunter Johnson and Emily Alandt, are watching the service via live stream.

She doesn't mention that they aren't there in person partly because they are afraid Ethan's murderer is coming for them next.

Stacy also doesn't mention the starkly obvious fact that the other three victims' families are not holding public services for their kids out of fear that whoever did this might attend.

"My wife's biggest fear," Steve Goncalves later told ABC News, "part of the reason we didn't have a funeral, is because she couldn't be guaranteed that that monster was going to not be there."

Unlike the other families, the Chapins are not fearful. Chris Cammock, the local police chief, is a friend. There's a small police presence outside Ethan's service, but that's to cope with the crowd. The question of who the perpetrator was and what he might do next is just not something they think about.

"Nothing can bring Ethan back," Stacy says. Her focus now is exclusively on her living kids.

She concludes her eulogy: "Ethan was an amazing human and we're so lucky to get to call him son and friend. So thank you, all of you. I am not sure what tomorrow looks like in our family. I do know that the four of us will make it. It is going to change the look of what we've had for twenty years, but we'll do it. Ethan would want that for us. He would want that for all of you. He wants that for you kids. He wants that for his brother and sister. And that is what we, if there's anything to take away from this, it's to know that Ethan Chapin would want the very best for all of you no matter what it is. . . .

"It's incredible that a man so young has touched so many of us. May we continue to carry his kindness and his smile through all of our years, and when night skies are clear, wherever you are, look to the brightest star in the sky and send him your love. Certain people feel it. We love him. May he be your guiding light."

Nearly two years later, Stacy watched the video of the service and said, "I wouldn't change one thing."

Chapter 73

Rochester, New York
November 19, 2022

It's a cold, gray morning in upstate New York. The sun won't rise for another hour at least.

But Kristine Cameron, assistant principal at a local school, is already awake and sitting in front of her computer screen. On November 19, Cameron and her best friend from high school, Alina Smith, started the University of Idaho—Case Discussion Facebook group page. It's already become the fastest-growing page about a true crime in Facebook history.

Overnight, 3,000 people have requested to join.

In just a few weeks, it will have 200,000 members.

Many of these are fake accounts, but as page administrators, the duo has learned on the fly that it's essential not to reject people out of hand. It turns out that many of the local kids in Moscow who think they saw something important during the relevant time frame want to report that anonymously. They haven't used Facebook until now, preferring Instagram and TikTok. So they create Facebook accounts with fake names in order to reach Kristine and Alina personally.

The administrators have helped put many of these students in touch with the FBI.

"We had one girl contact us [via her aunt] and talk to us and tell us that she was hanging out with Kaylee and Maddie that day," Kristine said. Alina took the call. "They got ready together, they went to the football game together. They came back and they got ready together. They went to the Corner Club with the girls. They were hanging out, they were drinking, were having a great time. And then when it was time to go, Maddie and Kaylee left, went to the Grub Truck, and they went and they left and went home." Their house was kitty-corner to 1122 King Road.

"The amount of guilt that you could hear in their voices," Kristine said, "and how they were talking and 'Oh, I wish I would've stayed with them. Oh, I wish they would've come over to our house.'"

Kristine and Alina have founded and administered true-crime Facebook pages before. In fact, they have ten of them. They have one about the 2007 disappearance of Madeleine McCann. Another about the 2021 murder of Gabby Petito. Others about the 2022 killing of toddler Quinton Simon and the 2019 so-called doomsday-cult murders committed by Lori Vallow Daybell and Chad Daybell. And more.

Their goal is to create an audience for a true-crime podcast they hope to start. Alina has had several high-level meetings about it. So far, their pages have attracted a few thousand followers each.

It had been Alina, based in Prosper, near Dallas, Texas, who pushed to create a page about the Moscow murders because she'd seen someone else start a Facebook page and quickly garner 4,000 members.

This struck a nerve with Kristine, who knew the founder of that group and who describes herself as "supercompetitive."

"Okay," she said. "We'll do it."

She'd known right away that the Idaho case was "different," in a league all by itself when it came to attracting Facebook followers.

Four victims meant four times the chance that someone might sympathize or connect with one of them. Plus, the victims were particularly appealing. Bright, smart, attractive; "four young people that had their whole lives ahead of them," Kristine said. "And they were so insanely popular and they were on social media and their house was so lively and...they were like the life of the party anywhere."

But the speed at which the page took off shocked even the two administrators. Within ten days, they found themselves interviewed on NewsNation by Ashleigh Banfield about the findings and discussions on the page around the Venmo activity of the four victims, including one transaction from the sister of a guy Ethan had Venmoed that was time-stamped 3:30 a.m.

Kristine attributes the success of the page to the vacuum created by the police.

In the Gabby Petito case, "you'd see the police [asking], has anybody seen this girl? Does anybody have any videos? Does anybody have any pictures? The police were out asking for public help and assistance, whereas this case was very different. The Moscow police were very tight-lipped. They held all of their information close to the vest."

Their Facebook page seems to fill the void left in the narrative by the Moscow police's reticence. On it, no stone appears to have been left unturned based on the few nuggets out there. Almost everyone has an opinion about Hoodie Guy, about Bethany, Dylan, Jake, Jack, Emily, Hunter...

There are so many different theories as to who committed the murders and why that people are getting into fights.

"You had to deal with people [fighting] in real life," Kristine recounted. "And when I say real life, I mean people going onto other people's pages, people going into people's messages and threatening them."

Somebody on the page phoned Kristine's employer and accused *her* of being inappropriate online. Her boss called her in: "What did you do? What did you say?" And her boss wanted to see the page.

Another time, she was asked to call the HR department of a guy's workplace after a woman on the page claimed she was underage and that he (also on the page) was soliciting her. (He was not.)

It has become all-consuming for both of them. Alina is in the midst of getting multiple procedures for an injured back, but she works on the page day and night and gets to know some of the members personally.

Kristine wakes up at five a.m. so she can work on the page before going off to school. Even there, she sneaks in more work on the page, and when she gets home, she doesn't even try to handle the house or the kids. She leaves all that to her husband.

There's more to do than anyone might guess. Behind the scenes, Kristine and Alina are flooded with messages and calls from young people claiming to be friends of the victims — and who do *not* want to post.

"So now those people who are talking to us, all right, they're not posting about that. They don't want the fame . . . They would private-message us and say they would talk to us. They wanted somebody to talk to and they didn't want to talk to police. They didn't want to talk to their other friends. They wanted an adult to talk to, to just go through what they were going through. They needed somebody to talk to. Literally, we were therapists. We were a go-between, between police and the FBI. We were Facebook starters. We were page starters. We were everything rolled into one."

One person is watching all the Facebook chatter with more than idle interest.

On the other side of the country, Alivea Goncalves asks to join the page so she can monitor all of it from her parents' house in Rathdrum. She reads all the frenzied speculation blaming Jack DuCoeur. She reads that people think Kaylee and Maddie had secret OnlyFans accounts. She reads all the theories about Kaylee's Range Rover, about how she afforded it. She reads that people believe her dad, Steve, must be promoting something because he's on TV so often. She reads that there is a rift among the victims' families.

Even though it doesn't seem terribly effective, she appreciates the firm hand that Kristine and Alina try to take as administrators: **STOP the name calling, STOP the belittling**, they wrote in a post to their tens of thousands of members on December 3.

>‼This is a space to discuss and theorize NOT attack other
>members‼ ‼You will NOT agree with everyone and most

likely will not change their mind so politely disagree or
MOVE ON!! ✔ We will no longer warn you. You will simply
be removed.

As Alivea reads and reads, an idea starts to form in her mind.

This page could be a great resource. A great place to ask people for tips. A great place to send videos. And a great place to start setting the record straight.

Chapter 74

Moscow, Idaho
November 24, 2022

The FBI trailer that will act as the agency's mobile command center pulls up to the Moscow police station on Thanksgiving Day. The truck is so enormous, it looks like it might not fit through the gate. It does. Just.

TV cameras film the arrival, of course.

In this week's press conference, the chief and his team try to strike a more media-friendly tone, even addressing the fake news out there.

"We have heard that Kaylee stated she may have had a stalker. Detectives have been looking into that and to this point have been unable to corroborate the statement, although we continue to seek information and tips," Captain Roger Lanier said, reading from his script, adding that, contrary to online rumors, the victims had not been bound and gagged.

Just a few days later, the team obtains a search warrant for Kaylee's Tinder account.

Kaylee's wounds had appeared to reflect the possibility that she had woken up and tried to either fight off her attacker or call for help and then she was somehow stifled. Broadly, this will make its way into the public consciousness, courtesy of Steve Goncalves, who cites the coroner and blames the police for not sharing more details.

But the public certainly does not know that two days ago, the forensics team sent a sample of the DNA they'd found on the knife sheath to Othram, a DNA sequencing and genomics lab in Texas. That's because the investigators had run the DNA through CODIS, the FBI's database of fingerprinted individuals, and it had come up empty. So now, using the new methodology of investigative genetic genealogy (IGG) that has sprung up around the popularity of public genealogy sites, Othram will try to build a family tree around it. But the process could take days, maybe weeks.

Investigators have also sent off 103 pieces of evidence, including hair, fingernail clippings, and footprints, to local labs. Law enforcement's interview team has spoken to more than one hundred people so far.

The chief's victimology teams are building detailed profiles of the four victims they are getting to know as well as they know their best friends: Xana, the charismatic extrovert; Ethan, the all-star laid-back athlete; Maddie, the quieter only child; Kaylee, the exuberant go-getter.

At least one of them was a target. Which one? Why?

The chief still hasn't got a suspect, so it's understandable that he doesn't yet have a handle on a motive: "I think you're always looking for the why all the way through your investigation," he said. "Typically, the why doesn't just jump out to you because you have to piece the whole picture together. And really every piece of something that you get, or every warrant you do, there might be a nugget in that piece that gives you a little bit more of a clearer picture. And maybe not, maybe you get nothing out of it. Maybe whatever you put in for didn't give you any fruit at all."

There's one critical development in the case the chief doesn't share with the media.

The team monitoring CCTV cameras is homing in on the white car seen doing three passes around the King Road house between 3:29 a.m. and 4:00 a.m. At 4:04 a.m. it appeared to make a three-point turn near the residence, go back and forth on King Road, then take Queen Road, which had a turnoff going behind the house. The car reappeared at 4:20 a.m. and left at high speed.

Yesterday the FBI vehicle specialist got a better shot and identified the vehicle not as a Nissan Sentra but as a 2011, 2012, or 2013 white Hyundai Elantra.

So, on November 25, the day after Thanksgiving, the chief approves a message to local law enforcement agencies to be on the lookout for this specific car.

Four days later, in the early hours of November 29, over in Pullman, Washington, WSU police officer Daniel Tiengo searches for white Elantras registered at the university.

He sees that one, a 2015 model, belongs to a student named Bryan Kohberger.

A colleague of Tiengo's, Officer Curtis Whitman, spots the actual vehicle in a Pullman student-housing parking lot. He logs it.

But white cars are ubiquitous. So are Hyundai Elantras. So, since this car appears to be a model from the wrong year, the Pullman cops don't pass this up the food chain to Moscow. They don't yet know that the FBI vehicle specialist has in fact now conveyed to his agency that it's possible, given the shape of the fog light and rear reflectors in the available images, that they should extend the date range of the Hyundai Elantra to as late as 2016.

Meanwhile, Fry has got his hands full managing another screwup with the media, possibly even worse than the first. This one's from a surprising quarter.

On November 30, Bill Thompson gave a rare interview to a TV reporter named Brian Entin, a rising star at NewsNation.

Entin and his crew stormed into town like a tornado. Of all the national reporters, he's the one getting access. He's gotten to the Goncalves family and to Aaron Snell. And, somehow, he gets to Bill Thompson. Who made a rare mistake when Entin asked him about the use of the word *targeted*. Some of the students and the victims' families, Entin said, have been frustrated, not understanding what that word meant. Could Thompson explain?

Thompson told Entin in a recorded video interview that *targeted* had perhaps not been the right word to use. He said that investigators believed that whoever did this was still at large and was specifically looking at the King Road *residence,* but they could not yet say who might have been the target. Entin posted the video of the interview to Twitter.

But then, just a day later, Thompson spoke to KTVB's Morgan Romero and gave a different explanation—he said that one of the *victims* was definitely a target, although he did not specify which one.

Hours later Thompson wrote a letter to Romero walking that back. She tweeted a quote from it: "Investigators do not believe the murders were random, but we cannot unequivocally state the residence, or any occupants, were specifically targeted. I apologize for any confusion."

Piling onto the bonfire of confusion, Moscow police posted a "clarification" to their Facebook page:

> Conflicting information has been released over the past 24 hours. The Latah County Prosecutor's Office stated the suspect(s) specifically looked at this residence, and that one or more of the occupants were undoubtedly targeted. We have spoken with the Latah County Prosecutor's Office and identified this was a miscommunication. Detectives do not currently know if the residence or any occupants were specifically targeted but continue to investigate.

Chief Fry knows that the PR damage is done. Under pressure from the media, who themselves are under pressure from the Goncalves family and others to get answers, Bill Thompson misspoke.

All that progress Fry made with Aaron Snell just got undone and more. Thompson's office puts out a statement saying he will be giving no further interviews.

The image of the Keystone Cops running Moscow has been reignited in the national media, Pete Yachmetz, a security consultant and former FBI agent, tells the *New York Post*. "What is also happening now is the police, by providing imprecise comments, are creating an erosion of public confidence in them . . . That's unfortunate because in the end public confidence is needed to solve this crime. The public is very concerned there is or may be a killer in their midst and they see no progress in the investigation."

The *Post* quotes Steve Goncalves telling Fox News right after Thanksgiving that he was frustrated because the police hadn't spoken to him in three days. "We're the same family that found the original timeline. We're the same family that broke into the phones. We tried everything in our ability." (In fairness, Goncalves has another source of stress he keeps private: The family has been getting threats in the mail and online. Steve is concerned for the safety of his youngest daughters. But when he tells the police this, the reaction is underwhelming. "Tell them to be aware of their surroundings" is the unsatisfactory response.)

When Evan Ellis interviews the chief in the midst of all this, Fry blows off a bit of steam. He tells Ellis that he's discovered the national media, disappointingly, is focused only on the story and money.

But for him, this is not about those things. It's about lives. Four human lives and families.

He doesn't tell Ellis—at least not on the record—what he thinks privately: He has tremendous sympathy for the Goncalves family, but he wishes they would say less to the media. It makes police less inclined to share developments with them. Because the one thing that would ruin the investigation is for someone to know too much about it—and talk about it on TV.

Chapter 75

Christ Church pastor Doug Wilson is ready for the trolls when they come.

For two days after the murders, everyone had been united in shock. But he'd known that wouldn't last. "It took two days for the old fault lines to reappear," he said.

So now he's sitting back and reading the online hate mail linking his congregation to the murders. "We get slandered regularly and so it's just all in a day's work," he said of the speculations and accusations.

Ever since Wilson's father started Christ Church in Moscow, in the 1970s, the institution has been a bête noire for the town. Wilson accepted, with equanimity, the seeming local consensus: He and his church are an irritating, possibly even evil, cultlike presence in their midst.

"I know they think I kick puppies on my lunch hour," he said matter-of-factly during one such lunch hour as he sat in his book-lined, windowless office in downtown Moscow, Diet Coke on the desk.

Partly the friction stems from money. The church is so rich that even though it has around three thousand members—perhaps 10 percent of the town's population—it's bought up most of Moscow's prime real estate and filled Main Street with church-owned schools and businesses: New Saint Andrews, the church college; the K-12 Logos School; the Sword and Shovel bookstore; Bucer's coffeehouse. The church even has its own bar: Tapped.

Wilson knows that most Muscovites refuse to patronize these businesses. He quite enjoys hearing about their resistance, especially one comment: "It's a shame, too, because they've got all the best stuff."

The Kirkers, as members of Christ Church are known—a reference to the church's local nickname, "Mother Kirk"—stand out for their blond Caucasian looks and preppy attire. The men wear button-down shirts and jackets; the women all wear skirts—a distinction that feeds into the perception of misogyny. The liberal town finds the church's attitudes toward women antiquated at best, repugnant at worst.

UI professor Kelly Quinnett remembers a 2019 campus talk entitled "Toxic Matriarchy," given by conservative pastor Christopher Wiley, with a Q and A session moderated by Pastor Wilson, in which Wiley argued that modern society was suffering because women "have basically gotten too much power." Quinnett was livid that they'd hold such a discussion *on* the UI campus.

During COVID, the police and the Kirkers clashed badly, and lawsuits are still flying.

Three of the Kirkers were arrested in September 2020 when congregants gathered outside city hall, unmasked, and sang psalms in protest of the city's mask mandates. Donald Trump even tweeted about it, writing **DEMS WANT TO SHUT YOUR CHURCHES DOWN, PERMANENTLY. HOPE YOU SEE WHAT IS HAPPENING. VOTE NOW!**

But just a few weeks later, two of Wilson's teenage grandsons, Seamus and his older brother, Rory, who was a scholarship student at Columbia, were detained and charged with multiple misdemeanors for placing hammer-and-sickle SOVIET MOSCOW stickers on city utility poles in the middle of the night. They were dressed in hijabs and flip-flops at the time.

Their father, Wilson's son Nate, a screenwriter, was asleep. But he was phoned, awoken, and then arrested, charged with helping to make the stickers. The charges against him and his younger son were dropped, but the Columbia scholarship student, Rory, wound up being convicted of one charge of affixing a sticker to a pole.

He's appealed the ruling, and the appeal is on the desk of Judge John Judge. The litigation has cost his family north of six figures.

So as Doug Wilson reads all the news reports criticizing the Moscow Police Department for its handling of the murders, he senses an opportunity. This could be great PR for the church. And very helpful for his grandson's litigation.

He starts to type his weekly newsletter to his congregation.

> There are three things to remember. The first is that the police are currently engaged in a crucial task that God has assigned to them, and we should be doing nothing but praying for their success in it.

But then he gets to point two—the opportunity for the litigation around his grandsons.

> Second, you are all aware of the fact that it was this same police department that arrested some of our members for singing psalms legally…and lawsuits are in progress. But this is all being pursued biblically and out of true principle, and does not want to unjustly tar those good cops who had nothing to do with it. So if we give way to any carnal gloating or glee over the fact that our police department is now receiving very critical attention from all over the world (which it is), then we have become part of the problem.

Finally, he focuses on the larger PR opportunity the murders offer to the church and the community. It's imperative that his congregants do not screw it up.

And last, we need to take a few steps back and look at the big picture. Our little town keeps finding itself in the limelight, and it has to be acknowledged that something strange is happening...*Meet the Press* came and did a story on what was happening here in Moscow, tagging our town as the place where the Christian Nationalism thing is going on. And then these sensational murders happened.

When he's finished, Wilson sits back, pleased with his handiwork.

He knows there will be eye rolls in the town, but who cares? The pastor describes himself as having very thick skin.

He regularly invites local law enforcement and other civic leaders to lunch in a back room of the church. They refrain from talking about the lawsuits, but he subtly and unsubtly reminds them of the church's importance in the community.

It's not unhelpful, Wilson thinks, that the church owns the building that houses New Saint Andrews College, which has a CCTV camera positioned above the Grub Truck. He gathers that there's video on it of Maddie and Kaylee walking toward the truck with a guy in a hoodie, talking about someone named Adam on the night of the murders. It's been handed over to the police—a useful reminder to law enforcement of the upside of the church's presence in Moscow. Until recently, that building had sat there empty, no camera. Wilson tells people that Moscow was on a downhill trajectory until Christ Church and its businesses came along.

But Wilson would like to be much more than just an economic solution for Moscow. "Our desire is to evangelize the town," he said.

So the murders, though tragic, are an opportunity for him to step in and preach the need for his church to fill the moral and spiritual vacuum.

The house where the students were murdered, 1122 King Road, was in "a seedy area," Wilson said, "not somewhere I'd want my daughters living"—making the point that seediness, which stems from godlessness, brings about trouble. And, in this case, murder.

Chapter 76

University of Idaho — Case Discussion Facebook group page
November 29, 2022

Kristine Cameron and Alina Smith, the two administrators of the University of Idaho — Case Discussion Facebook group page, start to notice some unusual posts from a member going by the name Pappa Rodger.

They have no idea who the user is in real life.

His avatar is cartoonish, creepy, seemingly digitally created. It's a profile of a man with graying hair in some sort of military uniform.

Pappa Rodger garners attention very quickly with a startling opinion: **Of the evidence released, the murder weapon has been consistent as a large, fixed-blade knife. This leads me to believe they found the sheath. This evidence was released prior to autopsies.**

Until now, amid all the theories and speculation on the page, no one has mentioned a knife sheath.

Pappa Rodger gets pushback, and he argues with people who disagree with him.

A user named Dustin Stubblefield responds: **Due to the number of victims and assuming each victim was stabbed multiple times I'm sure that there was visible evidence of a [knife] guard. For all we know the** investigators on the scene wiped a couple stab wounds clean to look for bruising. I think it's far more logical than finding a sheath. Sheaths are usually attached to a belt.

Pappa Rodger writes back: They don't clean bodies at a crime scene. The amount of blood must have been tremendous.

> Stubblefield: Who knows. Finding a left behind sheath seams like a stretch, though.
>
> Pappa Rodger: Why? They are very specific about the weapon but vague about every other detail.
>
> Stubblefield: I think it's more likely they did closer examination on the wounds on scene than you think...
>
> Pappa Rodger: Curios, why are you debating the sheath theory so hard?
>
> Stubblefield: Because who would carry a sheath?
>
> Pappa Rodger: Who would carry a large exposed knife?

A picture of a Ka-Bar knife is posted for everyone to study.

> Pappa Rodger: How did the killer hold the knife prior to entering the scene in your opinion?
>
> Stubblefield: I would guess he carried it in his hand from wherever he came from. A knife in a sheath could cause him problems.
>
> Pappa Rodger: Which hand?
>
> Stubblefield: I don't freakin know lol. Why would you even ask that?
>
> Pappa Rodger: So a knife wielding person walked from where? And, entered this house at what point with a large knife in hand?
>
> Stubblefield: How in the hell would I know that?

Pappa Rodger: Do you carry a knife?

Stubblefield: Dude give it a rest. You sound like a psycho.

Members start messaging Kristine and Alina asking who the heck Pappa Rodger is. Why is he so arrogant? And why is he focusing on the knife sheath?

Kristine and Alina wonder if Pappa Rodger is ex-military, given his strange profile picture and his seeming expertise in crime.

They notice that he posts fairly regularly, sometimes multiple times a day. And his questions and opinions seem to contain a certain macabre insight. Who is he?

I believe the killer(s) came from the high side of the house. They were covered in blood after the attack.

I feel like blood ran down a few places but it has been suppressed. The kitchen was dripping blood but they won't admit it.

Did the killer(s) drive or walk to and from the scene? Thoughts?

Why did the killer choose a knife as the weapon of choice?

Did the killer stop at 4 victims out of exhaustion, convenience, or lack of knowledge?

Why do we think the dog was spared?

Why did the killer choose that house over all the others in the area?

How long do we think the killer was in the house?

Do we think the killer took anything from the house?

Kristine googles Pappa Rodger to see if there's any clue as to this person's real identity. All that pops up in her search is the incel martyr Elliot Rodger, the twenty-two-year-old student in Santa Barbara who wrote a manifesto and in 2014 videotaped his plans to murder a bunch of people as revenge for all the women who wouldn't sleep with him.

Kristine clocks this, but the connection seems too vague — just the spelling of the name Rodger — for her to do anything dramatic like report him to the police. But neither she nor Alina likes his arrogant tone or the darkness of some of his thoughts, so they decide to keep an eye on Pappa Rodger's posts.

One reason they are particularly sensitive to the content and tone on the page is that Alivea Goncalves, Kaylee's sister, is in regular touch and has become a contributor. Kristine had reached out to her on Facebook Messenger and Alivea responded with her phone number. A relationship developed between Alivea and the two founders. But there was a bump when Kristine asked Alivea to participate in a Vice documentary about the Facebook page founders and Alivea said no, bluntly.

But Alivea and Alina continued to talk. Alivea has mentioned that she's pregnant but she wants to keep that a secret. There's too much else going on for that to be a focus.

The two have an unofficial arrangement in which Alina passes on any video or tips submitted that Alivea might find useful, and Alivea sets the record straight about Kaylee and the Goncalves family directly on the Facebook page.

No, Kaylee was not on OnlyFans.

No, Steve Goncalves is not promoting any product on TV.

No, there was no "deal" for Kaylee's Range Rover.

No, the family never said this attack was targeting Kaylee.

Finally: No, I do not know who killed her. I wish I did. & I can promise that I will find him & I will know. But I am still getting there piece by piece.

Chapter 77

Moscow, Idaho
November 30, 2022

D ean Eckles chose this date deliberately. The first Wednesday after Thanksgiving is Chapter Day, when Greek life reconvenes on campus. "We knew the fraternity and sorority community was going to turn out massively for this," Eckles said.

It's snowing. It's *really* snowing. Seven or eight inches.

He cannot believe his good fortune. He used the weather as an excuse to move tonight's candlelit vigil for Ethan, Xana, Maddie, and Kaylee indoors, inside the Kibbie Dome. But the weather isn't the real reason he made the switch.

Chief Fry told him last week that it would be much harder to secure the venue, maybe impossible, if it was outside. The Kibbie Dome has magnetometers at the entrances. It's entirely possible the suspect may try to show up. They need to be ready.

So Eckles gave up his vision of an iconic outdoor ceremony and notified the students of the change — but he cited the weather as the reason, not wanting to scare anyone.

Idaho's governor, Brad Little, is also coming.

Eckles arrives an hour early to go through last-minute checks. He sees a crowd of about thirty young people all dressed alike. Despite himself and the gravity of the situation, he chuckles. They're undercover FBI agents. "I don't know who told 'em to dress like college students," he said, "but they all looked like lumberjacks... plaid shirts, blue jeans, and boots."

Still, Eckles immediately feels better. He doubts anyone can get past this bunch.

He's not yet met any of the victims' families, and soon some begin to arrive.

The Chapins barely make it in time due to the weather. Even without snow, the drive from La Conner to Moscow is a good six to seven hours.

I-90 is closed, so Jim takes Highway 2. "I don't even know why it was even still open. It was just me and a couple of other people on the road," he said. "It's heavy snow. Crazy. I wouldn't want to do that again."

Stacy remembers that other awful drive from La Conner to Moscow just two weeks earlier. And she remembers something else. She wants to make an apology.

"I really chewed out someone on your staff that day," she tells Dean Eckles when they shake hands, recalling the angry phone call.

"I know," he tells her with a smile. "It was me."

The Chapins are ushered through a separate entrance and up to a press box, sky-high, where they can watch the students filing in.

And where they can be surrounded by FBI agents.

From this height, Hunter sees the Sig Chi brothers, all dressed up in coats and ties, walk to the front. He's instantly touched. "I knew my fraternity was coming, but I didn't know how many of them," he said. "But every single person came."

He asks Jim and Stacy if he can go stand with his brothers. They ask law enforcement. The answer is yes, but with a caveat: He has to take his FBI detail with him. A young woman with long, shiny black hair, clad in boots, jeans, and a green plaid shirt, follows him.

The Sig Chi brothers are confused to see Hunter with a stunning woman who does not take her eyes off their friend for even a fraction of a second. His brothers don't believe that she's an FBI agent until she sees they are all looking at her and she flashes her badge. The shocked expressions on their faces is something Hunter Chapin savors. A moment of fun in an otherwise bleak universe.

When the service is about to start, Stacy and Jim head downstairs, agents in tow, and meet Steve and Kristi Goncalves.

Steve is practicing his speech on behalf of Kaylee and Maddie, but he stops to shake hands. He shows Stacy a photograph on his phone of a man with glasses.

"Have you seen this guy? It's Maddie's dad, Ben Mogen," he says. Steve seems surprised that Ben is there to speak about Maddie. Maddie was raised by her mom, Karen, and her stepfather, Scott Laramie. They had full custody. So Steve has never met Ben.

But Karen and Scott Laramie, grief-stricken, are skipping the vigil. So are the Kernodles. Maddie's grandmother—Deedle, as Maddie called her—later said that she stayed home out of fear.

But the vigil is televised, so even those who are absent can watch. After introductions from Dean Eckles, Stacy Chapin takes the stage. And in her inimitable, articulate style, she finds a way to touch everyone there.

Her message is about life, not death. She draws a portrait of the Chapin family, a family, she says, probably not unlike any of theirs. They play games; they eat dinner together when they can; they listen to country music; they spend their weekends following their kids to various sporting events. She tells the students she's not going to dwell on that awful night. No one can change the outcome. Ethan would want them all to carry on. To keep pursuing their dreams and reaching their goals while cherishing the time they have together because "you can't get it back."

Steve Goncalves is up next. With his wife, Kristi, by his side, he strikes a soft tone as he describes himself as the girl dad constantly amazed by the perspectives of his daughter. He talks about Kaylee and Maddie's friendship, taking comfort in the fact that the two besties died together. But he also makes Kaylee and Maddie a promise: "We're gonna get our justice," he says toward the end.

That night, the Chapins' chief concern is the well-being of the Sigma Chi brothers. Since November 13, their fraternity house has been besieged by media knocking and drones flying overhead. (Even on this visit, Stacy's best friend, Susie DeVries, who has come with them, wakes up in her hotel to find what she later realizes is a member of the press washing her window.) Part of honoring Ethan's legacy, Stacy and Jim believe, is looking after the fraternity brothers he meant so much to.

So Hunter messages the house in a group text that the family is coming over to be with them and they need to put their phones in a basket and pull down the blackout shades. There's money, he says, for pizza and beer.

They gather in the lodge. In the same room where Ethan and Xana spent their last night partying.

Cocooned in a safe space, far from prying eyes and lenses, insulated against social media, the brothers, still in their suits, and the Chapins stay up all night talking about Ethan. Laughing. Some of them get extremely drunk. Some of them cry. Nobody cares.

They are living on borrowed time, safe for just one night to let rip. This is their moment of catharsis, their moment to connect, remember, and treasure Ethan, and they are going to make the most of it.

Chapter 78

Post Falls, Idaho
December 2, 2022

The chapel is overflowing with people, many of whom Emily Alandt recognizes but a lot of whom she doesn't.

She and Hunter Johnson are back in Idaho for Xana's memorial service and to get their stuff from Moscow. Emily had refused to go to the vigil at the university. She was too frightened to go to something huge and public like that.

And she'd said no when Jazzmin, Xana's sister, asked her to speak at the second vigil in Post Falls the previous night. It was being live streamed and she didn't want to find herself blowing up even more on social media. Her mom is now following a Facebook page that's a case-discussion board to try and get ahead of all that.

But Emily said yes to Jazzmin when she asked her to speak at Xana's memorial because the family wants to keep that small.

It hasn't turned out small, Emily thinks. Looking around the church, she figures there must be at least a hundred mourners. And there's a side room with another fifty chairs. People are standing because there's nowhere to sit.

Emily sees the Chapins and the Sig Chi brothers. They all look wrecked. It's been a heck of a few days since Thanksgiving. There was the vigil at the school. Then a vigil in Post Falls. And now this. There's Josie and Linden. They are more together now than they were before. Dylan is there too. No sign of Bethany.

Emily doesn't recognize Xana's mother, Cara Northington. Why would she? But Cara is there, out on bail. (She'll be rearrested when she fails to report to court afterward.)

The service itself is surprisingly religious. Everyone is often asked to pray. Emily hadn't known that Jeff Kernodle was religious, but you never can tell.

When it's her turn to speak, she pulls out her phone. She spent last night writing out what she'd say. She wants it to be real. She doesn't care what people think. Xana didn't care what anyone thought. So this is it. This is her moment to say everything she feels about Xana, her best friend.

And so she begins.

> Hi, my name is Emily Alandt. I would like to start by saying how honored I am to be up here getting the chance to speak about someone who I got to call my best friend.

She tells the story of Xana introducing herself to the Pi Phis, explaining that her name is pronounced "'Xanax' without the *-x*." How Xana was the light and energy source in every room.

> I remember the moments. And after all, it is the moments we are left with. For all the moments I have been blessed to share with her, I am grateful. Death ends a life, but not the relationships of that life. We get to keep the moments and relationships. There was a silly sweatshirt she would wear with Eeyore on it and I found a quote from Winnie-the-Pooh...that says, "How lucky am I to have something that makes saying goodbye so hard."

Xana's length of life was shorter than any of us could have imagined or wanted, but the depth of her life was grand. You can look at Xana's short life as a success. If you made your life about happiness and the happiness you give to others, then she was successful in what truly matters. May you rest in peace, my best friend, Xan.

When she's done, she and Hunter say their goodbyes to everyone. Then Emily heads with her parents to the airport. They're going back to Mexico for five long weeks. Hunter will come as often as he can.

Emily needs to get far, far away from everyone. She needs to finally sit with her grief. But as she looks back at all her friends, Xana's friends, Ethan's friends, it occurs to her that she'll miss them. In fact, she needs them. And five weeks without them is going to be very tough.

Chapter 79

Moscow, Idaho
December 15, 2022

F or once, in the morning meeting, the Chief hopes that they might be getting somewhere with the DNA found on the knife sheath.

It's been a meandering process.

Othram labs had checked the sample against DNA in public geneology databases such as FamilyTreeDNA. Those results had led to "low matches" with four brothers.

The Idaho State Police had reached out to one of the brothers, requesting he give a DNA sample so that Othram could keep working to build a family tree. But he had refused.

So the team had conferenced. On December 10, Idaho State Police had asked Othram to stop work and hand over its findings. The ISP had then turned those findings over to the FBI to take the step of running the DNA profile through GEDMatch and MyHeritage, two genealogy databases which purport not to permit law enforcement searches.

The FBI can legally do this because, as later noted in court records, there is a loophole in Justice Department policy that permits government agencies to use *discretion* when searching data provided to websites that do not have customers' permission to share it.

The chief doesn't know all the details, but it turns out he is feeling optimistic with good reason.

Four days from now, on December 19, the FBI gives "a tip" to Brett Payne. Payne will later say that the name provided is not one they'd previously associated with the investigation.

The name is "Bryan Kohberger."

Now the investigators can look at Kohberger's vehicle records, which show he owns a white 2015 Hyundai Elantra.

The Moscow team will look at the video they've gotten from cameras around King Road, to see if the white car that appeared to drive around the house several times that night could be a 2015 Elantra. And it turns out that, yes, it could.

And when they do a video canvass in Pullman—where Kohberger lives—for the night of November 13, they can see that at 2:44 a.m. the car is headed north on Nevada Street. But less than ten minutes later, it's headed south on State Route 270, the road that connects Pullman to Moscow.

And when investigators check Kohberger's name in their databases, a police body cam shows that on August 21, a Bryan C. Kohberger was detained in Moscow at a traffic stop—and that the car had a rear Pennsylvania license plate LFZ-8649 that was set to expire on November 30. It had no front plate, which is permissible in Pennsylvania but not in Idaho or Washington. The car they'd captured on video had no front license plate.

Further DMV records will show that on November 18, just five days after the murders, Kohberger registered the vehicle in Washington and received new license plates, front and back, as is required: CFB-8708.

From there, locating the car will be relatively easy. The new plate showed up on a license plate reader in Loma, Colorado, on December 13. And on December 16, CCTV footage put the vehicle in Albrightsville, Pennsylvania, where, according to databases, Kohberger's parents live.

They will also note that Bryan Kohberger's driver's license photograph shows a man with dark hair and dark bushy eyebrows—the description that Dylan Mortensen gave of the masked man she had mistaken for a fireman on the night of the murders.

Obviously, Fry isn't going to start smiling in his press conferences. He'd like to. "I'm not a downer person," he complains to Julie, his wife.

But he's hopeful.

And no one passes on anything to the victims' families.

Chapter 80

Moscow, Idaho
December 2022

When Steve Goncalves pulls up to the house of attorney Shanon Gray, he feels so at home, it's weird.

The Grays' house is on five acres outside of Moscow. Like the Goncalves, the Grays have five kids. Like Steve Goncalves, Gray's initials are SG. His license plate is 7GS, a sometime Goncalves family password.

Gray is covered in tattoos and wears a trucker hat. He drives a maroon Mercedes G-Wagen and complains that the Moscow cops are endlessly stopping him because of it. Even before Steve knows anything about Gray's career, he decides he's going to hire Gray to be his lawyer.

He'll later say that it wasn't really his decision at all. "The girls"— meaning Kristi and his daughters Alivea, Autumn, and Aubrie—had already decided. They'd told him the family needed a lawyer because they were worried Steve would go and say something he shouldn't.

"They know I'm willing to break rules," he said. "I don't want to catch the wrong person, but I don't want to sit in a line of five people and wait for my turn to figure out justice." He added, "There are things that we can request and things we can do to get to the truth faster. You have to fill out forms to get this evidence released to you. I don't know how to do that."

Jack DuCoeur's aunt Brooke Miller knows Gray's wife, Tiffany, an Instagram influencer whose account describes the ups and downs of their large family. Miller introduced the Grays to the Goncalves women, but they sent Steve to close the deal.

Steve applauds the dynamism his girls showed in getting Gray, though he might have gone in a different direction and hired a civil lawyer. Gray is a criminal lawyer.

To Steve, there is much to appreciate about Gray, an unlikely lawyer who cannot let a perceived injustice drop. He feels positive about Gray's "prosecution experience . . . more experience than Thompson"—specifically "way more murder cases," he said.

"I'll spend as much money as I got to to make sure that we get to the bottom of this," Steve said.

The girls have in fact already thought about how to pay Gray—*and* a private investigator. To get out in front of any controversy over the Goncalves family online fundraiser that Brooke has advertised on the University of Idaho—Case Discussion Facebook group page, Alivea posts: **By no means do we expect anything at all but for those looking to specifically help with legal and independent investigation fees, this fundraiser has been started for us.**

Steve wants Gray, a former prosecutor in the Multnomah County (Oregon) DA's office who's aggressive and "not afraid of a microphone," to go shake some trees to pressure the cops and Thompson.

Steve explains that his frustration with the cops started to build on the third day following the murders, when, thanks to Alivea, the Goncalves family discovered who Kaylee had been in touch with on the phone, had gotten hold of the Grub Truck video, and had been in touch with the rideshare driver, a fraternity house–designated driver.

Steve says he asked the cops: "Do you know about the food truck? Do you know about the Uber driver?" When the answer to both was negative, he says he exploded. "These guys don't even know what the fuck's going on."

The family expected to be interviewed by police. Instead, they received a questionnaire to fill out about Kaylee. They'd also gotten hold of video of the crime scene from a neighbor that the cops didn't pick up from them. And they'd asked the owner of a local vape shop, where Kaylee had talked about a stalker, if he'd given the CCTV footage of that to the cops. The answer was no. And now it was too late. The recording had looped. So when Bill Thompson appeared to be muddled about whether the house, a victim, or no one had been targeted, Steve snapped.

On December 13, Steve told Fox News Digital he'd hired Shanon Gray because he was frustrated with the police's lack of communication and what he saw as missteps in the investigation.

"I have a lawyer for a reason," he said. The police talk to his lawyer now. "They've messed up a million times," he continued. "But I don't get to say that because what experience does Steve have? He doesn't know. He's just a dad who woke up one day and had his life turned upside down."

Gray started giving TV interviews in which he said he sat down with investigators and Thompson and asked for more transparency and accountability.

When Chief Fry first saw Shanon Gray on the news, he was bemused. *Who is this guy?* he wondered. Most people in Moscow had never heard of him. The more the police chief sees of Gray, on TV and off, the less he trusts him. It doesn't help that back in January, Gray was suspended from the Oregon State Bar for misconduct. (He was reinstated thirty days later.)

Gray moved to the outskirts of Moscow from Portland earlier in the year. In one of life's ironies, he bought the house next door to Nate Wilson, the screenwriter son of Christ Church pastor Doug Wilson and the father of the two boys arrested for putting SOVIET MOSCOW stickers on lampposts in the middle of the night during COVID.

Nate Wilson is completely mesmerized by his new neighbors. Gray's wife, Tiffany, strikes Nate as an "emotional, passionate" person, and he listens raptly to Gray's life story, which includes an earlier career as a bouncer in a bar and a row with the Moscow City Council over a halfway house opposite the junior high school that lacked, he felt, appropriate oversight.

He told Wilson he'd uncovered all sorts of corruption and self-dealing inside city hall, but Nate never gets to the bottom of that story, partly because Gray is always on the road, defending clients in Coeur d'Alene and Kootenai County. And now Gray is swept up in the murders, because he started representing the Goncalves family.

Gray is, understandably, given his stalemate with the police, very sympathetic about the Wilson family's clashes with law enforcement. Nate remembers finding it difficult, borderline impossible, to trust that the MPD could get anything done.

The chief wants to help the Goncalves family. He wants to get justice for Kaylee.

They are getting closer with the investigation. But the battle lines have been so clearly and aggressively defined by Gray that the police chief feels unable to share much, if anything, with them. It's a shame.

Chapter 81

Rochester, New York
December 16, 2022

It's dawn and Kristine is looking at the Facebook page, aghast.

She posted an exclusive video that has news programs calling her constantly; her phone is ringing off the hook.

It shows Maddie and Kaylee on the sidewalk, en route from the Corner Club to the Grub Truck. Hoodie Guy is accompanying them, a little bit off to the side, but it looks as though he's there to help. The two women are not walking entirely steadily.

Kaylee asks Maddie: "What did you say to Adam?"

Maddie replies: "I told Adam everything."

Everyone on the Facebook page and in the media is now fired up about the identity and role of Adam.

Oh God, Kristine thinks. This is not good. Not good at all. The opposite, in fact, of what her intention had been.

The point of posting the video was to show everyone that Hoodie Guy—Jack Showalter—apparently had good intentions that night, not bad. She wanted to provide much-needed context to the Grub Truck Twitch video in which he seemed to stare at them and follow them for no reason. This new video showed there was a perfectly good reason: He'd been walking with them all along.

The video had been given to police soon after the investigation began by someone who worked at Saint Andrews, but nothing was released to the public. Kristine had gotten this video from a man who did not want his name out there or his connection, via his girlfriend, to New Saint Andrews College, the building on which the camera perched.

The source had followed the online mania and the speculation about Hoodie Guy and wanted to help clear his name. At first he'd wanted Kristine to show a still, but they ultimately decided that the best choice was the simplest: just play the video.

Prior to posting it, Kristine sent the video over to Alivea Goncalves. It turned out that the family knew who Adam was.

He's Adam Lauda, a close friend of Jack DuCoeur—and Maddie and Kaylee. The former high-school basketball star bartends at the Corner Club.

The video has gone viral because of the mention of Adam.

"Who Is Adam?" That's the headline run by major media outlets—including Fox News and *Inside Edition*—and it's the topic of numerous posts on the Facebook page.

Marc Trivelpiece, the owner of the Corner Club and Adam's boss, is livid.

Not just because he's gone overboard to protect Adam and all his employees from media intrusion but because weeks ago police interviewed them all, and they figured the way to protect the investigation was to stay quiet.

He knows at once where this video came from: New Saint Andrews College, the school founded and owned by Christ Church. Which makes him even madder.

"They like chaos," he said of the church. "Anything that can get the people who are dead set on being in Moscow to loosen their grip and make it easier for their people to come in, they're going to do it."

Appearing on Fox in a split screen with Shanon Gray on December 17 is Steve Goncalves, who surprises Kristine by saying, "We've had that film for a while."

Even so, she's glad he's doing this interview to set the record straight about Adam.

"I believe the business reached out to us directly after they had given it to the police," Steve says, though his attempt to calm the waters once again roils Kristine, who'd thought she had an exclusive.

The video, Steve says, "was kind of comforting to us because it's just two girls having a good time, talking about, you know, asking about their bartender, just being girls on their way to the Grub Truck...We did the obvious due diligence and looked into that, and it was pretty clear that this individual was not a part of the investigation as far as a suspect."

Phew, thinks Kristine.

But even as the speculation about Adam is dying down, another problem appears: Pappa Rodger. This Facebook page is meant to be a place to discuss the murders, not rant.

His posts continue to needle other members. It's not just his arrogance. It's some undefinable feeling of aggression. He keeps making snide comments like **Why is proof so hard for you?**; **Help me help you**; **Maybe you should consider post-secondary education?**; and **Do you have emotional issues?**

On December 14, he posted about law enforcement: **Fight me...LE is no closer to solving this than they were 30 days ago?**

Two days later: **The killer has a sexual dysfunction. Thoughts?**

And in another instance of seeming overconfidence, of possibly having peculiar insight into the case, when he was asked how long he suspected the killer was in the house, Pappa Rodger answered: **15 minutes.**

On December 22 he posted: **The killer is not in the victims immediate circle.**

And on December 24 someone asked: **You think the assailant has left the area?**

Pappa Rodger replied, **Likely.**

Sitting in his office at the police station, Chief Fry is interested in following this. The team has appointed an investigator to track all the social media discussions about the case, including the Facebook page.

By now the police have a good idea of who their suspect is.

And Pappa Rodger is right. The suspect is *not* in the victims' immediate circle. And, yes, he has left the area.

The question for the investigator is: *Why* is Pappa Rodger right?

Is it because he knows the suspect?

Or because he *is* the suspect?

Chapter 82

Moscow, Idaho
December 19, 2022

I t's evening when Brett Payne gets the phone call from the FBI suggesting that a "Bryan Kohberger" might be worth looking into.

It's the call he and the team have been waiting for. "The DNA from the knife sheath was the one thing we had that we thought was a very strong piece of evidence," Payne will later say.

The next morning, via Microsoft Teams, the FBI walks him through how they constructed the family tree and why they believe Kohberger should be looked at. Payne doesn't know much, if anything, about investigative genetic genealogy. He's never used it before, so he finds the details they give him "above [his] head."

But that doesn't matter. What matters is that the tree includes the Kohberger family, based in Pennsylvania.

On December 23, the investigators have enough information for Payne to apply for a warrant to pull Bryan Kohberger's phone records to check the location of the cell towers pinged by his phone in the early hours of November 13.

Payne learns from AT&T records that Kohberger's cell does indeed appear in the broader area early that morning:

2:42 a.m.: Network near Pullman picks up the cell phone
near his house, heading south out of Pullman

2:47 a.m.: Phone disappears from the network

4:48 a.m.: Phone reappears on a network covering I-95 south out of Moscow

5:30 a.m.: Phone shows up on the Pullman network again

9:00 a.m.: Phone appears to leave the Pullman network

Between 9:12 a.m. and 9:21 a.m.: Phone shows up on the network around 1122 King Road

9:31 a.m.: Phone is back on the network covering Kohberger's home in Pullman

In fact, the phone, when they retrieve it, will also show that an hour later, around 10:30 a.m., while he's still at home, Kohberger takes a strange mirror selfie in what appears to be the bathroom in his apartment; the bare shower rod, empty towel rack, and white tilework are visible in the background. His dark hair damp, he's grinning and giving a thumbs up, his face deathly pale. He's wearing over-ear headphones and a clean white dress shirt, buttoned all the way to the top.

In order to see if Kohberger had stalked the King Road house or anyone in it, Payne and the team get another warrant and review earlier records of the phone's calls as well as its locations. Since Kohberger opened the account in 2022, the phone appears to have been close to the King Road house on at least twelve occasions. All except one occurred late at night.

So, finally, the puzzle is coming together.

Now it's time to find a way to prove the very compelling, but still circumstantial, theory that Bryan Kohberger is their man.

The simplest and most obvious way to do this is to check his DNA and see if it matches the DNA on the knife sheath.

The FBI reaches out to its Philadelphia field office.

Plans for a surveillance operation in the area are set in motion.

The chief knows better than to count his chickens. But this year, Christmas feels more bountiful than he had dared hope. He even manages to take the whole day off to be with Julie and the family.

And because he's feeling optimistic, he writes back to his emailer in Florida, the one who tells him this will be unsolved like the JonBenét Ramsey case:

"I want to wish you a merry Christmas. God bless you."

The guy writes back: "You better hope God blesses you because if not, you're going to go down in history as one of the worst."

We shall see, thinks the chief. *We shall see.*

Chapter 83

Rathdrum, Idaho
December 28, 2022

Alivea, Steve, and Kristi Goncalves are seated together on their black leather couch, tissues in hand. A large photograph of Kaylee hangs behind them.

They are giving their first in-depth interview, not to a reporter from a news network but to a cybersleuth from New York, Olivia Vitale, a brunette in her twenties.

They've chosen Olivia rather than a journalist from an established news network, Steve says, because, in going through Kaylee's TikTok, he learned that Kaylee watched Olivia's interviews under her moniker "Chronicles of Olivia."

Could this be a sign that Olivia is the chosen one to find whoever killed Kaylee?

"It feels like…this is Kaylee-approved…And if that can play a role in solving this crime, then that makes it a lot better. That helps with the process of healing," he says on camera.

Toward the end of the interview, Alivea explains that she has taken it upon herself to be the Goncalves family's own cybersleuth. Her mother,

Kristi, tried for a week to follow University of Idaho—Case Discussion Facebook group page but quit because it made her too upset. But Alivea understands what a treasure trove—a hive mind of research—exists online.

Alivea speaks slowly and emphatically to the camera: "I'm in every group I can be. I monitor every post. Because what if he slips up there? What if he's *in* one of those groups? What if he says something that's a little too close, that gives me a bad feeling? That's why it's a long shot, but it's what *I* can do. *I* can take that time. I can read these posts. I'm physically capable of doing that. So I will."

Alivea devotes all her waking hours to the work, because who knows what—or who—she will find.

The same day that the Goncalves film with Olivia Vitale, the chief and his colleagues field a query from NBC about a Texas-based self-described psychic and TikTok cybersleuth.

Ashley Guillard, creator of "Ashley Solves Mysteries," has now posted hundreds of videos accusing University of Idaho associate history professor Rebecca Scofield of orchestrating the murders.

Professor Scofield has never met any of the four victims. She and her husband and young children were in Portland, Oregon, when the murders occurred, but this doesn't matter to Guillard, whose "evidence" is based solely on her "clairvoyant" insights.

She keeps posting that Scofield had had, at some unspecified time, a romantic relationship with Kaylee, and when she was jilted, she hired a hit man to prevent the affair from ever coming to light. Guillard identified the hit man as Jack DuCoeur.

Scofield hired a lawyer in Boise, former US attorney Wendy Olson, who wrote twice to Guillard asking her to cease and desist with the lunatic claims.

But the psychic doubled down and posted even more.

On December 21, Scofield sued Guillard for defamation. The suit claimed that her family's safety had been put at risk.

So, today, NBC is on the phone to the police, asking if Scofield is, in fact, a suspect.

By now Fry, Snell, and the communications team know better than to bother squawking in disbelief when the crank questions come.

They give a measured statement: "At this time in the investigation, detectives do not believe the female associate professor and chair of the history department at the University of Idaho suing a TikTok user for defamation is involved in this crime."

"I know I said at one point, 'There are no dumb questions,'" Fry later said. "But I was wrong. There are."

Chapter 84

Pullman, Washington
December 28, 2022

The WSU police chief, Gary Jenkins, is finishing up for the day when he sees that James Fry is calling his cell phone.

"Can you meet at our police department?" Fry asks.

Jenkins and Fry are old friends. Jenkins was recently reassigned to WSU, but prior to that, he ran the Pullman Police Department for twelve years.

It's highly unusual for Fry to be as secretive and tight-lipped as he's been about the Idaho Four, as the victims are coming to be known, but the chiefs have helped each other out on dozens of cases. Jenkins knows what his friend is trying to prevent: somehow tipping off the murderer.

So, as he drives over to the Moscow police station, he assumes Fry's holding a second multiagency briefing, similar to the one where they asked for help searching for the white Hyundai Elantra.

But when Fry meets Jenkins at the front door of the station, the WSU chief senses this is different.

Jenkins follows Fry upstairs and into the conference room and sees a sea of faces. He realizes the entire team of investigators is gathered there, waiting for him.

What they are about to tell him, Fry says, is completely confidential, not to be shared even with his agency.

In that instant he realizes why he's there.

They've found whoever did this.

And this person is at WSU. On his turf.

His heart sinks.

Brett Payne says, "We think we know who the suspect is, and he's in WSU housing."

And then he says his name: "Bryan Kohberger."

Odd name, Jenkins thinks. But it's an odd *familiar* name. It rings a bell, and then it comes to him.

"I know that name," he tells the people in the room.

He sees astonishment on their faces.

"I think I interviewed him for an internship position when I was Pullman chief. I probably have his résumé and cover letter in my files."

He goes straight back to his office and sends them over.

Payne and the team receive them, and their contents make it straight onto Payne's draft affidavit, the one he'll submit providing evidence to justify an arrest warrant for Kohberger. It already contains what the police have discovered about the path of the Hyundai Elantra, Kohberger's cell phone records, and what Dylan Mortensen saw that night.

Payne now adds to it the following:

> Pursuant to records provided by a member of the interview panel for Pullman Police Department, we learned that Kohberger's past education included undergraduate degrees in psychology and cloud-based forensics. These records also showed Kohberger wrote an essay when he applied for an internship with the Pullman Police Department in the fall of 2022. Kohberger wrote in his essay he had interest in assisting rural law enforcement agencies with how to better collect and analyze technological data in public safety operations. Kohberger also posted a Reddit survey which can be

found by an open-source internet search. The survey asked for participants to provide information to "understand how emotions and psychological traits influence decision making when committing a crime."

While Payne is writing, Jenkins is sitting in front of his computer, already running his to-do list through his mind. He's getting ready for what he'll say when he's allowed to share what he knows and for when his team gets the green light to write the warrants for the Moscow team to search Kohberger's home and office.

Thank God he'd spoken to the guy in charge of camera security along Stadium Way, the main street in Pullman.

Soon after the murders they'd agreed it might be worth holding on to the footage of the night of the murders beyond the regular retention of sixty days.

He sees in his databases that the Pullman cops pulled over Kohberger in October. And he now sees that his guys, Officers Tiengo and Whitman, had identified the car a few weeks back.

WSU's community is going to freak out when Kohberger is arrested. Jenkins knows this. He's got a team of counselors on standby for the cops; he'll almost certainly have to offer their services to the university.

He goes back to his database. What else was there about this guy that was missed?

There was a break-in near his apartment reported recently. Wasn't there some story about a student being followed to her car?

What else?

His train of thought is interrupted by his phone. It's Fry, thanking him for Kohberger's résumé and cover letter. "No problem," says Jenkins.

"Oh, and Gary, one more thing," says Fry, letting out a small chuckle: "Aren't you glad you didn't accept his application?"

"More than you know," replies Jenkins.

Chapter 85

Albrightsville, Pennsylvania
December 27, 2022

G et in. *Get the garbage. Get out. Don't be seen.*
Don't be seen.

The FBI surveillance team can tell Kohberger is skittish. And that he knows what he's doing.

It's pitch-black, freezing.

The agents are cloaked by night and by the dense woods of the Poconos. It's the time when most people are sound asleep, particularly in the dead of winter.

And yet, astonishingly, at four a.m., Bryan Kohberger walks out of his parents' house, carrying garbage and wearing nitrile gloves. He dumps the bag in his neighbor's trash can. Then scurries inside.

But a few hours later he's back out again, gloved and depositing more garbage in his neighbors' trash cans.

Back and forth. He carries out bags several times in the hours to come. Always wearing gloves.

The agents are ahead of him, though. They know time is of the essence.

In the early hours of the morning, they fish the garbage out of the Kohbergers' bins and the neighbors'. According to the law, once trash is placed in a bin or on the curb, it is public property. They fly it to the Idaho state lab.

By December 28, they've got what they need.

They alert Pennsylvania's state police, stationed at Stroudsburg, to be ready.

Bryan's DNA was *not* in the trash. He must have worked overtime to ensure that. But his dad's DNA is.

And his dad's DNA shows a likelihood of his being the father of the person whose DNA is on the knife sheath—a likelihood that, according to the lab, would not be shared with at least 99.9998 percent of the male population.

That's enough for Payne to finish his probable-cause affidavit, sign it, and walk it over to the courthouse for the signature of Judge Megan Marshall.

From there it's emailed to Pennsylvania.

Justin Leri and Brian Noll, two veteran troopers in Pennsylvania's Criminal Investigation Division, fill out the paperwork they need to get a judge to sign the arrest warrant and the other seizure warrants. At 4:35 p.m., Judge Margherita Patti-Worthington of the Monroe County Court of Common Pleas signs them.

Now it's go time.

The Pennsylvania State Police Special Emergency Response Team (SERT) gets ready for a night raid.

Chapter 86

Rochester, New York
December 29, 2022

It's 7:10 p.m. and Kristine is hunched over her laptop watching Pappa Rodger cross a line.

He writes to one woman: **Please elaborate you attention whore.**

And to another: **You are full of donkey excrement.**

Kristine has asked a friend, Deb Cully, to oversee the page when she and Alina are busy. Deb's technical title is page moderator. She calls Kristine. "This guy's going crazy," she says. Deb has had to delete four of his posts in the space of a few minutes.

Kristine tells Deb to go ahead and ban him.

"We have strict rules about name-calling other people, belittling other people, swearing at them, or trying to meddle in their real life," she said.

But when you ban someone, you delete the footprint of all their posts.

This is not something that worries Kristine in this moment, but later she will wish she'd screenshotted absolutely everything he ever posted before they banned him.

An hour later she sees that he's created a new Facebook page, called Moscow Idaho Murders Anything Goes.

It's a collage of Instagram photographs, chiefly from Maddie's account, although there are a couple of pictures of Kaylee.

Oh, well, Kristine thinks. Pappa Rodger is trying to compete with her. Let him try!

But the next day he goes dark. No posts. Nothing.

When Kristine looks at her Facebook messages to find their correspondence, she sees the messages are gone, as is his creepy picture.

Now, *that* is weird. That doesn't need to happen after a ban.

She doesn't know if he deliberately styled himself after Elliot Rodger or what his deal was.

On December 30, the news bursts onto TVs around the country: The police have made an arrest. In Pennsylvania.

When Kristine compares the features of the guy in handcuffs on her TV screen to the profile picture of Pappa Rodger, she sees an uncanny resemblance.

And she starts to wonder...

Was he right here under her nose all this time?

Is Bryan Kohberger also Pappa Rodger?

Chapter 87

Albrightsville, Pennsylvania
December 29, 2022

The emergency response team readies the explosives, the flash-bangs they'll use for "dynamic entry." It's the only way to handle dangerous arrests.

"You've got to protect the team," Fry said. "It's all about creating a diversion."

He did his part to divert Kohberger by giving a short statement earlier that evening in his office. On camera he announced that 1122 King Road would be visited by a cleanup crew on Friday to deal with biohazardous material. He also thanked the public for the tips—almost twenty thousand had come in. His entire statement took one minute.

If Kohberger was watching—and chances were, he was—he'd have no idea from the chief's grim expression and matter-of-fact delivery that outside his window, around forty highly trained members of the Pennsylvania State Police SWAT team are getting ready to enter his parents' house.

Fry, on the other side of the country, knows from personal experience exactly how this is going to play out.

Back in 2011, Fry's ride-along partner, Paul Kwiatkowski, stood on a ladder looking into a room at the Best Western hotel where a UI assistant professor of psychology, Ernesto Bustamante, was holed up with six guns; he had just shot dead his student Katy Benoit, with whom he'd had a romantic relationship. The cops wanted to get inside the room before he could shoot himself or someone else. They had shot canisters of gas through the window to persuade him to come out. Kwiatkowski's goal was to explain what was going on and calm the professor down.

But with no warning, the SWAT team threw a flash-bang through the front door into the gas, temporarily blinding Kwiatkowski and almost knocking him off the ladder. The chief climbed up the ladder to rescue his friend, who recovered.

But Bustamante had killed himself by the time the cops got into the room. That was not ideal.

So Fry knows the playbook they'll likely use in Monroe County.

The team in Pennsylvania would use flash-bangs as a distraction. They'd likely throw one through the front door or run a diversionary device through, say, the back window or the kitchen. The combination of the loud bang and the bright light usually stunned the occupants and gave the team time to get into the room.

The team in Pennsylvania wound up doing more than this to guarantee access. It was later determined that they'd blown out several windows *and* several doors.

They find Bryan Kohberger awake, dressed in shorts and a shirt. He's standing in the kitchen wearing medical-type gloves putting trash in ziplock bags.

They surround him at gunpoint, zip-tie his hands, and stuff him in a police car.

Then they ransack the house and his car for anything and everything covered by the warrants.

A few hours later, Kohberger is sitting in the Monroe County jail. He's been swabbed for DNA. After initially waiving his right to counsel and agreeing to speak with law enforcement without a lawyer, he'd changed his mind and asked for one.

At approximately 7:15 a.m. local time, Gary Jenkins accompanies the

Moscow PD team with warrants to search Kohberger's apartment in Pullman and his office on campus.

And at one p.m., James Fry ascends the podium at city hall. With Bill Thompson behind him on the left, he's finally able to say the words that he hopes will deliver the knockout blow to his numerous critics.

"Last night, in conjunction with the Pennsylvania State Police and the Federal Bureau of Investigation, detectives arrested twenty-eight-year-old Bryan Christopher Kohberger in Albrightsville, Pennsylvania, on a warrant for the murder of Ethan, Xana, Madison, and Kaylee."

Later that night, Fry's Florida emailer writes: "We'll see if you got your right guy."

Fry wonders if this guy will still be skeptical once Kohberger is in custody in Idaho and he's read the probable-cause affidavit.

Because if ever a document demonstrated good police work, Fry thinks, this is surely it.

PART FOUR

On the Run

Chapter 88

Moscow, Idaho
November 13, 2022

The drive west from Moscow to Pullman on Route 270 can take just minutes.

On the back roads, it can take hours.

When Brett Payne's affidavit became public, it explained the police's belief that Bryan Kohberger took the circuitous route.

According to the affidavit, after the murders, Kohberger's Elantra left Moscow, headed south toward Genesee, then turned west to Uniontown— which is not so much a town as a shack surrounded by miles of cornfields.

If WSU kids have been drinking in Moscow and don't want get pulled over by the cops, they'll risk the back roads, well known to be deserted during the day, unlit at night, and treacherous with snow and ice in winter.

But Rand Walker, the Moscow therapist, opined that to someone who has committed murder, the road's most dangerous facets could become conveniences. He suggested that a person could toss a murder weapon into the surrounding snow-covered fields, and the chance that anyone would find it was negligible.

That early morning, according to Payne's affidavit, it took Kohberger over an hour to make his way back to Pullman—fifty minutes longer than it took to drive the eight miles on 270.

But he stayed home for less than four hours.

At around nine a.m., according to Payne, he left Pullman and returned to Moscow.

Not just to Moscow, but to the very scene of the murders.

Every criminologist knows that the more emotional the crime, the more likely it is that the criminal will revisit the scene.

Kohberger's phone pinged on the 1122 King Road network between 9:12 and 9:21 a.m.

It was the last time that the cops saw his phone use the Moscow cell network.

And then, the cops believe, he went home.

His cell phone records showed him arriving back in the Pullman area at 9:32 a.m.

But Kohberger wasn't done driving for the day. Not by a long shot.

Just three hours or so later, his cell records suggest, he made the forty-minute trip from Pullman to Clarkston, Washington, via US Highway 195, where cameras saw him at Kate's Cup of Joe coffee stand and then, at 12:46 p.m., at the Clarkston grocery store, Albertsons, where he purchased unknown items and left at 1:04 p.m.

Students of local crimes—and Kohberger was most certainly one of those—knew that Clarkston was a good place to throw things into a river.

Twelve years earlier, Charles Capone strangled his estranged wife and threw her body into the river. It was never found. Bill Thompson got the conviction only after an accomplice talked.

Next, Payne wrote, Kohberger returned to the country roads he had been driving the night before.

His phone pinged in the rural backwoods of Johnson, Washington, two hours from Lewiston, between 5:32 and 5:36 p.m. Then it vanished from the network for two and a half hours, from 5:36 p.m. to 8:00 p.m.

Payne didn't account for what happened in those hours.

But Kohberger's defense attorney, when he got one, wrote in court papers that the police never found the murder weapon, nor did they find any of the victims' DNA on his clothes or in his car.

In fact, the knife sheath appears to have been his only mistake.

Gary Jenkins said, "From what I've heard of his activities afterwards, he was pretty sophisticated in knowing how to get rid of DNA and whatever else he needed to do.

"I don't know if he went to Lewiston, but he certainly did a lot of driving around."

Chapter 89

Pullman, Washington
November 14, 2022

Ben Roberts has his mind on end-of-term exams, so he barely notices that the spot where Bryan Kohberger usually sits in class in Wilson-Short Hall is empty today.

Ben's head is filled with projects and deadlines. Plus, he's just bumped into someone in the financial technology program who has news of four horrendous homicides over in Moscow. University students stabbed in their bedrooms in the middle of the night.

That's completely horrible, Ben thinks.

He tries to put it out of his mind. Goes back to focusing on his classwork.

But later, members of the cohort, and Ben, will think hard about Bryan's absence that day and what it meant.

They clocked it because they decided they needed to create a paper trail, a record of what Bryan said and did. Just in case something unexpected happened. If he were to lodge a complaint against one of the professors, for instance.

"We all felt he was creepy," Ben said, "but harmless."

Bryan is weird. But he's not *evil.*

But the next day and the day after that, Ben starts to see a slight change in Bryan. He becomes a bit lighter, more animated. Ben ascribes it to the end of term coming and the "filters" coming off. Something about his appearance is a little looser. He's grown stubble.

Ben also hears that Bryan's grading of the undergraduates' papers is changing dramatically.

Everyone—women included—starts getting high marks. Bryan stops writing essays on their essays. Some of the students are shocked. But also relieved.

Ben hears the gossip, but he doesn't pay too much attention to this at the time. None of the cohort does; their focus is on exams and grades. They came here to get graduate degrees so they could find good jobs. Ben assumes that's what they all want.

Bryan must too.

But when Ben thinks about it, he realizes Bryan doesn't talk much about his plans for the future.

Still, Ben assumes he has them.

Why wouldn't he?

Chapter 90

Pullman, Washington
November 17, 2022

S ome of the WSU kids have skipped town early for Thanksgiving.

The murders over in Moscow have freaked everyone out.

So the receptionist at the medical center is glad when one of them, at least, keeps his scheduled appointment.

The kid's name is Bryan Kohberger.

He comes in in a North Face jacket. Tall, thin, pale. Eyes that bug out.

He's a talker. Goes out of his way to chat to all the staff. Charm them. He stands out.

The receptionist doesn't usually remember anyone's name, but she'll remember Bryan's. Her boss doesn't usually comment on any of the patients, but even she says, "He's so nice and charming."

The receptionist agrees.

Before he leaves, Bryan schedules an appointment for next spring.

"See you then," she tells him.

She and her colleagues will look forward to that.

Chapter 91

Pullman, Washington
November 18, 2022

S o what do you think about the murders in Moscow?"
Peggy at the state department of licensing in Pullman is making small talk with the tall, thin WSU student at the front of the line who has come to exchange his Pennsylvania plate for two Washington plates for his white Hyundai Elantra.

His name, according to the forms, is Bryan Kohberger.

She and her five colleagues regularly make small talk with their customers. They pride themselves on running a government outfit that's got some character. They allow pet dogs to run around. They don't want their customers to have a run-of-the-mill experience just because it's vehicle licensing.

They want the experience to be memorable, fun even. They've got a reputation they are proud of.

So Peggy doesn't hesitate to get into the murders with this guy in order to pass the time.

"Horrific, isn't it?" he replies.

She later says that there was nothing out of the ordinary about their conversation.

He's as happy to chat as she is. Frankly, it makes people feel better about what happened to blow off steam together. It's a productive coping mechanism.

The guy says he's as shocked as they all are. Nervous, too, that the murderer is on the loose. He wants to know what she thinks. Who would have done that? Is the murderer among them? What about what the cops said?

It's such a perfectly normal exchange that, given the circumstances, Peggy doesn't think twice about it.

But then, after he's arrested, when she sees his face on TV, it hits her.

The guy she had that perfectly normal chat with about the murders was changing his plates.

To try to get away with it.

She can hardly believe it.

Chapter 92

Pullman, Washington
December 2, 2022

At 1:45 p.m., Rose Perez, a local hair stylist, sees that one of her regulars, Bryan, is coming in for his usual: "skin-fade thirty-five-minute hair appointment."

No big deal, she thinks.

Bryan has always been nice. Polite. He started coming to her in July. Since then, he's popped in every few weeks and become one of her regulars.

He left her a voicemail yesterday asking if she could fit him in the next day. She was able to see him at Powers Barbershop, just off the main street in Pullman, where she works most days.

So today he shows up, and as she clips using the scissors and the blade, they talk the way they usually do. She learns he'll be heading home to Pennsylvania for Christmas soon. But he plans to be back in January.

It's a routine visit on a routine day.

But in four weeks, Rose won't think anything about it or him was routine. When she sees his mug shot on TV, she falls on the floor.

"It's crazy to find out I interacted with this person," she later said. "I touched this person's hair. I made this person look and feel good about themselves."

Like everyone whom Bryan ran into over the next few weeks, she wonders if she missed any signs.

But Bryan is a good actor.

He's confident.

And the Pullman police have no idea that the suspect is in their midst. Or what he looks like. Or, in fact, anything, because for once, in an unprecedented fashion, Moscow hasn't been looping them in or sharing any details—and that makes them unhappy.

Glenn Johnson, the Pullman mayor at the time, later reflected: "Everyone was so frustrated. 'Where's the information?' they kept asking."

The Pullman cops have an unwritten rule never to have less than half a tank of gas in their cars, in case Moscow needs them to pursue someone who committed a crime there.

But now the Pullman cops are sitting in their cars, idle. They have nothing to go on.

When WSU police chief Gary Jenkins considered how Bryan resumed his normal activities in Pullman in the days and weeks following the murders, he believed his actions denoted a growing confidence.

"I would think with every day that went by that he wasn't caught that his chances were getting better and better [that he wouldn't be]," Jenkins said.

But cockiness, it turns out, can be misplaced.

Chapter 93

Pullman, Washington
December 2022

Iℓt's one of the last classes of the semester, Criminal Justice Processes and Institutions, a course taught by Dr. Craig Hemmens in Wilson-Short Hall.

The topic of the recent murders in Moscow is brought up for class discussion.

For instance: What is legally on the table for the murderer when they've caught him?

Idaho has the death penalty; Washington State does not.

The murderer surely would have known this.

Ordinarily, Bryan would be front and center, speaking more than most of the others.

But one of Bryan's classmates—someone who has four classes with him that semester and is used to listening to his monologues—notices that he doesn't speak at all. Not once in three hours. He's got nothing to say on a topic that has the class revved up.

This is extraordinary, the classmate thinks.

The classmate assumes Kohberger is ill or tired or something. Ben

303

Roberts, another classmate, remembers dimly that Bryan said he was extra short on sleep in December.

But it doesn't occur to anyone that their homophobic, misogynistic classmate is anything other than deeply weird.

Ben wonders if Bryan is feeling the pressure of being the only one in their cohort from the East Coast, if he's found it hard to adapt to Pacific Northwest culture.

"He is running into an entirely new group of people who are now his peers," he said. "He doesn't have any seniority over anybody. He doesn't have any authority...He is trying to adapt to a new social structure on the opposite side of the country. And the West Coast does things somewhat differently from the East Coast."

Weeks later, Steve Goncalves—his blood boiling at the thought of "this Pennsylvania kid who came out here on purpose to kill us"—said something similar.

"I know my history...the East Coast feels like they're the superior coast," Steve said. But he's determined not to let this atrocity undermine the very reason he moved his family here, his desire to provide a safe home for his family.

So his goal is to make absolutely sure prosecutors get a conviction so the world can see that Idaho is still the sanctuary he believes in.

"We have farm towns and trusting people," Steve said. "But he underestimated us."

Chapter 94

Pullman, Washington
December 9, 2022

B ryan is blowing up again at Professor Snyder.

Only two days ago, it had seemed as though Bryan might have eked out a Hail Mary.

He and Snyder, along with graduate director Dale Willits and Dr. Melanie-Angela Neuilly, so the cohort hears, had met in Wilson-Short Hall to discuss Bryan's progress following the improvement plan that had been emailed to him on November 3.

The plan that told him to be more respectful to women—his professors, his peers, and his students.

"While not perfect, we agreed that there was progress," Dr. Neuilly wrote to Bryan, yet the committee still decided it had to terminate him.

Because now, just two days after that promising meeting, Bryan is losing it—for the second time this semester—with Snyder in the professor's office.

When Ben and Bryan's cohort hear about this, they are mystified about how anyone could rub the affable, easygoing professor the wrong way.

"To use very coarse language for a second," Ben said, "if you fuck up badly enough that you wind up on a PIP, a performance improvement plan, as a graduate student, you have done something terribly, dreadfully, miserably wrong."

But Bryan cannot control himself in front of Snyder, apparently.

The rest of the class has seen what happens to Bryan when he's angry. He goes bright red and clenches his fists so hard that his knuckles turn white.

Chief Jenkins heard that one of the thorny issues under discussion is the allegation by a woman student that Bryan followed her to her car.

But the discussion spins out of control, way beyond civility, into something angry.

Two days later, on December 11, Dr. Neuilly wrote to Bryan requesting a meeting—at which he must have known she would fire him. And he would lose his funding.

She later wrote in her termination letter of December 19 that she'd requested the meeting because, during his "altercation" with Professor Snyder, "it became apparent that you had not made progress regarding professionalism."

Bryan will receive this letter when he's back home, in Pennsylvania, so the rest of the cohort is in the dark as to what happened.

As far as they know, he'll come back in January. But they aren't giving much thought to him and his difficulties.

Top of mind for them is the troubling fact that there have been these horrific murders in Moscow, and the police seem to have no clue who did it.

So everyone just wants to get the heck out of Dodge for the holidays.

Chapter 95

Pullman, Washington
December 12, 2022

Deola Adetunji, a WSU criminal justice undergrad, is puzzled when she looks at her end-of-semester grade.

She sees that Professor Snyder's TA Bryan has posted that she got a B.

He's wrong, she thinks. He added up her scores wrong. She deserves an A. So she emails him and tells him he needs to fix it.

She's never had a one-on-one interaction with Bryan before. She's seen him in Professor Snyder's class three or four times, but not recently.

It seems that he has stopped coming to class. She doesn't know why. She assumes he's got his own stuff to take care of.

When he *was* in class, he was strangely restless and flitted around unnervingly. One time Professor Snyder asked him to move because, the professor said, he didn't like people standing behind him while he taught — so Bryan hovered somewhere by the door. It was awkward.

At 10:58 p.m., Bryan emails Deola back. "I have adjusted the settings to only count your ten highest scores. This should have a positive impact. Let me know if you have any questions."

Good, she thinks. *That's taken care of.* And she doesn't think about Bryan Kohberger anymore.

Until she sees his mug shot a few weeks later.

And then she thinks that if he committed the murders he's been accused of, it's both odd and interesting that he bothered to answer her email about her grade.

Chapter 96

Indiana
December 15, 2022

At 10:45 a.m. on the third day of the four-day cross-country trek east from Pullman, Washington, to Albrightsville, Pennsylvania, father and son hear sirens on I-70 outside Indianapolis.

Bryan pulls over and waits for the officer to get out of the cop car and approach from the shoulder.

Michael Kohberger is in the passenger seat, a buffer between the officer and his son.

If Bryan fears the worst, he hides any inner turmoil. His face is pale, as usual. But his hands are on his lap, relaxed.

The sheriff's deputy is disarmingly cordial as he asks for Bryan's license.

"You were right up on the back end of that van. I pulled you over for tailgating. Is this your car?"

Bryan nods.

"Where ya headed?"

Now Michael injects himself into the conversation, which goes strangely circuitously.

Michael: "Well, we're coming from WSU —"

Sheriff's deputy: "What's WSU?"

Michael says, "It's Washington State University." Then he explains there's just been an incident there involving a SWAT team.

Bryan interjects: "I go to the WSU university, basically."

No one has answered the deputy's question, so he asks again: "So you're coming from Washington State University and you're going where?"

Michael tells him, "We're going to Pennsylvania." He adds conversationally and with emphasis: "We're slightly punchy from hours—days!—of driving."

Sheriff's deputy: "What did you say about some SWAT team thing?"

Michael: "There was a mass shooting and everything..."

Sheriff's deputy: "Interesting."

Michael: "Well, it's *horrifying,* actually."

Sheriff's deputy: "So y'all work at the university there?"

Bryan: "I actually do work there."

Michael (with pride): "He's getting a PhD."

Sheriff's deputy: "Yeah, I hadn't heard about that incident...just yesterday or..."

Michael explains that just an hour and a half ago, they learned that a SWAT team was called in to deal with a gunman hostage situation at WSU. The situation is "still wrapping up." He says he thinks they did shoot somebody.

Bryan again interrupts his dad. "Not sure about that, actually."

This conversation has gotten far, far away from tailgating.

The cop has got other things to do today.

"Interesting," he says.

He lets them go.

Not ten minutes later, the Kohbergers hear sirens again. They are still on I-70.

This time it's the Indiana State Police.

Again, the trooper explains he's pulled them over because Bryan is tailgating.

If Bryan senses anything strange or threatening about this second stop, he hides it well. This time Michael looks slightly nonplussed when the officer appears at the passenger window.

But again, the officer is quick to let them go: "I'm not gonna give you guys another ticket or warning if you just got stopped. Just make sure you give yourself plenty of room. It's all about how fast you're going, okay?" Then he asks, "Where y'all headed?"

When they answer, he laughs. "That's a long haul. You guys scared of airplanes?"

For weeks, months, years, in fact, after Kohberger is arrested, it's reported that the Indiana stops were not random. It's reported that the FBI already had Kohberger in their sights. That the FBI had a single-engine plane tracking him. That the FBI hadn't looped in Moscow to what they knew.

Many articles mention this, and Chief James Fry gets irritated every time he reads one. Because it's not only off base; it's completely nuts. He's pissed that the only leak, the *only* leak in the entire investigation, came not from any of the people who worked directly with him but, he believes, from the Pennsylvania branch of the FBI.

"So tell me this. If they can't keep their mouth shut that we're getting ready to arrest a person . . . do you think they can keep their mouths shut about a plane tracking the killer all the way across the United States?" he asked sarcastically.

Yet again, in his view, the media knows nothing and wants to make a buck off something. "It makes a great story," he said wryly. It's also completely untrue.

"If that truly would've happened and I would've found out about it, you would've probably seen the roof of the police department come off."

The boring truth of it is, as far as Fry knows and as a spokesperson for the FBI has, unusually, stated on the record, the stops in Indiana *were* random.

The timeline of the investigation indicates that law enforcement had not yet homed in on Kohberger on December 15. Brett Payne hadn't even heard the name "Bryan Kohberger" until the FBI phoned on December 19. He didn't try to obtain warrants for Kohberger's phone records until December 23. It was only in the days right before Christmas that the threads connecting the touch DNA on the knife sheath, the right model of white Hyundai Elantra, and its new license plate and owner came together—and then the phone records all pointed to Bryan Kohberger.

On December 15, when the Kohbergers were pulled over, law enforcement still didn't have him.

The Kohbergers arrived in Pennsylvania on December 16 without being stopped again, and Fry's team was later able to see that the car had reached home.

But in that moment, Kohberger was still safe. He was still below the radar of Fry's team.

Although that was changing by the minute.

Chapter 97

Albrightsville, Pennsylvania
December 28, 2022

Bryan gets in the car—he's cleaned every inch of it, inside and out—and drives to the end of Monroe County and back.

He doesn't know it, but he's got eyes on him every second.

The car and his phone are being tracked.

There's a team of Pennsylvania state troopers in the woods surrounding 119 Lamsden Drive, surveilling it around the clock. They've been there since yesterday at dawn.

They've seen him depositing the garbage in his neighbors' bins.

Bryan has no idea that they've taken the family garbage or that a forensics lab will determine that there is a 99.9998 percent chance that the DNA collected from the trash belongs to the father of the person whose DNA was on the knife sheath found beside Maddie at 1122 King Road.

He has no idea, basically, that it's game over.

Chapter 98

Albrightsville, Pennsylvania
December 29, 2022

When FBI agents storm the Kohberger family home, blowing the door down and the windows out, raiding it and Kohberger's car, they have warrants for anything and everything that could connect him to the murders at 1122 King Road.

Pennsylvania state trooper Justin Leri signs his name to each of the two long lists that go into the "FBI's Receipt of Property" document, which will be made public months later.

From Bryan's car, they take:

Swabs, Ziplock bag with pink zipper, 7 quarters, plastic baggie with green zipper, 36 dimes, 32 nickels, 8 pennies, gloves, receipts, car insurance card, car registration, hiking boots, Comfort Inn room key holder and stay information, tire irons, shovel, goggles, floor mats, reflective vest, used water bottles, wrench, door panel, seats and seat cushions, headrests, seatbelt, visor, fiber, brake pedal, gas pedal, phone charger, band aid, wrappers, maps, document, seat belt, boot.

From the Kohberger family home they take items that quite obviously could connect Bryan to the "firefighter" of Dylan Mortensen's half-awake dream: an assortment of clothing, including black face masks, hats, gloves, boots.

They take his phone, laptops, hard drives, computer, the black-box Samsung car-navigation system, as well as three knives—including a large, sheathed Taylor Cutlery knife—a gun (a Glock 22), and three magazines. They also take a flashlight, two bags with a "green leafy substance," an AT&T phone bill, and a large Craftsman shop vacuum.

More tantalizingly on Leri's list are items that are not fully explained but that could suggest a possible motive for murder. It's the inclusion of these that catches the attention of cybersleuths when the list is made public, months later in March.

For instance, the list intriguingly mentions a book—it doesn't give a title—with underlinings on page 118.

All the online forums—the Facebook discussion page, Reddit, TikTok, Instagram, and more—will debate for days if this could be underlining on page 118 of Elliot Rodger's manifesto.

On that page, Rodger wrote of how he came to select the date of his "day of retribution," his act of misogynistic terrorism. After ruling out Halloween because of the heavy law enforcement presence, he decided it "would have to be on a normal party weekend, so I set it for some time during November."

Then there's the item on Leri's list of a drawing referred to as "A Man's Mind." Could this be a reference to a well-known black-and-white poster of a man's face in profile with a naked woman erotically arched backward, cleverly drawn into his frontal lobe? The name Sigmund Freud is scribbled underneath.

That's the question posed by cybersleuths, who post the drawing side by side with page 118 of Rodger's manifesto and suggest—to much agreement—that both point to the mind of a misogynistic incel who planned a murder that was more or less a copycat of Rodger's 2014 killing spree as vengeance for all the women who would not sleep with him.

Other miscellaneous items are harder for the online community to analyze.

These include a "note to dad from Bryan, a note in his desk," a "note from Bryan to Montana," a criminal psychology book, other criminology books, a maroon notebook, documents, and the DeSales University handbook.

As the items are being seized and documented, on the other side of the country, in Pullman, at 10:38 p.m. PST — 1:38 a.m. EST — Chief Jenkins gets the call from Moscow he's been waiting for.

Kohberger has been arrested in Pennsylvania.

Some of Fry's team, led by Sergeant Dustin Blaker, are already en route to sit outside Kohberger's Pullman apartment while Jenkins's crew paper and serve the warrants.

By 7:15 a.m., the paperwork is done. And while Jenkins's team watches, the Moscow team goes in looking for evidence that ties Kohberger to the King Road murders.

They take, according to papers filed in court:

> One nitrile type black glove
>
> 1 Walmart receipt with one Dickies tag
>
> 2 Marshalls receipts
>
> Dust container from "Bissell Power Force" vacuum
>
> 8 possible hair strands
>
> 1 Fire TV stick with cord/plug
>
> 1 possible animal hair strand
>
> 1 possible hair
>
> 1 possible hair
>
> 1 possible hair
>
> 1 possible hair strand
>
> 1 computer tower

1 collection of red dark spot (collected without testing)

2 cuttings from uncased pillow of reddish/brown stain
    (larger stain tested)

2 top and bottom of mattress cover packaged separately
    both labeled "C"

Multiple stains (One tested)

When this list is published, it isn't just the internet forums that focus on the "possible animal hair strand," along with the bloodstains and human hair, as being of vital importance.

Steve Goncalves wonders if the hair could belong to Murphy, Kaylee's goldendoodle, now in Jack's care. "She loved to sleep with Murphy, so the question I want answered is who put Murphy in a separate room that night?"

If it was Bryan Kohberger, well, Steve thinks, *that could have been a costly mistake.*

Chapter 99

Monroe County, Pennsylvania
December 30, 2022

They hold him in the Monroe County Correctional Facility in Strouds- burg, about twenty-five miles from his parents' home. And they talk to him for nearly fifteen minutes.

Bryan Kohberger is charged with four counts of first-degree murder for Xana, Ethan, Maddie, and Kaylee, and one count of felony burglary for breaking into 1122 King Road.

They've swabbed him for DNA several times. Presumably the samples are in a lab being analyzed right now.

But Bryan knows no more than that about what law enforcement has on him. According to Idaho law, Brett Payne's probable-cause affidavit must remain sealed until the suspect is back in the state.

At first Bryan says he doesn't need a lawyer. He's calm. When he's asked if he knows what murders they are talking about, he says of course.

"Yes, certainly I'm aware of what's going on. I'm ten miles away from this," he says.

And then, suddenly, he changes his mind. He asks for a lawyer.

While he waits, he's given a dark green blanket-like suicide-prevention vest to wear. As a Fox News reporter explained: "Suicide-prevention vests are used to 'ensure warmth and comfort' while not obstructing the wearer's movements, according to PSP Corp, a maker of tactical and suicide-prevention gear. The vests also cannot be rolled or torn and prevent inmates 'from using the fabric to create a weapon or hanging mechanism.'"

On the morning of December 30, Jason LaBar, the chief public defender for Monroe County, comes to see Bryan.

LaBar said that he was astonished when he first got the call. Of course he knew about the murders—but for the suspect to be in Monroe County? "I did not expect that."

LaBar finds that his new client is calm in all of their four meetings over the next three days. Unusually calm, given the circumstances.

Bryan tells the lawyer that he was "shocked" when the agents burst into his parents' home waving guns in his face.

LaBar said that in his experience—and he has quite a lot of experience—every defendant reacts differently.

Kohberger seems to want to chat; it's as if he's got a story he wants to tell LaBar. But the lawyer cuts him off.

"I really wanted to make sure that [Kohberger] understood that I didn't want to know about the facts and circumstances."

LaBar explains to Bryan that he's there only to handle the extradition proceedings. That someone in Idaho will be appointed to act as his criminal lawyer. That the only way for Bryan to learn why he's been charged with these crimes is to fly back to Idaho. Only then will the probable-cause affidavit, the document filed by the police with enough in it to justify the arrest and search warrants, be available to him. LaBar is just as in the dark as his client.

LaBar is almost surprised by how quickly Bryan agrees to waive his rights in Pennsylvania and be extradited. His client wants to understand what the police think they know. "He was very candid with me about the extradition," LaBar said, which made his job easier.

So did Bryan's obviously high intelligence and working knowledge of criminal law.

LaBar works with Bryan on the wording of what he, in his role as chief public defender, will say to the media; journalists noted that it did not explicitly state that he was innocent.

On Saturday, December 31, LaBar issues that statement.

> Mr. Kohberger has been accused of very serious crimes, but the American justice system cloaks him in a veil of innocence. He should be presumed innocent until proven otherwise—not tried in the court of public opinion. One should not pass judgment about the facts of the case unless and until a fair trial in court at which time all sides may be heard and inferences challenged...
>
> Mr. Kohberger is eager to be exonerated of these charges and looks forward to resolving these matters as promptly as possible.

Chapter 100

Monroe County, Pennsylvania
January 3, 2023

Dressed in a red prison jumpsuit, Bryan walks into the Monroe County Court of Common Pleas in Stroudsburg for the extradition hearing. He looks three times at his family.

The person he gazes at directly is his father, Michael.

Bryan even smiles — faintly.

As Judge Patti-Worthington questions him as to whether he's fully understood that he's waiving his rights in Pennsylvania and will be flown to Idaho to face four charges of murder, Maryann Kohberger collapses.

A court official rushes over and provides Kleenex. Mrs. Kohberger's eyes are so swollen from crying that she can barely see as the proceedings finish.

Two nights ago the family released a statement that they had worked on with LaBar.

> First and foremost we care deeply for the four families who
> have lost their precious children. There are no words that can
> adequately express the sadness we feel, and we pray each day
> for them. We will continue to let the legal process unfold and

as a family we will love and support our son and brother. We have fully cooperated with law enforcement agencies in an attempt to seek the truth and promote his presumption of innocence rather than judge unknown facts and make erroneous assumptions. We request privacy in this matter as our family and the families suffering loss can move forward through the legal process.

After the judge signs the extradition order and they've said goodbye to Bryan, who walks out of the courthouse flanked by guards, the Kohberg-ers return to their home with its blown-out windows and doors.

Privacy is something they will find they have lost.

Chapter 101

The single-prop plane makes two refueling stops, first at Willard Airport in Savoy, Illinois, then in Rapid City, South Dakota, on its journey from Pennsylvania to Pullman.

A sea of law enforcement, members of the Latah County Sheriff's Office, arrive at 5:15 p.m., ahead of the 6:23 scheduled landing.

It's pitch-dark when Bryan gets out, cuffed, but the flashes pop and media can see his distinctive features as he towers over the officers flanking him. He's got a dark winter jacket on over his red prison clothes.

Agents load him into a black SUV and make the eight-mile drive to the Latah County jail beside the courthouse in Moscow, where they book him. Then he waits in a small cell for a lawyer and for the wheels of justice to start turning, moving him toward his eventual trial for mass murder.

As far as law enforcement knows, it's Kohberger's first time back in Moscow since his brief visit to King Road four hours after he allegedly committed the murders.

This time, he's here to stay for the foreseeable future.

PART FIVE

Blame Game

Chapter 102

It's late, after ten thirty p.m., and the Chapins are headed to bed.

Stacy is showering when Jim hears her phone ring. He looks at the caller ID. He knows something big must have happened for Tyson Berrett to be calling so late.

"Stace, you need to come get this," he yells.

Stacy comes out and hears from Berrett that they have just arrested a guy named Bryan Kohberger.

She and Jim go to Hunter's and Maizie's bedrooms and tell them the news.

That night, for the first time in weeks, Jim Chapin sleeps well. They all do.

Kohberger's arrest can't bring Ethan back. But Maizie and Hunter are headed back to UI in a few days, and Maizie was worried that whoever murdered Ethan was still around campus, lurking.

Stacy and Jim assured her that the UI campus right then was probably "the safest in the country"—but privately, behind their closed bedroom door, they expressed to each other that maybe Maizie was right to be concerned.

So the fact that the police have arrested someone comes as a huge relief.

They have no idea what his connection to Ethan is, and they are not interested in finding out. The bottom line is that their son is in a jar in their basement and nothing can change that.

But when Jim sees Kohberger's face on the news, weirdly, it resonates.

"He just looked like a bad guy... the long, drawn face... he just... fit the picture that I had in my mind," he said later.

Jim is glad they've got him. He wants this guy to pay. And he feels certain that he will, no matter what happens next.

"Stace will shoot me for saying this... but... there's three ways you can look at it. He's either going to go to jail for life or he is going to be put to death or he's going to walk out the front door. And I'm okay with any one of them. Because the outcome for him is going to be the same."

What he means is that Kohberger is not likely to survive even if he gets off.

This is Idaho, after all.

"You really think Steve Goncalves," Jim asked months later with a wry smile, "is going to sit back while he walks around freely?"

The answer is no.

Chapter 103

Rathdrum, Idaho
December 29, 2022

There's relief for the Goncalves family too, of course, after Tyson Berrett tells them the news.

Tomorrow is the joint memorial for Kaylee and Maddie. Now the family can focus on the service without the fear that their murderer is watching.

They have no idea what the connection could be between the girls and the guy the police have captured, this criminology PhD student at WSU. And what's the deal with WSU? How and why did the school protect him if he'd been the menace he seemed to be on social media?

Steve hears from Alivea, who is plugged into social media, about all the red flags Kohberger exhibited; students started posting them once the arrest was made public. The more he learns, the angrier he gets.

Just because this was a school environment, it seems to him, this guy—Steve doesn't like to say his name—got protections he would not otherwise have had. WSU hasn't published any of the disciplinary problems the school faced with Kohberger.

Steve Goncalves isn't going to stop with his own investigations just because they've got him in custody. "Half of the stuff that I found and dug up on him...that shit hasn't [come] out...And it pisses me off. They've really clammed up," he said.

Steve plans to keep up the pressure on the prosecution the same way he did on the cops.

He's going to search the dark web for any piece of data he can find. He's going to look for this guy's cell records, his social media posts. He's going to leave no digital stone unturned.

Steve wants to make sure, absolutely sure, that Bill Thompson gets a conviction.

Anything less would not be serving Kaylee.

Chapter 104

Pullman, Washington
December 30, 2022

Journalist Evan Ellis is live on air that Friday when he sees a text from Chief Fry:

Holding a press conference at 1 pm.

There are many press conferences held by the Moscow PD these days, so Ellis doesn't pay much attention. This was a mistake, he later realizes, because the chief had never given him a heads-up about any of those.

Ellis is still on air when the news breaks in Pennsylvania. It's a leak: Agents there have arrested Bryan Kohberger, a WSU criminology PhD student.

Oh, shit, Ellis thinks, experiencing a rare feeling of shock.

The murderer had been walking among them.

He needs to report. If Kohberger was at WSU, he's been living in Pullman. And if he's been living in Pullman, the Moscow team is going to be raiding his apartment right around now.

Ellis phones a source in law enforcement and asks where in the area he might "bump into" out-of-state authorities executing a search warrant.

The source tells him, "I'd go to the Steptoe Village Apartments."

Ellis arrives just as the raid is getting started and records it for his Facebook page.

But even as he clocks the scene in front of him, his mind is racing to what comes next.

Based on his experience, he fears that the administration at WSU, his alma mater, will go into communications lockdown. "My wife works there and she shows me some of the crap that WSU sends out [internally], which is: 'Do not say anything. Do not talk to anybody... This is not happening. You're not talking.' And of course, they can't prevent people [from doing] it, but they're extremely vindictive up there and everybody is scared."

Ellis and the WSU vice president of marketing and communications, Phil Weiler, have long had a contentious relationship. "I fight with WSU on a weekly basis," he said, "about hiding information and shutting out the taxpayers... It's completely disgusting and sad, but WSU has been doing it for years."

Today is no different, he thinks. *In fact, it's worse.* Evan phones Weiler. He texts him. He emails. Nothing.

At noon, the school issues a statement.

> Law enforcement officials in Pennsylvania have arrested Bryan Christopher Kohberger, a Washington State University graduate student, in connection with a quadruple homicide that took place in Moscow, ID in November.
>
> "On behalf of the WSU Pullman community, I want to offer my sincere thanks to all of the law enforcement agencies that have been working tirelessly to solve this crime," said Elizabeth Chilton, chancellor of the WSU Pullman campus and WSU provost. "This horrific act has shaken everyone in the Palouse region.
>
> "We also want to extend our deepest sympathies to the families, friends, and Vandal colleagues who were impacted by these murders," Chilton said. "We will long feel the loss of these young people in the Moscow-Pullman

community and hope the announcement today will be a step toward healing."

This morning, the Washington State University Police Department assisted Idaho law enforcement officials in the execution of search warrants at Mr. Kohberger's apartment and office, which are both located on the WSU Pullman campus. WSU Police are working closely with local, state, and federal law enforcement officials as they continue their investigation.

Kohberger had completed his first semester as a PhD student in WSU's criminal justice program earlier this month.

Ellis thinks this isn't good enough.

Where is the transparency? Accountability for hiring Kohberger? Any apology?

He posts a Facebook video that afternoon in which he repeats Weiler's name three times for effect: "We have reached out multiple times to WSU spokesman Phil Weiler for more information on Kohberger as a WSU student. Phil Weiler has failed to return any emails, texts, or phone calls in regard to this arrest of a WSU student, doctoral student in criminology, and any more information from WSU on this suspect has been denied at this point with no response from Mr. Phil Weiler, the spokesman at Washington State University."

He later tells his listeners that part of his frustration with the college is based on history that goes back two decades.

Bryan Kohberger is *not* the first high-profile criminal connected to the WSU Department of Criminal Justice and Criminology.

On Route 270 between Moscow and Pullman, Evan tells his listeners, there's a road sign commemorating three WSU fatalities. In 2001, a twenty-two-year-old student, Frederick Russell, was charged with the vehicular homicide of three WSU students and of injuring four others in a horrific crash on that highway. Fred was drunk at the time.

His father, Gregory Russell, was the head of the criminal justice department.

Fred was arrested, but three days before he was due to stand before a preliminary hearing, he escaped, accompanied by a WSU criminal justice graduate student and Russell family friend. He spent six years on the lam and was featured on the US Marshals' Most Wanted list before being captured in Ireland.

Evan doesn't hide his disgust.

"This is how deep it goes with that dumpster fire of an institution that I went to," he said.

As it happens, the mayor of Pullman, Glenn Johnson, who is a regular on Evan's show and a friend of his, also knows the story of the Russells.

Mayor Johnson, who holds a master's degree in journalism and a PhD in mass communications, shares Evan's frustrations with WSU's stonewalling. That the school where he taught classes in subjects like television news and communications management for thirty-five years before becoming mayor employed the guy arrested for the Moscow murders is a bridge too far, he thinks. *Something* needs to happen at that school. *Something* needs to change.

So when he finds himself in an emergency meeting with WSU chancellor Elizabeth Chilton, he says: "Elizabeth, in case you hadn't been told, this is the second time there's a bad story coming out of WSU's criminal justice department."

He figures she probably does not know about the Russells because she's new. She started in January 2022.

"So, the point is," he says in conclusion, "this"—he means Kohberger—"is the second black eye [for the WSU criminal justice department]."

He adds with a flourish: "You only have two eyes."

Chapter 105

Pullman, Washington
December 30, 2022

In fact, the Washington State University administration is in total meltdown.

Inside Wilson-Short Hall, phones are ringing off the hook as the news of Kohberger's arrest spreads like wildfire.

Professor Snyder is bombarded with calls. So too is Professor Willits.

The last people either one wants to engage with right now are members of the media.

Willits is distraught. It was he who admitted Kohberger.

A day or so later, he runs into WSU chief of police Gary Jenkins in the corridor, and Willits almost collapses.

"He was about ready to break down," Jenkins said. "He said, 'I just feel horrible. I'm the one who accepted him in this program.' So he felt responsible."

As Evan Ellis predicted, the administration's mandate—don't "give interviews"—comes down very quickly from on high to the faculty and the students in the department of criminal justice. That's the message in the email that Ben Roberts and the other members of Kohberger's cohort receive from WSU administration.

Ben and the others are in transit back to Pullman after the holiday break when they receive the email. Which is shortly followed by a bombardment of emails and calls from the media. Kohberger's class list is on WSU's website for a further twenty-four hours before the department takes it down, citing privacy.

The students immediately reach out to one another, torn between shock and disbelief.

What had they missed?

And, worse, as advanced students of criminal minds, *how* had they missed it?

"I can't think of a group of people who would be better positioned to see this sort of behavior, the red flags associated with it in their own ranks," Ben said, "and we just completely didn't see it."

Several of them struggle with the idea that Kohberger was just there, in their midst, sharing office space and classes.

"It's one thing to study criminology from the relative safety of academia's ivory tower," Ben said, "but it's quite another [to] have a quadruple homicide on your doorstep."

So when the graduate students arrive on campus, WSU administrators are ready for them; there's a meeting attended by staff and students in which they learn they will receive psychological support from counselors loaned out by Gary Jenkins's police department.

It's much needed. The group feels not only blindsided by what happened but betrayed. And the curt answers they get from faculty in the meeting don't help much.

"We enter into criminology because we want to make the world a better place," Ben said. "There's a general interest, not really in taking the reins of power, but in figuring out how those reins of power can affect people and how you can service the system to be better. And so when you see somebody run off and do the exact opposite of that and make the world a very, very dark and ugly place for somebody, it sort of really is the ultimate betrayal of everything that I think a criminology program stands for."

Making things worse is that the group is now under siege on campus.

Journalists pose as students. The cohort winds up locking their offices because random strangers mill around, holding out their phones, wanting a quote.

The cohort locks down. They decide that to protect the members' sanity—and for practical reasons of getting on with their work—they'll follow the case and they'll talk to investigators when they inevitably come to question them.

But they no longer want to discuss Bryan Kohberger, even among themselves.

Chapter 106

Moscow, Idaho
December 30, 2022

Dean of students Blaine Eckles gets up at around six a.m. and sees
he missed a call from Captain Tyson Berrett the night before, at
around eleven.

It's rare that he misses phone calls. Usually his wife, Shelley, gets the
phone if he can't, but they'd both fallen asleep.

He texts the police officer: **Hey Tyson, what's up?**

Before he gets a response, he sees a news flash. Moscow PD is holding a press conference. They've arrested a suspect in Pennsylvania. He
attends Washington State University.

Eckles feels like a huge weight just lifted off him. "Once we learned
that the alleged perpetrator wasn't from our community, that was such a
relief," he said. "Just knowing... what it meant for our students... I knew
they'd feel more secure."

He texts Jenna Hyatt, the dean of students at WSU.

In the weeks since the murders, he's gotten to know Jenna well. The
outreach he's received from her has been so overwhelming that he's
ashamed that UI hasn't done more for other campuses in tragic times.
She's sent counselors to man the UI counseling center so that the UI team

could attend the vigil. She's sent care packages galore. He considers her a good friend.

So now he texts her, sympathizing: **The tidal wave that just hit our campus is about to hit you.**

Whatever she needs, he wants to help.

Chapter 107

Moscow, Idaho
December 30, 2022

exi Pattinson, daughter of local lawyer Mike Pattinson, is pissed.
She's on TikTok on her phone, watching all these videos that WSU students are making about Bryan Kohberger.

Apparently the guy was a TA? He was *hired* by WSU?

WSU has a reputation, locally, for hiding bad news. Lexi knows a lot about this because her mom works there, so she's heard the stories.

"Their hazing is much worse than ours," she says, explaining that WSU's Greek life, unlike the University of Idaho's, is not regulated by the Interfraternity Council. (Three weeks after Kohberger's arrest, nineteen-year-old WSU student Luke Tyler dies in his bed—a "suicide" after being badly hazed—and the school does not issue any statement. Lexi's mom tells her that the staff is very, very upset.)

She can see on TikTok that Kohberger's former students are talking about all the red flags: his harsh grading of women, his rude remarks to women in class, his aggression, his stalking of someone, his social difficulties.

So where is a statement from WSU about the school's role in this?

"He was their hire, a teacher, a TA," Lexi said after learning about

Kohberger's past disciplinary problems. "They haven't even addressed that aspect. And I think that's disgusting and that reflects on a lot of the community. I know my mom and people that work there were pissed."

Her mom will wind up leaving.

The only silver lining—and it's a very, very thin one—is that Kohberger's arrest removes a question mark Lexi had about the possible role of someone she went to Moscow High School with: Emma Bailey.

Emma lived near the King Road house and would, months later, face drug-related charges in connection with the suspicious death of another UI student. (Prosecutors dismissed the case.)

When the Vandal Alert went out about an unconscious person and then Lexi heard about the murders, she was worried that drugs and Emma were involved.

But when she learned it was a knife attack and that drugs were not involved, she stopped suspecting Emma. When Lexi sees all the stuff floating around on TikTok about Kohberger and his strange behavior, she's relieved that he's not from Moscow.

Even so, as she looks around at the enhanced police presence and the way everyone now locks their cars and doors at night, she realizes that the imprint Kohberger made on Moscow is going to last for a very long time.

"People think they know how it affected our town," she said, "but [they don't]. It isn't the same. We lock all our doors...all our car doors... our little town isn't as safe as we thought it was."

And in her mind, WSU is primarily to blame.

Chapter 108

Montana
December 30, 2022

Moscow's mayor, Art Bettge, is spending the holidays in his off-the-grid cabin in northwest Montana, and one morning, there's an unexpected knock on the door.

It's one of his neighbors. She tells him there's been an arrest in the case.

Bettge treks with her to her cabin to borrow her Starlink internet connection. He contacts the city council and gets a sneak peek at the arrest and extradition documents. He immediately understands why it took a few weeks for the investigators to get to Kohberger's DNA.

"The public does not realize how long DNA analysis takes and believe results should be available in TV-crime-show time frames," he said. "In my day job as a food scientist–biochemist, I know better."

He quickly gets up to speed on Bryan Kohberger.

Thank God the guy is from Pullman and not from Moscow, Bettge thinks.

And where the hell has Pullman been on this, anyway? Have they not been looking out for white Elantras? That was out in the public.

And as for WSU . . .

For WSU, he thinks, this comes at a tricky juncture. The school has lost its footing—that's the common view in the area.

"I think they've sort of forgotten why they're supposed to be there," Bettge said. "You're a land-grant university, which means you should be primarily involved in research associated with agriculture, mining, forestry—issues like that."

Instead of which, the school has focused on football; the athletic department has run up a twenty-million-dollar debt. And now the Pac-12 Conference has been depleted because, apart from Oregon State, all the other schools have left. There are rumblings that the faculty is about to deliver a vote of no confidence in the administration.

Bettge is going to sit back and watch this unfold—with a little bit of schadenfreude.

There's a lot of connectivity, for obvious reasons, between Moscow and Pullman—they share an airport and an aquifer but also an unspoken rivalry. After all, they are in different states. Each houses a different university.

It's a source of pride to the Muscovites that many people who work in Pullman live in Moscow, even though it means they have to pay the 5.8 percent Idaho state income tax. (Washington has no income tax.)

Muscovites believe Moscow has a community spirit, a downtown with lots of bars and restaurants, and that Pullman, situated as it is on four hills, does not.

"You go to Pullman [at] lunch, noontime, things are happening. Go back at about six thirty or seven o'clock at night...it's like tumbleweeds are blowing gently down the streets," Bettge said. He launched into a joke he said he probably shouldn't tell, but what the heck:

"What's the difference between Pullman and yogurt? The answer is that yogurt has live culture."

Bettge says that the sudden switch in focus will turn out to be costly for Pullman.

"I don't know why, but WSU and Pullman were both completely and utterly unprepared for the attention to shift" in their direction, Bettge said. "They were caught flat-footed."

Chapter 109

Puerta Aventuras, Mexico
December 30, 2022

Emily Alandt comes down to the kitchen in her pajamas. Hunter Johnson and her parents are already sitting there talking.

"They found him," her mom says, and she hands Emily her phone.

Emily looks at the photo. She's never met this guy. She and Hunter feel certain that neither had Xana or Ethan.

Josie and Linden check in, and it turns out they never met him either. It's mystifying.

Josie immediately searches for Bryan Kohberger on Instagram, but she's too late. If he had a real footprint there, it's gone.

But there's a plethora of fake accounts.

She even gets a DM from one of them: **Hey, it's Bryan, sorry for killing your friends.**

Although she's heard the news she's been hoping for, Emily doesn't feel the emotional release she expected to. Although "there was someone arrested, there was no fear that had left my body," she said.

She doesn't really believe it can be this guy, some random stranger.

It's the one possibility she hadn't thought about: Why would someone unconnected to any of her four friends have murdered them?

"Just like everybody else out there," she said, she "expected it to be someone they knew."

Over and over again she reconstructs the events of that night—this guy entering the house—and replays them in her mind.

Why Xana? Why did he ignore Dylan?

"I have wondered a million times over why he walked away and didn't look in the other rooms...if Xana and Ethan, if Maddie and Kaylee, why not the rest?" she said. "I also just try to keep a positive mindset and say, 'Thank God, not the rest.'"

Chapter 110

Lehigh County, Pennsylvania
December 30, 2022

Josh Ferraro is on edge, waiting for the news.

Last night, Grace, a friend he works with at the Swim-In Zone, a local pool, told him that her dad was part of the state police team staking out the home of the suspect in the Idaho Four killings.

She tells him that it's a former DeSales student.

Josh is shocked.

He went to DeSales. He studied criminal justice, then spent three years as a corrections officer. So he feels like he has more understanding than the average person about why people commit serious crimes.

The people he's seen locked up, they look like average Joes. They *are* average Joes, in fact, for most of their lives. But underneath... underneath there's an itch. And these people spend their lives waiting for the chance to scratch it. They put themselves in places where the opportunity is readily available.

On December 9, for the heck of it, Josh made a TikTok video suggesting the profile of whoever did this is a single male between the ages of twenty and thirty. That's because, he theorized, Moscow was a college town, and the suspect would need to blend in.

Still, when the face and name of Bryan Kohberger flash on his TV screen, he's taken aback. Something about that name rings a bell. But that face—he doesn't remember that face.

Until he checks his phone and sees old emails.

"Oh, shit!" he says.

It's the Ghost. His lab partner on a biology project. The strange guy who showed up promptly for classes, then vanished into his car and drove off to one of an assortment of jobs. The guy who didn't speak to anyone except the professors. Who occasionally hung back to talk to Professors Ramsland and Bolger.

When Josh last saw the suspect's face, it was fuller. Different.

Josh is shocked.

Nothing about Kohberger stands out in his memory as a red flag. Nothing.

Quiet, yes. Strange, yes. Awkward, yes.

But a murderer?

"There's nothing, there's just nothing to the guy, except he was a good student," Josh said.

He reaches for his phone and texts as many of his classmates as he can find. Does anyone remember anything peculiar about Bryan Kohberger? Anything that would indicate he'd turn into a mass murderer?

They ask one another the same question:

When they look back, what did they miss?

Chapter 111

Center Valley, Pennsylvania
December 30, 2022

DeSales University professor Katherine Ramsland is deeply frustrated.

As soon as the news breaks that the suspect arrested for the murders of the Idaho Four was once a student at DeSales, the university issues an edict to the faculty:

No one who taught Bryan Kohberger is to say anything.

So the expert in forensic psychology and extreme offenders finds herself in a truly ironic situation. She's the author of seventy-two books, more than a thousand articles, and a *Psychology Today* blog called *Shadow Boxing,* the tagline for which is "a blog that probes the mind's dark secrets." And yet she's not allowed to write or talk about the one murder case she has personal knowledge of and for which she may or may not be called to testify—the case involving her former student Bryan Kohberger.

Her inbox and voicemail are cluttered with endless media requests that she has to decline.

She reads media reports describing her classes, like her Psychological Sleuthing class in the crime scene house where she staged murder scenes using dummy bodies and fake blood and asked the students to act as detectives.

She reads recollections of Kohberger as one of the better students, someone who evidently wanted to impress Ramsland by reading her books, including her most well known, *Confession of a Serial Killer,* about Dennis Rader, the BTK Killer.

In articles discussing her classes—including her course on spree murderers like Elliot Rodger—her students tell the media they remember Kohberger dedicating himself to the assignments, in particular to Rodger's YouTube video, which was on the syllabus.

Classmate Brittany Slaven remembered that he was so "advanced" that she once peeked at his paper when stuck on a test, knowing he'd have the correct answers.

Brittany said they spent weeks learning from Ramsland, via the acronym IS PATH WARM, the characteristics that law enforcement should look for to detect a murderer-in-waiting:

I—Ideation

S—Substance abuse

P—Purposelessness

A—Anxiety

T—Trapped

H—Hopelessness

W—Withdrawal

A—Anger

R—Recklessness

M—Mood changes

What if Kohberger had copied Elliot Rodger? The character similarities were there all along. Ramsland's students tell the media they learned from Ramsland that psychopaths like Rodger and Rader are very hard to detect.

Chad Petipren, another student of Ramsland's, said that he remembered Kohberger as a normal guy. Bryan sometimes mentioned going to church and Bible study, but when Chad asked him questions about the Bible, Bryan didn't always know the answer.

But look at Dennis Rader and what Ramsland taught them, Petipren said. "Rader had a son, he had a child . . . It's like he became a normal person for years. He could have been my church president."

Until, that is, Rader went out and committed murder.

Chapter 112

Saylorsburg, Pennsylvania
December 30, 2022

That little prick! He was in my house all the damn time!"
When Mark Baylis sees Kohberger's image on the TV, he swears. Suddenly it all makes sense.

If the guy is capable of murder, he's certainly capable of burglary.

Baylis remembers Kohberger as clear as day, always lurking behind his son and nephew, never saying hello, staring into space.

He hadn't connected the dots at the time. But now he's sure of it.

Baylis dials the local state troopers and asks them to reactivate the investigation into the series of break-ins he experienced all those years ago.

He hadn't been able to figure out who was stealing items from him piecemeal, maybe up to twenty-five times, taking thirty thousand dollars' worth of rare coins, jewelry, and knives from his house out in the woods.

The worst of it was that, at the time, he'd worried it was some of the homeless veterans his charity aimed to help. That was a shitty feeling.

He'd known it had to be somebody who knew his property well, who could get close enough to watch the house and track his movements.

Someone who had the time to sit out in the woods, crumpling up the Reese's Peanut Butter Cup wrappings, dropping them on his land.

He just hadn't bothered to think about his son Jack's friends.

Until now.

This Kohberger guy was always around. Until he got into heroin. And then Jack had dropped him for a bit.

So Mark asks the cops if this time they could do their job, because he knows who was stealing from him.

But it turns out, it doesn't matter.

The case is no longer in their system. It's too old.

"We can't do anything," they tell him.

Mark's too busy to press further.

Looks like the little prick is going to get his comeuppance anyway.

Chapter 113

P oor Maryann!"

All Connie Saba can think of when she sees the news about Bryan is his poor parents.

All those struggles with Bryan, the arguments that he and Michael used to have on the phone when Bryan was in her house hanging out with her son, Jeremy.

Maryann trying to protect Bryan from Jeremy.

The silent breathing over Connie's phone after Jeremy died.

Connie wants to believe the best, but she can't.

She knows better than to phone Maryann. That woman is a closed book at the best of times.

And this is not the best of times.

Connie is going to pray for her.

Chapter 114

Moscow, Idaho
January 4, 2023

The Suburban pulls into the garage. The steel doors lock behind him. Bryan Kohberger walks down the twenty steps to the fluorescent-lit dungeon that is the tiny, underground Latah County jail.

It was state-of-the-art construction back in 1972 when someone with a sense of humor scrawled outside the newly built booking room: *Welcome to the Latah Hilton*. Decades later, the graffiti was removed.

Most of the inmates are there for the usual reasons: drugs, DUIs, domestic abuse, assault.

Technically, the jail—with a capacity of thirty-eight inmates—is too small to meet the state's legal requirements. There aren't enough rooms. The inmates are housed in a square around the common areas: kitchen, shower, and library. They're allowed just one hour a day, combined, to use the library and the twenty-by-ten-foot wired-in exercise yard. There's nothing else to do except watch TV.

It's a twenty-four-hour cycle of boredom with the odd flash of excitement.

In 1984, Leslie Rogge, the "gentleman robber" who was being held for federal bank robbery, walked out, aided by a map and a door opened by the jailer. He was not apprehended until 1996, in Guatemala. He's due to be let out in May 2034, at the age of ninety-four.

In 1992, William A. Davison, a twice-convicted murderer, escaped from the exercise yard. He was captured after a manhunt lasting a month.

The common shared cell for up to eight people is not where Kohberger goes.

Months later, a friend of Josie and Linden's who is drunk and booked there for the night sees Kohberger in a cell alone, per his "maximum security" status.

Jail staff are not going to take a risk with him.

"Inmates have wives and children too," Sergeant Brannon Jordan, the deputy who was injured in the fatal shooting of Officer Lee Newbill, said. "What he did is out of a horror movie.... In the prison world there's status that comes with harming someone like him."

The deputies' priority is to keep Kohberger alive.

They need him to face the wheels of justice.

"Nobody," Jordan said, "wants to fuck that up."

PART SIX

Warpath

Chapter 115

Moscow, Idaho
January 5, 2023

They bring Bryan Kohberger up from his cell into the tiny Latah County courtroom, and he sits in the defendant box within spitting distance of the Goncalves and Laramie families.

He's shackled and clad in orange prison clothes.

He doesn't turn to look at anyone. His only animated gestures are directed to Anne Taylor, his public defender, who sits easily beside him. Taylor has long, blond, shiny hair, and everything about her—clothing, posture, and demeanor—exudes a no-nonsense confidence. If she's ruffled to be representing America's most notorious suspect, she doesn't show it.

Taylor works for the public defender's office in Kootenai County, where serious crime is far more abundant than it is in Latah County. (In an irony that will soon come to light, one of her clients was Xana's mom, Cara Northington. Taylor avoided the conflict of interest by quietly filing for a withdrawal from Northington's case.)

Moscow is scarcely unfamiliar territory for Taylor. She attended the University of Idaho's law school—it's almost impossible to find a lawyer in the area who didn't. In fact, the man who gave Taylor her first job is now sitting a couple of feet away from her on the other team: Bill Thompson.

Judge Megan Marshall, the Moscow magistrate, is another part of the cozy UI law graduate circle, and she reads out the charges against Kohberger. Four counts of murder, one of burglary. She asks if he understands them—he says he does. She explains that the punishment is either the death penalty or life in prison. The prosecutor has sixty days to decide which one he intends to pursue.

Judge Marshall sets another court date a few days hence to determine the date for the weeklong preliminary hearing during which the prosecution will lay out its evidence to show grounds for a trial.

Steve Goncalves watches it all go down with a mixture of extreme emotions. He has not been eating or sleeping more than three hours a night. Kristi and Alivea have been telling him they are worried about him.

But it's tough for him to sit back and watch this guy with the strange eyes and the passive face, considering the fact that he's alive and Kaylee is dead.

Where is the justice in that?

Steve read Brett Payne's probable-cause affidavit—it was filed one hour before the court proceedings began—and there's a lot in it, undoubtedly. The highlight, clearly, is the DNA found on the snap of the knife sheath. It's going to be hard to argue against that. That's what his sources in the local FBI are telling him. DNA is the gold standard of evidence.

But Payne's affidavit says that investigators got to Kohberger's DNA via his dad's, so the defense could look for loopholes there—and Steve is worried.

Will the DNA evidence hold up as legitimate and legitimately obtained? Will the defense try to argue that Kohberger's DNA could have gotten on the knife sheath years before? Steve plans to do his own research on how long DNA could last there.

"I'm told that that version of a Ka-Bar has a special material for the button and it's copper-based, and that dramatically speeds up the deterioration of the DNA—tests have shown sometimes less than twenty-four hours to the max seven days," he said.

And what about the lack of an obvious link between Kohberger and the victims?

Kohberger wasn't part of Kaylee's circle, so will the lurid speculation that Kaylee had an OnlyFans page or some sort of secret life worsen?

Steve wants to protect Kaylee, be her mouthpiece now that she's unable to speak for herself.

But Judge Marshall just made that harder.

Ahead of Kohberger's extradition from Pennsylvania, Judge Marshall imposed a gag order stopping the police, investigators, attorneys, and anyone connected to the investigation from talking to the media. The point of this, obviously, is to protect the investigation.

But a few days later—without any public process or rationale—she refines the gag order to include the lawyers for the victims' families and witnesses.

Steve doesn't like this one bit. His attorney, Shanon Gray—and thirty news organizations—filed an appeal.

Steve's concern isn't simply that his First Amendment rights are being restricted, though that is a legitimate issue. It's that he has seen and felt the harm that occurs when there's a vacuum in the narrative. He's seen all the rumors about Kaylee on Facebook, which Alivea, thankfully, was able to quash. He's seen innocent people like Jack DuCoeur falsely accused until the police cleared them. Now there's no official check on the rumors and speculation about Kaylee and Maddie other than a trial that could be years away. Kohberger's defense can say anything in the courtroom—and Steve is helpless to speak out against it.

"All this misinformation will get out there and then it will just sort of become legend," he says.

He's so upset that he stays locked in his home office for hours, glued to internet conspiracies. Concerned, Kristi and Alivea come up with an idea to help him.

They decide to take control of a Goncalves family Facebook page and repurpose it. Now that Kohberger has been arrested, what had originally been set up to field tips will become a supportive online community, not only for the Goncalves family but also for other families going through similar experiences. It's a way, at the very least, to tell the world what *they* are thinking and feeling—a way to keep Kaylee and who she really was alive in the public imagination.

Chapter 116

Rochester, New York
January 5, 2023

It's the mention of the knife sheath Kohberger left at the scene that convinces Kristine Cameron that Bryan Kohberger and Pappa Rodger are one and the same.

When Kohberger was arrested and she saw his face on the news, she thought that he looked similar to the strange profile picture of Pappa Rodger. But, she'd told herself, that could just be wishful thinking.

Kristine also thought about the fact that Elliot Rodger targeted sorority girls. In particular, he targeted the Alpha Phi sorority. Kaylee's sorority.

"I was like, wait a minute. [Kohberger] killed all—he killed four people. Three of them are girls, three of them. He's never had a girlfriend..."

After the arrest Kristine waits for Pappa Rodger to resurface on the Facebook page and opine about Kohberger.

But he doesn't reappear.

And his silence starts a frenzy on the Facebook page.

People put up screenshots of his earlier posts about the murders and highlight the parts of Brett Payne's affidavit that jibe just a bit too neatly with them.

There's his obsession with the idea that police had found a knife sheath at the crime scene, his opinion that the killer had been in the house fifteen minutes, that he'd stopped after killing four out of exhaustion, that the house was targeted for a reason, that the killer was not in the circle of victims' friends, that he'd left the neighborhood.

Once again, the contents of the Facebook page enter mainstream news. On NewsNation, Ashleigh Banfield does several segments on whether Pappa Rodger could be Kohberger.

Kristine and Alina half expect to get a call from the FBI or the police. It's not every day that you find you've *become* the story you are covering.

The exposure is helpful, Kristine believes, for Alina and herself. It takes the duo a big step closer to building an audience for the true-crime podcast they want to host. Vice Media has signed them to an exclusive deal to report on Kohberger.

Kristine loves that she and Alina are joined at the hip. Both women believe their arrangement works.

Alina puts in many more hours than her partner on this Facebook page and the others they started because, unlike Kristine, she's home most of the time because she's struggling with medical issues around an injured back. Alina believes that Kristine is fully supportive of her predicament; one night when Alina was recovering from a procedure, Kristine refused an invitation to go on Ashleigh Banfield's NewsNation show alone to talk about Pappa Rodger, a sign of how robust their friendship and partnership is.

But Alina has often told Kristine that she cannot afford to continue to work night and day on the pages if they can't find a way to monetize what they are doing. Kristine, who has a full-time job, tells her she understands. Their friendship and partnership are "above any sort of monetary thing," Kristine believes.

"I would've put her first," Kristine later said.

But by then, it was too late.

Chapter 117

Troy, Idaho
February 2023

He's been out in the snow for hours.

There's something deeply therapeutic about wielding a chain saw through logs again and again. In the two months since Kohberger's arrest, Chief Fry has used this quiet time to think and heal, though even out here, on his land, he's never quite able to forget those insane six weeks between Thanksgiving and New Year's Eve.

Thanks to the gag order, he's no longer being pressured to speak to the press. Fry has said no to every media request: "Geraldo, Katie Couric, Dr. Phil—I turned them all down," he said.

For now, it's mostly quiet; both sides are preparing for the preliminary hearing.

At work, he's continuing with the investigation, looking closely at Kohberger's digital footprint and the victims' to see if they intersect.

To see if they can find the motive.

Meanwhile, there's a page on Reddit called Justice for Kohberger that the chief follows, "for humor" and with irritation, on which people insist that Kohberger was nowhere near the house on the night in question and conclude that Fry's wife, Julie, who was elected county clerk in November, is somehow controlling Kohberger's court schedule or giving her husband advance notice of hearings.

The chief adores Julie, his wife of thirty-two years—"when she speaks, she's kind of like EF Hutton," he said—so this Reddit nonsense irks him greatly.

One conspiracy theorist even concluded that the chief was the murderer and Kohberger was framed as a scapegoat.

Fry looks forward to setting the record straight. As he hoped, Brett Payne's probable-cause affidavit definitely quashed some of the police department's worst critics. He received a congratulatory letter from retired LAPD deputy chief John D. White, the chief investigator in the O. J. Simpson case:

> Dear Chief Fry, Congratulations on a job well done. I told my wife after your first press conference, "This chief knows what he's doing!" Your handling of the media investigation was a textbook example of how to handle big media cases.

And the guy who'd emailed him that this would be the next JonBenét Ramsey case turned around and congratulated him as well. "You might have got the right guy," he wrote.

After all their back-and-forth, Fry was curious about this critic. "Tell me about yourself," Fry replied. He learned the guy was seventy, had been in the oil business in South Dakota before he retired and moved to Florida, and had three kids.

It never ceases to astonish the chief how, when you cut through all the crap, people have more in common with each other than they think.

Even Pastor Doug Wilson came to sit in his office recently.

The cops had lost their legal battle with Christ Church over the psalm-singing arrests, and Christ Church was now suing the city for wrongful arrests and the selective prosecution of Wilson's grandson.

But the pastor was extending an olive branch because he'd heard that Fry received death threats from Christ Church congregants over the episode. Fry told him that, yes, he'd received death threats, but not from Wilson's congregants, some of whom were police officers.

"I don't care who people are. We get paid and we take an oath to serve all people," he told Wilson.

Fry wishes that Steve Goncalves felt able to trust his department more. The chief hates to feel at odds with the family of a murder victim; he doesn't know how it happened, but he can see that the Goncalves family feels mistreated by the cops, and they do not trust Thompson and his team either. That's upsetting to him.

Their lawyer, Shanon Gray, is vocal in the media. He's demanding meetings and wants to be kept in the loop about whatever the cops hand over to Thompson as part of his case.

This is often a problem in murder cases. Victims' families think they are owed information, and by law, they do have some rights, but to protect the investigation, they can't be told everything.

It's not a perfect system. The chief knows that. And he's upset that the Goncalves family has articulated how upset they are to feel left out.

Fry wants to see this case through. But the clock is ticking. He's fifty-four years old. He believes in change. And elections for county sheriff will be held in November 2024.

That's the one other job, apart from being police chief, he'd love to have, and by then, he thinks Captain Anthony Dahlinger will be ready to replace him.

Fry needs to think about the future.

So he's taking a moment for himself, out here in the woods, while he can.

He's learned the hard way: You never know what's around the corner.

Chapter 118

Moscow, Idaho
February 2023

It's around eight p.m. and pitch-black when Ava Wood hears the knock at the front door of her home at 718 Queen Road.

She installed a Ring camera after the murders and she can see a man standing there. He's dressed in a Moscow PD uniform, but since last November, she doesn't trust anything or anyone. She keeps her door locked and waits.

He knocks some more.

Eventually she speaks through the camera: "Who are you here for?"

He replies, "I'm here for Ava Wood."

Ava had three new locks and an alarm system installed after the murders, and now she unlocks and opens the door.

He hands her an envelope and speaks in a clipped, formal voice: "You're being subpoenaed for the *State of Idaho versus Bryan Kohberger* preliminary hearing in June."

Ava thinks her legs might give way. She starts to shake. She has never been subpoenaed before.

"This is the Bryan Kohberger case?" she asks. "Who is it from?"

The officer answers, "The defense. Anne Taylor."

The *defense*?

"Do I have to show up?" she asks.

"Yes," he tells her. "It's illegal to disobey."

As soon as he's gone, Ava slams the door and, in tears, phones her parents.

Luckily, her dad is a lawyer who specializes in bad-faith litigation. He advises her to phone Thompson's office and let them know she has been contacted.

She speaks to Stacie Osterberg, Thompson's assistant, who suggests she should find out what Taylor wants.

So in March, Ava and her dad do a Zoom with Taylor.

On the call, Taylor homes in on something Ava told the police the day of the murders: On Friday, October 14, at one a.m., she'd heard someone climb up the metal steps to her apartment, which was across the street from 1122 King Road, and try the door.

"You could hear the jingle of my doorknob. It's a finicky doorknob," she said.

But the door stayed closed because Ava had put in a dead bolt during her junior year.

She told police what she now tells Taylor, that at the time, she'd looked on Snapchat to see if any of her friends were in the area, saw one, Mason Bangeman, and texted him to ask if he had just tried to let himself in.

No, he'd said. So Ava asked him to check the street. She watched through her bedroom window as Mason and a couple of friends walked into view. He texted Ava that he couldn't see anyone.

So Ava went to sleep. She didn't think any more about it.

Until Xana, Ethan, Kaylee, and Maddie were murdered in the house across the street.

And then she wondered aloud to the police: Was the murderer the same person who had tried to get into her apartment four weeks earlier?

Anne Taylor asks her repeatedly to describe what she can see of the street from her home. Ava says she can see the front door of 1122 King Road and the street leading up to it.

Taylor asks her if the police ever got back to her about the October incident.

The answer is no.

After Kohberger was arrested and Ava read the probable-cause affidavit, she asked if anyone in law enforcement knew if October 14 was one of the twelve times Kohberger's phone had pinged in the King Road area.

No one will tell her.

It occurs to Ava that if Kohberger wasn't in the area in the predawn hours of October 14, the defense could argue there was another predator running around.

But if he *was*...

Ava guesses from Taylor's other questions that the lawyer is looking for holes in the accounts of the victims' friends.

Taylor asks Ava a lot of questions: "How well did I know Maddie, Ethan, Kaylee, and Xana? What kind of people were they? Did the roommates ever fight? Did they leave their house unlocked? Did I ever attend the parties they had? How close was I with Dylan and Bethany? Were we all in the same room at the police station? Did I know anything prior to the police being called or showing up? Did I know anything while sitting outside? When did [I] find out all four of them were dead? Did I have any knowledge of Kaylee or anyone having a stalker? Did I hear anything that night? What did I do the night before? Why was I outside that morning? How did I get wrapped into this whole situation?"

Taylor apologizes for putting Ava through this, which is decent, Ava thinks.

But Ava, who is back with her parents in California, really does not want to testify.

Texts ping back and forth among her friend group. Who else has received subpoenas for the preliminary hearing on June 26?

Two of Jack DuCoeur's housemates, including Adam Lauda, the guy in the Corner Club bar, received them. So too has Ethan's close friend

Peter Elgorriaga. He was with Ethan and Xana until the end of the Sig Chi party on November 13. Unlike Ava, Adam and Peter can't try to contest the summons because of their location. They live in Idaho.

In April, court filings show that Bethany was subpoenaed by Taylor. But because Bethany lives in Nevada, it's been agreed she can be interviewed there instead.

How is that fair? Ava, the California resident, wonders. She writes to Taylor's office asking if they will at least pay for her travel and accommodation.

They will.

When she attends graduation in Moscow in mid-May, she keeps thinking that her next trip to Idaho is going to feel a lot more stressful.

She's back home in California a few days later when she hears the news: She doesn't need to return to Moscow for a preliminary hearing because there won't be one. Bryan Kohberger has been indicted for the murders by a grand jury Bill Thompson convened in Moscow—in secret.

All the better for the prosecution, which won't have to show its hand and reveal its witnesses to the defense ahead of a trial.

Chapter 119

Moscow, Idaho
May 11, 2023

Emily Alandt is already in town for graduation when she gets the email summons from Bill Thompson.

He's convened a grand jury and she needs to testify.

No one can know.

She needs to get to the Latah County Courthouse on Sunday evening, when Thompson's team will prepare her for what to expect at the real thing on Monday morning.

Hunter Johnson received the same summons.

The only people they tell are their moms, Karen and Jessica, who are with them for graduation.

Emily has an immediate problem: She has nothing to wear other than her graduation dress. So Jessica, Hunter's mother, takes her to Target, where she purchases a respectable pair of pants. It's hard, if not impossible, to relax through graduation events, knowing what lies ahead.

As she walks into the courthouse on Sunday evening, Emily glances at a big steel door to the jail. She shudders.

Kohberger is down there.

She tries to push him from her mind.

She and Hunter are separated for their practice sessions. Emily's interlocutor is Ashley Jennings. Emily is nervous answering the questions. There are times when she screws up and starts over.

The next morning, she and Hunter find that it's not as easy as they'd hoped to slip away from their friends, who are pregaming.

"We've got breakfast plans with our families," they lie.

"Oh, so do a breakfast shot first!" is the reply.

That puts Emily on the spot. But nothing is going to induce her to drink.

Too much is at stake.

She and Hunter are driving, five minutes from the courthouse, when a member of Thompson's team texts them an alert.

There's media outside. Use the side door.

When Emily does find herself in front of a jury, she is grateful for the preparation. It's intimidating. But she can do it. They ask the exact same questions she's just rehearsed, and she answers them smoothly.

"Tell us about the events of November thirteenth."

She and Hunter don't know who else Thompson called for the grand jury, but Emily suspects that Dylan and Bethany may have testified on Zoom. She doesn't see either girl around campus when she and Hunter return to their friends, then ultimately walk for graduation with their respective classes.

All she knows is that on May 17, it's announced that Bryan Kohberger has been formally indicted by a grand jury for the murders of Xana, Ethan, Maddie, and Kaylee—which means there will be no preliminary hearing.

Emily has played her part.

"I'll call you when I need you. But meanwhile I want you to get on with your lives."

That was Bill Thompson's parting message to Emily and Hunter when they headed back to Boise. But for Emily, returning to normality is a struggle.

After the murders, she struggles to focus. She worries that her GPA will not be good enough for her to get into a physical therapy program, so she ends up not applying. She's lost sight of her goals. She feels adrift, no longer the person she was before the murders.

Hunter is an athletics coach at Centennial High School in Boise, so he, at least, has structure in his life.

Emily takes a series of part-time jobs, and eventually trains to be a dental hygienist. But she knows deep down that she needs to address the trauma of November 13. She needs to try to get past it.

She starts going to counseling and digging deep, learning to be alone, even though, thanks to Hunter, she seldom is. Her doctor recommends she try Eye Movement Desensitization and Reprocessing therapy (EMDR), but when she runs this past Thompson's team, they warn her that this would likely disqualify any testimony she gives at trial because EMDR can affect memory.

Emily isn't going to risk that, even though a trial could be many months away.

"I don't want to testify, but I'm willing to do whatever it takes," she says. She wants to see this through. She wants to get justice for Xana, Ethan, Kaylee, and Maddie.

Then—and only then—she will do the therapy.

Chapter 120

Moscow, Idaho
May 22, 2023

Bryan Kohberger keeps his eyes forward, fixed on district judge John Judge, who is taking over the case after the indictment.

He answers "Yes," over and over, when the judge asks him if he understands the charges and the penalty for each one.

If found guilty, Kohberger faces either life imprisonment or the death penalty for each of the four first-degree murder charges.

"Ms. Taylor," the judge says, "is Mr. Kohberger prepared to plead to these charges?"

She rises and answers, "Your Honor, we will be standing silent."

The judge pauses. "Because Mr. Kohberger is standing silent," he says, "I'm going to enter not-guilty pleas on each charge."

If John Judge is surprised, he doesn't show it, but standing silent is not something that happens often. Many suspects don't even know there is an option besides pleading either guilty or not guilty. Even local attorney Mike Pattinson wasn't aware of this option.

But Anne Taylor is a very practiced criminal lawyer. And Bryan Kohberger knows more about criminal law than your average suspect.

There are two reasons, media commentators say, that someone who has said he understands the charges and issues would stand silent.

The first is if there are ongoing negotiations around a plea deal. Few people believe that that is the case here. Everything seems to indicate that Kohberger wants his moment of fame.

The second has to do with public perception. In high-profile trials, defendants might want to avoid sparking further public outrage by saying "Not guilty."

It's a nuance that likely occurs only to someone who thinks and cares about the PR ramifications of the court proceedings.

Bryan Kohberger, it is reported, cares greatly about the PR ramifications of his case. He watches TV coverage of it as much as he can in his jail cell.

Steve Goncalves complains publicly and often about Kohberger's privileges.

"We've got to get this guy. I don't want him ever, *ever* getting vegan meals, his own TV, his own phone, video conferencing his mother," he said. "I got family members that are military, they come home all messed up in the head. All they get is the VA. . . . And this is the way we treat our murderers? Our mass murderers that kill people? Vegan meals, TV, room and board?"

It's absolutely outrageous, Steve thinks. *But so much about the legal process is.*

Most people have no idea how frustrating it is to be in his shoes. Most people don't think about how little agency a murder victim's parents have.

But on his family's Facebook page, he's starting to hear from other victims' parents who say they wish they'd been more proactive and involved in their children's cases. He's getting messages of support from families all around the world.

It's hard to juggle his day job doing IT at the hospital and all this, but curating the page brings the Goncalves family together. It gives Kristi purpose on her down days.

The encouragement spurs him on.

Chapter 121

Moscow, Idaho
Spring 2023

Half a mile away from Kohberger's jail cell, in his office on Jackson Street, Christ Church pastor Doug Wilson closely follows developments in the Kohberger case and the implications for his family, especially his grandson Rory and his conviction for illegally affixing a sticker to a pole.

"This is just personal theory, connecting dots," he said. "I think that the judge [Marshall] did not want to throw the Moscow officials under the bus by finding in favor of Rory...because that would make the cops look bad. That would make the city of Moscow look bad in the middle of this."

His argument might not have gotten much traction with anyone other than his own congregants if it weren't for the fact that, after Kohberger was arrested, Marshall played into his hands by imposing the controversial gag order on the victims' families' lawyers.

When thirty media organizations and the Goncalves attorney, Shanon Gray, filed appeals against Marshall's gag order, Wilson felt deeply gratified. Now he isn't the only one who thinks Marshall has obstructed people's First Amendment rights.

This could be very helpful to Rory's case, he thinks.

"Just, not to put too fine a point on it," he said, but "Judge Marshall was the one who put the gag order on them, and she was the same person who excluded my grandson's defense. So it's the same. This is a small town. We're talking about the same people."

Wilson hoped that, given the public pressure, Marshall's superior, district judge John Judge, would be sympathetic to Rory's appeal. "We had heard rumors," he said, that John Judge "was not happy with the city of Moscow."

But it's May, and suddenly the district judge is under pressure of his own, because following the grand jury indictment, he's taking over Bryan Kohberger's case. It's by far the biggest one of his career, most of which he spent as a lawyer in private practice.

Later that spring, Judge John Judge denies Rory's appeal.

Doug Wilson is annoyed but unsurprised. He thinks that Judge, like Marshall, has no interest in issuing a ruling that could further harm the reputation of the Moscow PD in the wake of the murders.

John Judge is from the same network as all the local judges and lawyers. He is a UI law school graduate, just like Bill Thompson, Megan Marshall, Anne Taylor, and even Cathy Mabbutt, the coroner.

Wilson, now clear in his own mind that whatever happens in this case has a direct bearing on Rory's, intends to fight on. The Wilsons will appeal Rory's case all the way to the Idaho Supreme Court. They will sue in federal court too. They will spend whatever it takes; they've already surpassed six figures.

"If Kohberger is acquitted, let's say, and let's say he's acquitted because of a botched handling of evidence... then our allegation that the cops botched *this* case is... the second verse," Wilson said.

But, he added, "If it comes out that he was caught and he's convicted because of sterling police work—and we all would applaud it; including us, we would applaud it—then our allegation that the cops were Keystone Cops mishandling all of this becomes more of an uphill climb. It is obviously related, either way you go."

So whatever happens, Wilson will be watching very closely.

The way he sees it, the fate of his grandson—and, to some degree, his church—hang in the balance.

Chapter 122

Moscow, Idaho
May 12, 2023

I t's the Friday before graduation and the eve of the six-month anniversary of the murders.

It's also a few days before the celebration of the first "Maddie May Day." May 25, Maddie's birthday, will now be an annual holiday that Maddie's aunts, Katie and Rachel, helped create. They've bought a domain name, built a website, and extended an invitation to all: "Join us in continuing Maddie's mission by completing random acts of kindness. We can't wait to hear the stories that emerge as we all remember Maddie on this day and every day."

Deedle, as Maddie called her paternal grandmother, Kim Cheeley, is proud of her daughters for coming up with the idea. And she's excited to go to Moscow that evening with the Laramies and her son Ben Mogen and other family members to spread the word about Maddie May Day.

She's got cookies and a note about the new holiday for the Moscow police officers and the university staff.

"We wanted to thank the police department," she said. "I feel they've done an amazing job keeping their cards close [to] their chest and going about their business and doing what they had to do. I know that you're not supposed to say this out loud, but I feel they have their man."

When she arrives at the police station, gifts in hand, various officers come in and out of the room as she shares the cookies.

Deedle is gratified. Until, that is, nearly two weeks later, on May 25, Maddie's actual birthday. On that day, she reads in the *Idaho Statesman* that "the families" of Maddie Mogen and Kaylee Goncalves have filed tort claims notices with the city of Moscow, the University of Idaho, the Idaho State Police, and possibly—it's suggested but not confirmed—WSU. The paper quotes the Goncalveses' lawyer, Shanon Gray, explaining that the families have filed, as legally required within six months of the original incident, to reserve their right to sue. They haven't sued yet, but they might in the future.

"Filing a tort claims notice is really just a safeguard," Gray tells ABC News. "It's a safeguard to protect the interests of the families, the victims, and really the whole community around, because if something goes wrong or was done improperly, then someone is held accountable for that."

In May, Steve phones Stacy Chapin to tell her ahead of time that he is filing the tort against the cops and university. He explains, "This is nothing against you." And he means it. It isn't even against the police, in his mind. He's creating a layer of protection for Kaylee and Maddie. It isn't personal.

Stacy doesn't take it personally, but she is quietly upset on behalf of the police and the university.

Deedle is devastated. "It broke my heart," she later said.

She is mortified as she reads on and discovers that the Goncalves family filed theirs on May 2 and 3, but the "Mogen family" filed on May 11— the day before she showed up at the Moscow police station with her basket of cookies.

The "Mogen family" designation wrongly insinuates she had a part in this. She wants to set the record straight. She would *never* consider suing the police or the university.

"That is not us," she said. "We've been so thankful to the university, to the police department, and have been treated like royalty through this whole thing."

But Kim doesn't want to alienate Karen and Scott Laramie. During Maddie's short life, Deedle had consistent, unfettered access to Maddie because Karen and Scott allowed it. Ben was also made to feel welcome in their home. Even though he still had paternal rights, things could have been a lot less easy had Karen and Scott not been so generous and welcoming.

"I love Karen," she said. "We stayed really close for Maddie's sake. And Scott too. I really, really love both of them."

Nervously, she phones Bill Thompson's office and asks if she is bound by the gag order.

She is not.

Then she calls the *Statesman*.

She speaks to an editor and tries to explain she'd like to be separated from the Mogen family in future reporting. But she doesn't want to create a story about a fracture in the family, so when the editor asks her if there is an issue, Deedle treads carefully.

"Well, going forward, could we just make clear who you're talking about? That's all."

She hangs up and wishes it were all much less complicated. Maddie was such an angel of a person. Deedle has added an angel wing, in her memory, to the necklace Maddie ordered for her on Etsy that had both of their names.

She doesn't get why the Goncalves family seems to be making so many decisions for Maddie's family. She's puzzled about why Maddie's ashes are on their mantelpiece alongside Kaylee's. But she also knows that it's what Karen wants.

Deedle thinks, *If that's the case, then so be it.*

Karen has lost her only child. And poor Karen had also lost her mother in a car accident when she herself was barely an adult.

So whatever Karen wants, Deedle will roll with it.

Chapter 123

Moscow, Idaho
August 1, 2023

It's over a hundred degrees when Jim and Stacy Chapin arrive on the UI campus.

They are there to drop off Maizie and Hunter for the start of the fall semester. But what they haven't told their children, because they don't want to upset them, is that after they've settled them in, they have another stop to make. Opposite the Kibbie Dome, in a nondescript building that has no AC and no electricity, is everything Ethan left behind at 1122 King Road.

Jim is reluctant to go, but Stacy insists. "Damn it, I'm going to get my kid's stuff."

Dean Blaine Eckles has thought long and hard about how to make the hideous experience as easy as possible for all the parents. He's got bottled water and nitrile gloves on hand. He and a team have staged and divided the campus building to mirror the rooms of the King Road house.

"We had old desks, and we brought in tables and staged it kind of like a garage sale," Eckles said. "We didn't want them to have to worry about opening boxes and being surprised."

Eckles has deliberately made sure that the families all come on separate days. And he has security in place just in case.

The Chapins walk through a room labeled KITCHEN to see if there's anything of Ethan's in there, then they go into a room marked FOUR, which contains the belongings of Xana and Ethan. Some of Ethan's stuff is spattered with blood. It's upsetting to see it. Unsurprisingly, given the heat, the building smells rank.

"It was hell. I will not lie, it was hell," Stacy said later.

But she takes what she needs. She'll put the furniture in the storage unit she and Jim have kept in Moscow. And she brings the clothes back with her to Priest Lake, where she washes them and puts them away in the basement, beside Ethan's ashes. They don't need to overthink it now. But one day, she knows, when they are ready, Maizie, Hunter, and she and Jim will want to choose some pieces of Ethan's life to hold on to.

Going through Ethan's stuff is only one part of today's bittersweet experience.

Ahead of the trial—slated for October, just two months away—the court released 1122 King Road, meaning both the defense and the prosecution teams have no further use for it in terms of evidence.

Soon after the murders, the owner gave the house to the university, leaving it up to UI to decide its fate. In February, the school announced the house would be torn down.

The Chapins are fervently in favor of the house being demolished as soon as possible. Hunter can see it from his bedroom window at Sig Chi; so too can so many of Xana and Ethan's close friends, like Josie and Ava. Stacy and Jim believe no one needs to dwell on the horrific events of November 13, and the house is a horrible reminder.

"It needs to go," Stacy said, a position reflecting their larger, laissez-faire view of the unfolding judicial process. They don't want to spend a second thinking about Kohberger or a trial or any of the legal process beyond what they glean from Bill Thompson, whose staff phones regularly to update them.

Over coffee in La Conner one morning in March, as they watched the sun rise and, like every day, wiped away their tears, Stacy and Jim came to the decision that it was time to look forward, not back.

"Why would I want to waste my time looking at him?" Stacy said, referring to Kohberger. She has—for now, at least—no intention of showing up at any of the hearings or in the future at his trial. "Nothing is bringing Ethan back."

Out of devastation, the Chapins want to create something positive. To Stacy, that's *The Boy Who Wore Blue,* a children's book she wrote about Ethan with illustrations by Lana Lee. In June, she and Jim travel to New York, and she appears on the *Today* show.

The book's profits will go to the couple's nonprofit foundation, Ethan's Smile—also a new variety of tulip Skagit County farmers have named in Ethan's honor. The foundation plans to award scholarships to high schoolers applying to college.

While the Chapins have no interest in the judicial process or the efficacy of the system, Steve Goncalves is on a mission. He asks journalists and local sources in the FBI to help him with research, and on the Goncalves family Facebook page he refers to himself as a "private investigator."

From the data Steve receives, he becomes increasingly sure that Maddie was the target. As far as Steve can see, Kohberger liked Maddie's photos on social media. He liked Kaylee's too, but always in joint photos with Maddie.

He wants to figure out how Kohberger appeared to know the layout of the King Road house before entering it on November 13, so he strenuously objects in July when the university announces its plans to demolish the 1122 King Road house quickly. "Technology changes so fast," he said. "So you never know if they discover some new scan or some kind of new phone technology or whatever and they want to go back in there and retrace steps." (He has a point. Months down the road, there will be back-and-forth between prosecutors and Kohberger's defense debating the accuracy of the model of the house to be used at trial.)

Shanon Gray puts out a statement from the Goncalveses to that effect and says the Kernodles and the Mogens are united on this point.

Dean Eckles understands their frustration over the house, but his hands are tied. University administrators are worried that the house is not safe—investigators tore out pieces of walls and floors, and there are wires hanging out. And it's costing the school around six hundred dollars a day to pay for security. It's a liability.

Because of the Goncalves family's public opposition to the demolition, Eckles is concerned that there might be some sort of disruption when they arrive on campus to pick up Kaylee's belongings in August.

"I absolutely worried [that Shanon Gray] was going to get media there and try to make this a big deal," Eckles said later.

But the Goncalves family comes quietly, without Gray and without drama. They take their time looking through Kaylee's things.

Eckles feels for them. "I felt I had a really good relationship with [them] for the most part," he said. In person, he senses they are just decent people trying to grieve the loss of their daughter and advocate for her in the best way they know how.

By the end of August, all four victims' families have gone through the stuff. The Kernodles do it remotely.

Steve Goncalves is bracing for the worst. But out of the blue, the university announces that the demolition is postponed.

This is not entirely due to the pressure from the Goncalves family.

It's because of something that will come to frustrate Steve even more than the planned demolition of 1122 King Road.

It's because the trial date has been changed.

Chapter 124

Moscow, Idaho
August 18, 2023

Kohberger is clean-shaven, hair neatly trimmed, and dressed in a white shirt, striped tie, and gray jacket. He enters the courtroom through the side door and takes his seat at the defendant's table, where he and Anne Taylor appear to chat easily, too easily, almost as if they are discussing the weather.

Sitting in the gallery, Kristi stares at him. She wants him to look at her, make eye contact.

Her sister, Tami Buttz, *really* wants him to look over. Tami is wearing a black T-shirt on which is emblazoned in yellow and white lettering #JUSTICEFORKAYLEE. IDAHO HOUSE BILL 186. SHOTS FIRED.

A few months earlier, the Idaho House of Representatives passed a law that would effectively bring back the firing squad as a means of execution if state officials were unable to obtain the chemicals needed to carry out a lethal injection.

Tami's T-shirt—a photograph of her wearing it is later posted to the Goncalves family Facebook page with the caption **Damn it feels good to be a gangster**—is a reminder that Bill Thompson has put the death penalty on the table.

If Kohberger sees the T-shirt or the family, he doesn't react.

Even when the defense's first expert witness in this hearing talks about the science of investigative genetic genealogy, Kohberger's expression stays fixed. His attorneys will later argue in court papers that this is due to his Autism Spectrum Disorder diagnosis, and they will claim it could hurt a jury's perception of him. The media's pool camera keeps zooming in on him as if seeking something, anything. But it gets nothing.

In a preview of what may come at trial, depending on what the judge allows in, Taylor steers the focus to the DNA found on the knife sheath.

She wants the state to hand over to her the precise IGG methodology that was used to construct Kohberger's family tree—discovery that the state's lawyers say they don't have. And even if they did, they argue, the issue is moot, because they have Kohberger's DNA from a cheek swab, and it's an exact match for the DNA on the knife sheath. The IGG lab work simply gave them a lead.

Judge John C. Judge says he'll allow Taylor to pursue this avenue, even though it's "on the edge." He expresses his desire to be particularly cautious because "this is a death-penalty case. And if I deny...the presentations that one or the other side believe have some bearing on the case, it's probably more wise for me to allow it." Judge adds, "It's especially important in a case like this to have a record for appeal. So I'm not saying one way or the other how [my ruling] might fall, but I think it's important to preserve the record."

For the next two and a half hours, the courtroom becomes Taylor's theater. At least, that's how Steve sees it.

Thompson seems to have little to ask or say. Taylor calls three expert witnesses and peppers them with questions about the complexity of the science behind creating a family tree from trace DNA. One of them, as far as Steve can see, has no right to call herself an expert at all.

"How are you allowing her to become an expert on the stand and not even cross-examine her?" he complains privately afterward.

The experts discuss the room for error and also the issue of whether online genetic databases were accessed by law enforcement without authorization, which could lead to legal challenges down the line.

When you look at the two lawyers battling, it almost doesn't seem like a fair fight. Thompson is retirement age and looks it. Taylor is in her late fifties, young-looking, blond. She's quick on her feet. And she's aggressive. She asks the judge, for instance, to toss out the indictment based on numerous, far-fetched-sounding irregularities surrounding the grand jury process. She argues that too few jurors were called (thirty-two instead of forty-five), in violation of state statute. That the instructions they were given were inaccurate. Even that the questionnaires they received were misnumbered.

A former classmate of hers, Moscow lawyer Mike Pattinson, observed that part of Taylor's job was simply to buy Kohberger time. "It's a death-penalty case."

So when the disappointing if predictable news that Kohberger is waiving his right to a speedy trial comes down the pike five days later, on August 23, Steve is prepared.

It's a reminder, Steve says, that it's essential that the Goncalves family is there in the courtroom for every single hearing. He has so little control over the course of justice that his presence in that room, staring at the defendant, feels like the only powerful thing he can do. It's the only time he truly feels he's doing anything proactive for Kaylee and Maddie.

Chapter 125

La Conner, Washington
November 13, 2023

I t's the one-year anniversary of the death of their beloved child.

Jim, Stacy, Hunter, and Maizie Chapin, dressed in black tie, are welcoming their guests.

Over glasses of wine in early summer, Jim and Stacy thought very hard about what they wanted to do on this day. They wanted the evening to be upbeat. Positive. Celebratory, even. They wanted it to raise money for their foundation, Ethan's Smile. They wanted it to be intimate and private.

There are more media requests flooding in than ever, partly because of the anniversary, but also because Stacy's insistence on keeping the focus of Ethan's story away from the lurid end is becoming a focus in itself.

In October, the *New York Times* covered her weekend visit to Orlando, Florida, for CrimeCon, which billed itself as "the world's number one event for true crime and mystery."

Stacy had gone to the convention as part of a panel of victims' parents who, like her and Jim, were starting foundations as their children's legacies. Once there, she saw that a professor from Alabama was offering a seminar purporting to be a "forensic analysis" of Ethan's murder.

Stacy tried to attend, but walked out after a few minutes. After some deliberation, she returned to the packed seminar near the end of the session. She stood up at the mic during the Q and A.

"My name is Stacy Chapin, and I'm Ethan's mom," she said.

The room of thirty-two hundred people hushed, then broke into loud applause.

Her voice quavering with emotion, Stacy pressed on, explaining that she hadn't watched the presentation but had a message for the room: In their fascination with crime, they should not forget the victims.

"These were four of the greatest kids, and all of the great things that you read about them [are] legitimately true...Don't forget these kids. They were amazing, amazing kids in the prime of their life."

The moment goes viral on Fox News.

Whether she wants to do this or not, through her steady insistence that people focus on Ethan's life, not his death, Stacy Chapin is developing a brand: iconic supermom.

But now, on the one-year anniversary of Ethan's death, she and Jim want a press-free evening.

They accept an offer from a friend and neighbor in La Conner, Jeff Hellam, to use his Hellam's Vineyard wine shop and bar for a party.

As Stacy warms to the idea, she realizes she doesn't want just any party. If they are going to do this, they are really going to do this. The dress code is going to be black tie.

She thinks hard about a guest list.

Of course Hunter and Maizie will be there. Of course they will ask close family friends like Susie DeVries. And her cousins Kathleen and Stuart, and the PR executive who acted as their gatekeeper. And Melissa and Jeff and all the people who helped with the foundation. Dean Eckles sends two of his team.

There are also the people who have come to be part of the Chapins' growing family because of the tragedy.

One is Jazzmin Kernodle, Xana's big sister, of whom Stacy feels increasingly protective. Jazzmin has moved to Seattle with her boyfriend,

Pat. But because Jeff is in Arizona, Stacy worries that Jazzmin can feel alone at times. Stacy wants to support her.

The other person Stacy invites is the Moscow police chief, James Fry.

Even as she dresses for the evening in a long navy gown, Stacy isn't sure that the chief will be able to make it. After all, there's an anniversary vigil going on at the UI campus, and La Conner is a six-hour drive from Moscow.

But as everyone sips the fine wines, Chief Fry walks in quietly, his son JD beside him.

During her remarks Stacy asks the room to acknowledge him.

"We just cannot thank you enough for the work that you have done to right this atrocity. And we can't wait for it to be over so that we can talk about some of what we know and what some of us *really* know."

The chief smiles.

The Chapins, like Michelle Wiederrick, Joseph's mom, and Chrissy Dove, Sarah Parks's sister, are his kind of people. "We all have different personalities...Some of us are always going to take the bad and make some good out of it," he later said.

"And then there's people who take the bad and try to capitalize on it. And then there's people who take the bad and let it destroy them. And I think Stacy, the Chapins—look what they've already done. Thirty-three scholarships, over fifty thousand dollars given to kids."

He added, "After what happened to them? That's extraordinary."

Chapter 126

Rathdrum, Idaho
November 13, 2023

On the one-year anniversary of Kaylee's murder, the Goncalveses don't go to the vigil in Moscow.

Instead, they sit in their living room on their black leather couch, familiar now to America's many true-crime sleuths, and give TV interviews about Kaylee and their frustration with the excruciatingly slow and opaque legal path to justice.

"We said, 'Gather it up...we'll work with investigators and turn this around,'" Steve tells NewsNation. He repeats how, because "nobody knows her like her brother and sister," they were ahead of investigators on the Grub Truck video and reaching out to Kaylee and Maddie's driver.

"We went from being victims and became actively involved...and [that] could make a difference," Steve says.

They tell their interviewers that they do have some proof that their advocacy matters.

For one thing, 1122 King Road is still standing. And on October 31, the FBI reentered the home to create a new 3D map of the crime scene.

Because of the gag order, it's not clear to the public what drove the agency to do this. But it's an undeniable win for the Goncalves family. "I knew in my heart what was best for those girls and Ethan, and I knew what was best was to keep [the house] around, until they did more," Steve tells NewsNation's Brian Entin.

"There will be a point when I'll be like, 'Let it go.'"

But that isn't now.

The family shifts focus to another bone of contention: Kohberger's attire for court hearings. Once John Judge took over the case, he granted Anne Taylor's request to allow her client to appear in court unshackled and wearing a suit.

"He looks like a business executive," Kristi explodes. According to her research, "[I've] never seen another murderer or whatever he is at this point in a case not in handcuffs, not in shackles, one or the other or both, and in orange."

The absence of prison clothing is infuriating.

"It makes me sick that he sits there in his suit, and he sits there and taps his hands," she tells Entin. "He rocks back and forth...why is he sitting there in the judge chair with a fresh haircut?"

Bill Thompson explains to the family, via Gray, that the judge allowed this out of caution: If the defense argues successfully that Kohberger has been made to look guilty on TV screens around the world before he appears in front of a jury, it could be grounds for an appeal. But Steve assumes that with a case that's this high profile, there will be an appeal regardless.

Steve knows there's also a good chance that Anne Taylor will argue, due to the constant local media coverage of the case, that Kohberger will not be able to get an impartial jury in Moscow, and the trial should be moved. If it is moved, Boise, nearly three hundred miles away, would be the most likely venue. How is that fair to the victims' families?

"It just seems wrong," he says, "that an outsider comes here, does crime here...without that community having a voice and determining how the justice plays out."

That's why Steve chooses to be proactive.

"I want BK to look back and say, 'If there was one thing that really brought me down, [it] was messing with Kaylee's family. They wouldn't let up,'" Steve said. "I would never want him to get away with it."

He's toying with the idea of pursuing a federal case based on Kohberger having crossed so many state lines to commit the murders. Sources at the FBI have told him that this might be a possibility. Steve knows that's a long shot, but he's going to explore every avenue.

For the Goncalves family, nothing is off the table. "Our motto was 'Don't be victims. Don't ever be a victim.'"

Chapter 127

Moscow, Idaho
December 28, 2023

D emolition day is finally here, despite the Goncalveses' best efforts.
Last night Shanon Gray released a statement from the Goncalves
family with the headline "Please Stop the Demolition of the King Road
Home!"

"We feel that the University of Idaho and the court has put us in a horrible position to have to voice our opinions," the statement read. "We all
along have just wanted the King Road home to not be demolished until
after the trial and for us to have a trial date so that we can look forward to
justice being served. Is that really too much to ask?"

The Chapins have not commented. Nor has Ben Mogen.

But Kristi and Steve are not ready to so easily say goodbye to the last
place Kaylee had been on this earth.

Behind the scenes, Alivea, who is back in California and due to give
birth to her fourth child shortly, has been trying to get her parents to
back down and let it go. "This is not the hill you want to die on," she's
told them. "We will have other more important battles."

On the other hand, Alina Smith, the cofounder of the University of

Idaho—Case Discussion Facebook page, goes to great effort to join the protest.

She's flown in from Texas, arriving at 1122 King Road long before dawn.

But she cannot get close to the house. There's police tape everywhere.

"They had it so blocked off over there that nobody could get through," she said.

And other than the media, there's no one around—not even protesters.

"They put warnings out a good week or so ahead of time on these little billboards everywhere that if you think you're going to show up and protest, we're going to arrest you on the spot," she said. "They scared everybody away."

The demolition is scheduled for seven a.m., but the crew starts two hours early.

By the time the sun is up, the house is in pieces on the ground.

Kristine, the other cofounder of the Facebook page, is back in Rochester, New York. She is annoyed that she can't fly to Moscow to watch and take a video of the demolition with Alina, but she's got her family to deal with over the holidays.

Earlier in the month, the university stated—for the third time—that it planned to knock the house down on December 29, while the students were home for the holidays. UI president Scott Green told the *Idaho Statesman,* "While we appreciate the emotional connection some family members of the victims may have to this house, it is time for its removal and to allow the collective healing of our community to continue."

"That quote really stung," Alivea said.

Green's stance raised the demolition debate to a fever pitch. Members of the Facebook page are split, some for and some against.

Sympathizers with students who are distressed by the sight of the house debate those who favor preserving the premises for potential use in a trial. (In the recent trial of South Carolina lawyer Alex Murdaugh, the jury visited the family plantation where Murdaugh's wife and son had been found murdered.)

On December 20, Kristine and Alina did a TV segment with

NewsNation's Ashleigh Banfield to talk about the controversy around the demolition, and when Alina gets to Moscow, she tells Kristine that the trip is proving to be good PR for the page.

She's done a bunch of press, and she's met fellow cybersleuth Olivia Vitale, the creator of "Chronicles of Olivia" on TikTok. Olivia was the person to whom the Goncalves family gave their first in-depth interview a year earlier.

Alina tells Kristine, "I think we have an opportunity with her. She's, like, she didn't know half the stuff that you and I know. She's so interested in us."

Kristine is excited to learn this because she thinks that with all the work she and Alina have put into launching their podcast series, they are nearly ready.

On December 8, she posted on the Facebook page a photograph of Alina and herself captioned: **Your lovely administrators want to let you know our first podcast is in the works!! Enjoy your weekend but don't cause Alina and I to drink too much.**

By now Kristine has refined their podcast concept: "Two Sleuths, One Crime."

Alina, however, returns to Texas to bad news. Her husband has lost his job of twenty years.

Something is going to have to change, she thinks.

Unlike Kristine, Alina doesn't have a paying job. Running the Facebook page—and nine others like it—has been all-consuming for her. But she's got three kids, one with a disability, and she needs to carry her family while her husband gets back on his feet.

So she'll look for the right opportunity.

Kristine, she's sure, will understand.

Chapter 128

Moscow, Idaho
February 28, 2024

S teve is praying as he takes his seat in the gallery of the courthouse: *Let's get a date. Let's get a date.*

To the Goncalves family, attempting to set the trial date is beginning to feel like Groundhog Day.

Anne Taylor seems to be winning every tactical battle.

Each time, she presents a consistent visual: Kohberger sits up at the front, suited and stone-faced, next to Taylor and her colleague Elisa Massoth as the defense attorneys debate what evidence might and might not be admissible at a trial.

Each time, Taylor is the star of the show. She's on her feet talking and raising questions more often than any other lawyer in the room. Thompson barely says anything.

And the judge, as far as Steve can see, bends over backward to accommodate Taylor.

Last month, Steve, Kristi, and Shanon finally held an in-person meeting with Bill Thompson and his team, and they vented their frustrations about the lack of progress.

"We beat up on Thompson a little bit," Steve said. "On Friday [the judge] asked, 'What can I do to make sure that we get this case done before 2025? What would I have to do?' And Thompson said, 'You got to start setting dates.' And at the end of that court, what did he do? He didn't set a date. And we're like, 'That's your fault, Thompson.'"

Today, after yet another back-and-forth about how much of the IGG discovery the defense wants—Taylor asks the judge to allow three unnamed criminal investigators working for the defense to access the material—the meat of the session, finally, is a heated argument about a trial date.

Steve is hopeful at the outset of the dialogue.

John Judge and Thompson want to set it for March 3, 2025. But Taylor pushes back, managing to sound simultaneously calm and exasperated.

"Death is different," Taylor says.

The words punch Alivea Goncalves in the gut.

Taylor continues, "This is a capital case. I've heard the court say the court only wants to do it once and I've heard the court ask what I can do to speed things up."

She pauses.

"I need discovery. I need *all* of the discovery...when I ask for something I need to get it rather than have to go back and ask and ask and ask again.

"And I'm not trying to be mean about Bill Thompson," she says, looking directly at her former boss. "I'm just not. I think he tries his very best."

She blames the problem on agencies like the FBI, who, she says, hand things over piecemeal. "It's like if you wanted to play fifty-two-card pickup with a hundred thousand decks of cards and throw them in the air, and I have to go figure out how to put them together."

She wins the hour. No trial date is set. The judge adjourns with a further hearing scheduled for May to discuss a venue change.

Steve can barely believe it.

"So here we are stuck in this situation and we have a judge and a prosecution that's supposed to be defending us, acting like the biggest victim, and just keeps making us feel like a victim over and over. Every time we go into the courtroom, he just sits there and just lets her hit him and lets her dictate everything that's going to happen. It's so frustrating."

Steve feels he has got to do something—anything—to change the momentum. He's going to keep doing his own digging. If no one else can get a break in the case, he will.

"The discovery hasn't closed. If we do find something that they don't have, then they're going to have to put it in the case. And I don't care if they don't like the fact that somebody else found it that isn't part of Idaho...I don't know what kind of world we live in where we hide the truth."

Chapter 129

Moscow, Idaho
May 3, 2024

When it comes to saying goodbye to the police department he has served for thirty-one years, Chief Fry knows better than to try to get through it live.

Instead, he sits near the front of the audience in the conference room of Moscow's Best Western hotel, next to Julie and his kids, while the assembled guests watch him give the farewell speech he'd recorded on video a week earlier.

The raw, emotional, authentic performance would not be highly rated by his former press coach, Aaron Snell. And it's all the better for that.

The chief's voice cracks and he stumbles over his words as he runs through the very long list of people to thank.

"To everyone who worked the Idaho Four homicides, Idaho State Patrol, FBI, Moscow officers, Latah County prosecutors, and the Idaho attorney general's office: You are all the unsung heroes who did and continue to do a great job because of how you did your job. You have brought trust and respect back to the law enforcement community, to the Moscow police personnel. You truly are top-notch."

He runs through his list: Bill Thompson; colleagues; patrol; corporals and sergeants; command; his family—his kids, his sons-in-law.

And then, finally, he gets to Julie.

"God knew I needed a strong wife," he says, tears welling at the thought of the woman who kept his whiskey levels in check during the winter of 2022 and who has always been there for him.

He and Julie recently took the Birkman personality test, and James wasn't shocked to discover that the colors of his personality were red (for action, energy), green (for communication), and blue (for creativity), and that Julie's was yellow (for order).

"She completes me," he says.

Everyone in the room knows that this isn't farewell to James Fry so much as see you later.

Before he retired, the chief announced publicly that he would run for sheriff in November 2024. He'll be up against Richie Skiles, the incumbent, which is somewhat awkward because they know each other well. This is Moscow, after all. And both men are well liked. But if he doesn't win that, he'll find *something* to keep him in the mix.

Even so, the retirement of James Fry marks the end of an era, one in which the Moscow PD faced the most high-profile and arguably the most horrific challenge in its history.

The house at 1122 King Road may be demolished, but the people in this room bear scars that will last forever, long after Bryan Kohberger has finally faced justice, whenever and wherever that happens.

Exhibit A is Tyson Berrett, who is at the chief's retirement party. He has already told the chief he'll be having one of his own in July. Tyson is only fifty-two. But the stress of the demands placed on him during the winter of 2022 has taken its toll. He's done.

Fry later said that he regretted making Tyson the point person for all four victims' families. It was too heavy a burden for one man to bear in those ghastly six weeks between Thanksgiving and New Year's Eve 2022.

"I should have split it up," he said.

There's barely a dry eye in the room at the end of the ceremony when

Anthony Dahlinger hands James Fry his police radio to sign off—for the last time.

When the dispatcher utters the words, "One-oh-one is off duty for the final time," the room is silent.

"Heavy," says Dahlinger, the new chief, in conclusion. "Definitely, definitely a little heavy."

Chapter 130

Prosper, Texas
May 20, 2024

After breakfast, Alina goes to her bedroom to check her phone before taking her houseguests — a member of the Facebook page and the woman's seven-year-old son — to the airport.

She's away for about fifteen minutes.

When Alina returns, she's clearly distressed; her houseguest observes that Alina's face is unrecognizable from all the tears.

What's happened in those fifteen minutes is an argument over text message with Kristine, which has culminated in all the work Alina has done — on all ten of the Facebook pages she created and administered with her oldest friend — being eradicated.

It's devastating.

Alina is hardly in a fit state to drive, so her houseguests take an Uber to the airport. Once's she alone, Alina returns to bed and stays there for the next three days.

The fight between the two Facebook page founders began when Kristine texted Alina to ask if she was promoting a new case-discussion page about the recent controversial suicide of a Myrtle Beach woman, Mica Miller, whose husband was the pastor of a local church. Alina replied that she was.

Kristine responded that she couldn't believe Alina had started something without her.

Alina explained that she had joined a crime-scene collective as part of a victims' advocacy foundation because she believed it would result in paid work, which she desperately needed. Kristine, she thought, would understand. Alina had financial pressures, and Kristine was so busy with her day job that Alina wanted to forge ahead on this. She was worried that the podcast project might never happen.

But Kristine did not understand.

After a rapid-fire exchange of escalating, angry, expletive-filled texts, Kristine deleted Alina from every single page they had started together.

Just like that, the childhood friends were done. Over. But so too was everything Alina had worked on for years and years.

And almost immediately their dispute became public. Kristine posted to the Facebook page her side of the story of Alina's "betrayal." The post garnered twenty-eight thousand views and almost five hundred comments.

Not all of them were positive.

What does this have to do, some members asked, with the tragic murders of four young innocents in Idaho?

Alivea Goncalves was one of those members. She messaged Kristine that she felt what she'd written on the page was inappropriate.

Alivea felt very sorry for Alina. She knew firsthand how hard Alina worked. Alivea could see how consistently and often Alina had intervened on the page to squash some of the more outlandish conspiracy theories and victim-blaming.

Fearing that the page might be deleted suddenly in the midst of the fracas, Alivea joined another, smaller page, the University of Idaho Murders—Case Discussion as a backup. A couple of days later, Alina became its administrator.

It's not the outcome Alina had imagined when she and Kristine started their page and it took off so quickly.

And it's not what Kristine wanted either. The old page no longer accomplishes what it did at the height of the investigation.

Despite the building anticipation around the upcoming trial, there's less media interest in the Facebook page than there used to be.

Neither Alina nor Kristine is invited to go on NewsNation much anymore.

Privately, both women regret that the page's focus turned away from the victims and toward their messy personal affairs. But it's too late to mend fences.

Chapter 131

Moscow, Idaho
May 30, 2024

Yet again, Steve thinks this hearing is a complete waste of everyone's time.

Today, Anne Taylor kicks things off by interrogating Brett Payne about the surveillance video canvassing for the white Hyundai Elantra. She asks him to take her back in time to December 23, 2022, when he received Kohberger's phone records for the forty-eight hours around the murders and then issued a warrant for the six months prior to it.

Payne patiently explains that he deferred to the FBI expert, special agent Nick Ballance, to analyze the phone records and that the PCA (probable-cause affidavit)—no surprise—was put together based on input from the experts at command.

It's clear from the matter-of-fact way Payne answers Taylor's questions that he's describing the workings of a well-oiled investigation—all the different teams and experts do what they do individually, then click together.

But Taylor is looking to exploit any gaps in the machinery.

She homes in on the fact that investigators didn't create a central inventory for the thousands of hours of video surveillance. Rather, it's stored on different thumb drives. And because he was focused only on the video that was relevant for the PCA, the video with the Elantra in it, Payne doesn't know where all of it is.

Taylor wants the video they have of I-95, the main route back to Pullman, because the Elantra *doesn't* appear in it. (In Payne's probable-cause affidavit, he was careful not to specify which route Kohberger took from Moscow back to Pullman.)

Steve can see that the defense attorney is looking for any sort of hole.

It's an absurdly low bar, he thinks.

Worse, though, the technique plants seeds of doubt. Taylor is "poisoning the audience by saying that there's no connection, that there's no video," Steve said. "So when she starts doing that shit, I start getting impatient with Thompson and saying, you know, 'She's kicking your ass in there and you need to stand up for us.'"

Thompson *is* trying to push back. He's told the judge, "The characterization that we are just consciously withholding information to the defense is utter nonsense."

Indeed, at this point, Taylor concedes, the state has given the defense "a fifty-terabyte hard drive," more than 13,000 photographs, more than 15,000 video clips from businesses, and more than 8,000 video clips from residences.

But Steve doesn't think Thompson is doing enough to manage public perception. He's upset with how Thompson questioned one of the defense's expert witnesses on April 10.

"You acknowledged, falsely, that Mr. Kohberger allegedly stalked one of the victims. That's false. You know that to be false," Thompson said.

The defense expert confirmed that the information was false.

Steve is totally confused.

Maybe Thompson is being strategic, or maybe *stalking* has some legal definition that Steve isn't aware of. But as far as he knows — and Steve knows a lot at this point — Kohberger for sure looked in at the King Road house several times before the night of November 13. Steve has even gotten hold of a video of a car idling outside it for fifteen minutes. He isn't positive, but it looks similar to Kohberger's.

He's fairly certain from his own research that Kohberger showed up at the UI cafeteria. *And* that he was looking up restaurants with vegan options in the area. There's only one: the Mad Greek, where Maddie and Xana worked.

So how can Thompson say there was no stalking?

"Maybe there's some rule" around the term *stalking,* Steve reasons, where "you have to physically communicate. I don't know...But I do believe that these victims were selected. I think he picked them and he monitored them. He studied them. He hunted them. And every father and mother's understanding [is that] he stalked them."

Meanwhile, in court, he's got to sit through more mind-numbingly technical testimony from Sy Ray, a cell phone geolocation-data analyst, who says, essentially, there's stuff missing from the record, and the missing data—about "2 to 3 percent" of the location data from Kohberger's phone—could be important.

Steve figures he knows a heck of a lot more about cell phone data than this guy. What they *should* be getting into, Steve thinks, is the trial date.

And Kohberger's alibi.

In April, Taylor filed papers saying that Kohberger would use an alibi defense. She wrote that Kohberger "was out driving in the early morning hours of November 13, 2022, as he often did to hike and run and/or see the moon and stars. He drove throughout the area south of Pullman, Washington, west of Moscow, Idaho, including Wawawai Park."

"What kind of half-baked alibi is that?" Steve said. "I mean, stargazing? Give me a break."

Why doesn't Thompson try to get it thrown out as evidence? Steve doesn't get it. Not least because on the night of the murders, he's discovered, there was very little visibility.

The hearing ends with the state getting nowhere, as far as he can see. The afternoon session—to talk further about the IGG—is closed.

Steve hears through the grapevine that during the closed sessions, the judge reams out Taylor.

He would have liked to see that.

For the moment, he and Kristi use the only leverage they have: the media.

They issue a statement.

Wasn't this hearing supposed to address a motion to compel discovery? How did it evolve into an attack on the probable cause affidavit, the prosecution's witnesses, training records, and their evidence-gathering techniques? The court needs to take control of the case and the attorneys involved. As long as the Court continues to entertain anything and everything at every hearing, the delay will never end.

Chapter 132

Priest Lake, Idaho
June 2024

Its a beautiful day when Stacy Chapin gets the call from Bill Thompson's office.

Next week there's a hearing at which finally — finally — the judge will set a trial date.

It will likely be summer 2025.

Thompson would like for it to happen when there are no students around. He's pointed out to the judge that the high school is opposite the courthouse.

The news is something of a relief to Stacy, the first hint that maybe some sort of end could be in sight. Although by now, she knows better than to count her chickens. "You have to be in for the long haul," a prosecutor friend of theirs told her. "You have to let the defense put up everything."

And Stacy has been warned that it's possible the trial will not happen in Moscow, despite the best efforts of the prosecutors. The defense will continue arguing that the community is too small and too prejudiced to provide Kohberger with an impartial jury.

But where will they go when the trial takes place? Stacy starts to wonder. Will they stay at Priest Lake? Part of her wants to leave the country for three months. She knows that the press coverage will be intense, and that means reliving the horrors of November 13.

But after months of agonizing, she, Jim, Maizie, and Hunter decide they do want to be there to represent Ethan, especially at the opening, when the jury first convenes. They also want to be in the courtroom to support Hunter Johnson and Emily and all of Ethan's and Xana's other friends who will likely have to testify.

It will be a necessary but sorry interruption from the new normal that's finally emerging. Both Chapin kids are now so busy during the semester that their parents no longer feel they need to visit Moscow every other weekend.

Hunter and Maizie are set to graduate in May 2025. This summer, Jim is training Hunter to work with him in the machinery construction business. And Hunter also got his EMT certification. Maizie has been working as a server at Hill's Resort. After college, she's considering either training as a professional chef or studying nursing.

Public speaking, Stacy is finding, is a positive thing for her to do, provided it's in an appropriate forum that focuses not on the salacious aspects of the murders but on the family values that are Stacy's strong suit. She loves to talk about Ethan, but she's also beginning to realize that there's an appetite out there for the positivity that she and Jim are trying to create to remember him by.

In April, Stacy flew to LA to record an episode of *The Squeeze,* the mental-wellness podcast hosted by the actor Taylor Lautner, who starred in the Twilight films, and his wife, Taylor Dome.

When Lautner asked her what she felt about Kohberger's trial and the path to justice, Stacy said, "One of the greatest messages I feel like that we've done in handling this situation: Nothing changes the outcome. We cannot bring Ethan back. So you could spend a lot of time there or you can just realize that and figure out how to move forward."

And the Chapins *are* moving forward.

They like to walk around the lake and sit on the wooden bench engraved with their late son's name. "Ethan would be very proud," Stacy often says to Jim when they look out at the water and his beloved volley-ball court at Hill's Resort.

They like to come to this bench and sip mimosas as they watch the sun sink behind the mountains. Even better is when Hunter and Maizie are around on weekends. The entire family can all look at the lake and talk about Ethan in what was probably his favorite spot in the world.

They can find peace, even.

"The funny thing is, Ethan would be like, 'Well, of course my parents knocked it out of the park, that's just how we roll as a family,'" Stacy says to her husband, who nods in agreement. "We had a motto: 'Go big or go home.' And that's what we've done."

Chapter 133

Post Falls, Idaho
June 15, 2024

The black-tie crowd at the inaugural Make It Pink Gala is so large, it's hard to see everyone who's turned out to support the new Made with Kindness nonprofit that's been set up in honor of Maddie and Kaylee by Maddie's sorority friend Ashlin Couch.

There's a hiccup at the check-in desk. For the people in formal dress who are in a line that goes past the bathrooms and around the corner all the way to the elevators, it's a good thirty-minute wait.

No one minds. They are here for a good cause.

They can even buy the merchandise laid out on a table while they wait.

Tonight, even though people are there to support the Goncalveses and Laramies, the Goncalves family—seated around two tables in the middle of the room—mostly keep to themselves.

They lent Kaylee's name to the nonprofit, but because they know only a handful of people here, one might miss them in the crush. When the emcee mentions Kaylee and Maddie, Kristi puts her head in her hands and weeps. Steve puts his arm around her.

It's a bittersweet moment. Kristi and the girls have been looking forward to this; it's an excuse, Steve says, for them to get their hair and nails done and for him to put on black tie. And it's wonderful that there is now a scholarship in Kaylee's and Maddie's names. During the event, it's announced that Xana's name will complete the trifecta.

But they still haven't gotten justice for their daughter.

That night, Steve says he's heard the good news from Thompson that there's likely to be a court date set, finally, but his patience with Anne Taylor is as thin as ever.

He particularly objects to one line she repeatedly uses in court: "Judge, if we ever get to trial..."

If she doesn't want to get to trial, Steve says, well, Bill Thompson needs to press the judge—and find a defense attorney who does want to.

Steve is still pursuing his parallel investigation; he's seeking the answers to a million questions about Kohberger's connection to the King Road house.

For instance, he says, he'd like to know more about what Dylan saw that night. He feels certain he doesn't know everything about what she witnessed. Someone told him that she hid in a closet. Maybe she phoned someone? He's heard there's evidence on her phone that's important.

Steve is still pissed that 1122 King Road was demolished by the university when, as he puts it, "seventy-five percent" of the parents were against it. When the time is right, he'll be ready to look at his options for civil cases. He's on a roll.

Suddenly Kristi prods her husband. "Is that Blaine Eckles?" she says, shocked, looking across the room.

"It can't be," Steve says.

Post Falls is a ninety-minute drive from Moscow.

Blaine Eckles didn't tell the Goncalves or Laramie families he was coming.

And yet it is Blaine Eckles, sitting with a bunch of random strangers.

"I was a little curious to see how my presence would be received," the dean later said.

The Goncalves family is stunned, given the back-and-forth over the King Road house demolition.

Kristi and Alivea leap up and go say hello to him. And then they bring Eckles to their table. Steve and Eckles shake hands.

Eckles tells them that the university's Healing Garden, a project he spearheaded and has overseen to commemorate the victims and help the community grieve, is nearly done.

It's likely to open in August, at the start of the fall semester. Of course he wants the family there.

When Eckles leaves, readying for his ninety-minute drive back to Moscow, Steve Goncalves actually smiles.

"It's Father's Day weekend, and Eckles bothered to come."

In spite of himself and the fights, Steve is touched.

"Classy," he says.

Chapter 134

Brodheadsville, Pennsylvania
Summer 2024

As Connie Saba is shopping in the Rite Aid in Brodheadsville, she sees someone in the pain-relief aisle who looks familiar.

She stops. Is it someone she used to work with? And then she realizes... it's Michael Kohberger.

Bryan's dad.

"Connie?" he says. "Is that you?"

"How are you, Michael?" she replies.

He seems very pleased to talk to someone.

"My heart goes out to Maryann," Connie says. "How is she?"

Michael tells her that his wife doesn't talk to anyone, even on the phone. "We lead a very quiet life," he says. "We don't go out." And even when they are home, he says, they don't feel safe. "People," he tells her, "are watching our house."

"What people?"

"Government people," he says, leaving her slightly confused.

Then he says, "You know Bryan didn't do it, right, Connie?"

Connie thinks.

She says: "The Bryan I know wouldn't do it." She wants to be supportive.

It's then that Michael seems to remember that he hasn't spoken to her since Jeremy died.

"We were both shocked to hear Jeremy died," he tells her. "Maryann wanted to call you but she felt unable to." He doesn't explain why.

"Does Bryan know Jeremy died?"

"Bryan was away," Michael says. He doesn't say where. "We didn't tell him for months." But, yes, he knows.

"Bryan wasn't the same after the drugs," he adds. "He wasn't the same person."

Connie nods. But, she thinks, even on drugs, Jeremy had remained sweet and good-natured.

"But Bryan was framed," Michael says.

Connie is startled. Framed?

"Someone planted the knife sheath," he tells her. "The police didn't find it when they first went in. There were a lot of drugs in that house, a lot of people around. But they only looked at Bryan. You know how he likes to drive around when he's nervous?"

Connie doesn't, but Michael tells her, "He always used to get in the car and drive at night when he needed to think or he had some fog. He had to get away and just think. Or when he couldn't sleep, he would just drive around."

Michael adds, "Things will come out in the trial. Everyone will see."

The two go down memory lane, reminiscing about Jeremy's and Bryan's childhoods, the two boys running back and forth between their respective houses.

Connie asks after Michael's daughters, Amanda and Melissa. She's read news reports that Melissa was fired from her job, but she doesn't ask specifically about that.

Michael says they are good.

They chat in the aisle for at least an hour. Michael seems almost sorry to leave. She can tell he doesn't get to blow off steam much.

That night, she phones her daughter, Bridgette, to go over the whole extraordinary conversation.

Connie feels for Michael Kohberger. He clearly believes his son is innocent. She isn't sure if he's in denial or not.

But she can empathize with how a parent must feel in a situation like this, given everything the Kohbergers tried to do for Bryan.

"If it was my child," she later said, "I'd probably be the same way."

Chapter 135

Moscow, Idaho
August 21, 2024

It's blisteringly hot, but the Sig Chi brothers wear their suits nonetheless. They want to honor Ethan.

Stacy Chapin hugs each of them as they file into the new Vandal Healing Garden and Memorial for the dedication ceremony. She'd asked Blaine Eckles earlier if the guys could sit close to the Chapins.

It's the first time since the tragedy of November 13 that representatives of all four victims' families are together in Moscow.

The Goncalveses sit at the front to the left facing the podium. Ben Mogen is behind them. The Chapins and the Kernodles, represented by Jazzmin Kernodle and a couple of Xana's aunts, sit to the right.

James Fry stands at the back, almost unrecognizable in his jeans. Mayor Bettge is there. So are most of the Moscow PD. They are standing guard. There are still some true-crime maniacs around who are unhealthily obsessed with the King Road murders. Occasionally they surface on campus.

And, though few people talk about it, everyone is aware that sitting in a basement cell less than a mile away is the suspected murderer.

For Steve and Kristi, he's front of mind.

The hearing to decide the change of venue is only three days away. Kristi posted on their Facebook page: "All I can think about is the Change of Venue hearing this Thursday. I'm just sick about it...I wish I could snap my fingers and it would be over. The anticipation eats me alive. Please pray for us."

Today, though, the Goncalves family is not on defense. In fact, they are fully supportive of Dean Eckles and the university. Kristi even wears a T-shirt emblazoned with VANDAL STRONG. Steve Goncalves chats amicably with Chief Fry. He shakes Jim Chapin's hand. Dean Eckles hands him a folder of Kaylee's work. Steve and Kristi do several interviews with local media. They say that yes, it's hard to be here. But they are glad to honor their daughter. They think the healing garden is a wonderful idea.

Dean Eckles came up with the concept of the garden after the vigil. He knew that the university needed to memorialize the Idaho Four, and while they were at it, he thought, why not create a space to remember *all* the UI students who passed away too soon while attending college? There have been four student deaths since November 2022.

So the dean invited everyone to discuss where the space might go and what it could look like. More than a hundred students, among them Hunter Chapin, and faculty members came. Eckles created a garden committee that included not just landscape architects but representatives of the victims' fraternities and sororities: one from APhi, one from Sig Chi, and two from Pi Phi.

Dr. Shauna Corry, the dean of UI's College of Art and Architecture, developed a class focused on the creation of a template. "They identified plants that work with our temperature, our climate, time of year...They measure how dark it gets on what days of the year....They have done so much work," Dean Eckles said with pride.

Earlier, in the spring of 2023, the four families were invited to sit in on the class and give their input.

Stacy felt that it was one of the most cathartic experiences she and Jim had had since Ethan's death. The kids didn't ask them specific questions about garden design; they asked general, thoughtful questions, like "What does it mean to be a Vandal?" and "What are the words that describe Ethan?"

Ever the mother hen, Stacy felt a bond forming with these young kids, and she's thrilled to recognize many of them—wearing matching black shirts—on this big day.

Emily Alandt can't get to the ceremony today. The drive from Boise is too long, and Hunter Johnson is at work.

But she was asked to pick a flower for Xana. She'd suggested a Peruvian lily because the lily is Xana's birth flower and the Peruvian lily, Emily thinks, has the same sort of sparkle and spirituality as her late friend.

The Goncalves family will post on Facebook that they found it a deeply emotional, special day. They have buried the hatchet with the university for now.

It's hard to say which part of it is the most moving. Maybe it is the moment of silence for Ethan, Xana, Maddie, and Kaylee. Or maybe it is when Drew Giacomazzi, Ethan's friend and fraternity brother, speaks about each of the four victims, concisely describing their distinct personalities in a way no one will easily forget:

"Do more of what you love to honor Kaylee. Spread that love with random acts of kindness for Maddie. Be silly and do something spontaneous and fun to honor Xana. And tell stories with an abundance of laughter to live life like Ethan."

Chapter 136

Moscow, Idaho
August 29, 2024

The hearing to decide the change of venue lasts over six hours.

Steve is not hopeful that the trial will stay in Moscow, despite his best efforts to convey his feelings to the judge via Bill Thompson.

The expert witnesses that Anne Taylor produces—who testify that it would be impossible in tiny Moscow to find a fair and impartial jury—seem to speak out of both sides of their mouths, Steve thinks.

"One expert says you can call the jury and they can still remain impartial, and another expert says...you hear something and you can never get it out of your head," Steve said afterward.

But he's gotten the impression for months now that Bill Thompson doesn't really want to run the risk of having a trial in Moscow because of the university. The problem, Steve thinks, is that some of these people seem to put the university first, ahead of the victims. They all went there.

Thompson said in court it would be better to avoid having a trial when students are around. That's why he wants to have it in the summer. Steve was not pleased when he heard that.

"I mean, that's kind of a weird way to present four murders to a judge," he said.

He's also worried that the university timetable will give Anne Taylor some excuse to push the trial back beyond next summer. So even though he feels that it should be local and that it will be one heck of an inconvenience for him and Kristi if it gets moved all the way to Boise, he also figures it might not be all bad to get out of the cozy cabal that is Moscow. He'd welcome a new judge.

Today Judge John C. Judge, typically, punts making a decision at the hearing itself. He thanks both sides for their "really solid" arguments. "I would say that professionally this is the most difficult decision I've ever had to make," he adds.

On September 6, in the form of a written decision, the bad news arrives.

The judge writes that the defense has met "the rather low standard" of a basis to move venues. It isn't just that the media storm might have swayed jurors; there are the practical considerations of a tiny courthouse and staff.

The Goncalveses post their reaction on their Facebook page: "The family is incredibly disappointed in the Judge's ruling granting the change of venue. The only good thing about this decision is it will be Judge Judge's last decision in this case."

It isn't clear for a few days where the trial will be moved.

But on September 12, the Idaho Supreme Court orders it moved to Boise—Ada County—under the jurisdiction of a new judge, Steven Hippler.

Steve says that Judge Hippler is no stranger to capital cases. He's known to be strict and stern.

Good.

Chapter 137

Moscow, Idaho
September 15, 2022

B ryan Kohberger is flown three hundred miles south to Boise and booked into the Ada County jail.

There is the inevitable media fanfare around his trip.

Mike Pattinson considers this to be almost a literal weight off the minds of people in Moscow. Many of them might have wanted the trial held locally for emotional reasons—but no one liked the idea of Kohberger sitting underground, virtually beneath them.

It emerges that his exit is barely a day too soon. On October 3, it's reported that the Latah County jail might finally be closed because it does not meet code regulations. A new fire marshal has arrived in town, looked over the facility, and said that the fire sprinklers and electrical systems don't meet standards and the doors are too small.

Evan Ellis covers the story. He reports that rebuilding the jail could cost up to fourteen million dollars, minus the cost of the land. If city commissioners decide it's too expensive, Moscow's criminals might need to be housed in Lewiston instead. And the move could happen in just two weeks. "Thank the Lord Kohberger is not in there," Evan says, imagining the stink there would have been.

Being the cynical journalist that he is, he considers the timing—the election for sheriff is barely a month away—and thinks that it might be fortuitous for James Fry's campaign because the jail's failure to meet code regulations happened on his opponent's watch.

"Is [the new fire marshal] a Fry guy and trying to help him out or just a by-the-book guy and it's just coincidence?" Evan asks.

"I have no idea," he says with a laugh.

Chapter 138

Rathdrum, Idaho
September 28, 2024

Alivea and Kristi feel like they've hit a wall. They are going to need housing in Boise for three months, but they learn that there is no federal, state, or local assistance for families who have lost a loved one. The only option, they realize with input from Jack DuCoeur's aunt, Brooke Miller, is to start a Goncalves family GoFundMe page.

The family asks initially for fifty thousand dollars to house them for the three months they will need to be in Boise next summer for the trial. They explain there will be ten of them (as well as pets) for the long haul. They need the basics: money for housing, food, travel, and compensation for loss of work.

Money pours in.

But the trial date remains uncertain.

In his first hearing in Boise, Judge Hippler says he's leaning away from the June date set by the previous judge because he thinks it will be hard to pick a jury, given family vacation schedules. Thompson suggests May; Taylor suggests September.

Taylor hits her usual theme of being overloaded with discovery. She's received an additional three hundred ninety-eight gigabytes of information since August, she says, "and I can tell the court that nobody on the team has read every bit of that yet." She also has a new mitigation expert she needs to bring up to speed because this person replaced someone who passed away.

But in a sign, perhaps, that Judge Hippler has less appetite for delay than John Judge, he tells her she needs to get it done by the deadline he sets.

"There are twenty-four hours in a day, but if you use enough of those hours, enough days in a row, you get it done if you have to."

The judge delivers a stern lecture to both teams at the outset.

"I'd like to say I'm happy to be here, but why start with an untruth?" He adds, "I do expect—and this will come as no surprise to you—for you all to get along. I understand the stakes in this case are as high as they can possibly be in any case. But you are professionals. You have taken oaths, both as officers within your jurisdictions but also as attorneys before this bar. So I expect at all times for you to remain civil to one another, that you not engage in personal attacks, ad hominem attacks, that you not engage in theatrics, not misstate the facts or the law to the court, and that when you cite arguments in your briefs, if there is contradictory precedent, I expect to see that."

On October 9, Judge Hippler issues his ruling: The trial will start on August 11 and run through November 7.

The Goncalves family finally feels optimistic. The atmosphere in Judge Hippler's courtroom is palpably fresh, electric even.

Once they get to trial, Steve hopes events will be anticlimactic. He has reason to be hopeful. Steve's FBI sources have told him that when the agency is involved in a capital murder case, they secure a conviction over 93 percent of the time. The odds, therefore, of getting a conviction in a quadruple homicide—"Well, you do the math," he says.

A lawyer for the FBI has told Steve that in all his years of experience, he's "never seen a case where DNA has been found at the crime scene and it didn't lead to that conviction." A piece of evidence like that is "insurmountable."

Cathy Mabbutt, the coroner, and other investigators agree.

But there's one person in Moscow who is worried.

Mike Pattinson, the Moscow lawyer and Anne Taylor's old classmate, isn't so confident. "Anne's a sharp litigator," he says. He wouldn't want to bet against her.

Mike hopes he's wrong, but "if it's just a knife sheath that happens to have Kohberger's DNA on it, what does that mean?" he asks. Is the DNA by itself enough proof?

Taylor will argue that it isn't. She will also likely "challenge the process upon which [investigators] came about his DNA," Mike believes. She may even offer alternative theories or suggest that somebody—perhaps a crooked police officer—could have planted it.

So now the stage is set for the drama that will begin in August, the moment when Emily, Hunter Johnson, Bethany, Dylan, Ava, Jack DuCoeur, Adam, and so many others in the victims' circle will likely have to take their positions in the witness box and relive the horrific events of November 13.

As to whether Bryan Kohberger will be found guilty or be acquitted? That's a story for another time.

Epilogue

The orange NO TRESPASSING sign is the only indication that something terrible happened here.

The patch of land where 1122 King Road once stood is now strangely peaceful. Green shoots spring out of the earth. Birds sing.

Students come and go from the houses and dorms all around. But no one stops to gawk anymore. There's nothing to see, just a small field that's overrun with weeds.

Most of the students now on campus are of a different, younger generation. They have no memory of Ethan, Xana, Maddie, or Kaylee.

They have no memory of the parties, the laughter, and the life that once blazed here.

They have no memory of the deck where the inhabitants drank coffee and posed for Instagram photos.

But a stone's throw away, the four plaques in the Healing Garden ensure that no member of the Vandal family, past, present, or future, will forget the names of the four innocents who lived on this piece of green happily and hopefully.

Their names are Ethan, Xana, Maddie, and Kaylee.

Acknowledgments

We could not have written this book without the support of a crucial group of people.

Max DiLallo's ideas around structure and language were essential, as was his enthusiasm and energy.

Maxine Richter played a critical part in the early research.

Denise Roy is our incomparable editor at Little, Brown and we are so grateful for her quick, deft, detailed improvements.

Thank you also to Tracy Roe, for a superb and rigorous copyedit.

Eric Rayman is the eagle-eyed attorney who gave us great notes.

For their support and expertise, we thank Margaret Cannon, Brian Perrin, and the entire team at Little, Brown.

And to Mary Jordan, James Patterson's PA, for keeping the trains running on time.

Special thanks, as always, to our nearest and dearest for bearing with us through it all. Susan, Jack, Orlando, and Lorcan: You make it all worthwhile.

Notes

The notes for this book can be found at https://www.hachettebookgroup
.com/titles/james-patterson/the-idaho-four/9780316572859.

About the Authors

James Patterson is the most popular storyteller of our time. He is the creator of unforgettable characters and series, including Alex Cross, the Women's Murder Club, Jane Smith, and Maximum Ride, and of breathtaking true stories about the Kennedys, John Lennon, and Tiger Woods, as well as our military heroes, police officers, and ER nurses. He has coauthored #1 bestselling novels with Bill Clinton, Dolly Parton, and Michael Crichton, told the story of his own life in *James Patterson by James Patterson,* and received an Edgar Award, ten Emmy Awards, the Literarian Award from the National Book Foundation, and the National Humanities Medal.

Vicky Ward is a *New York Times* bestselling author, a magazine columnist, and an investigative reporter. She is the author of the bestselling books *The Liar's Ball, The Devil's Casino,* and *Kushner, Inc. The Idaho Four* is her first book with James Patterson. Read her Substack newsletter, "Vicky Ward Investigates," at Vickywardinvestigates.com.

For a complete list of books by
JAMES PATTERSON

VISIT
JamesPatterson.com

 Follow James Patterson on Facebook
JamesPatterson

 Follow James Patterson on X
@JP_Books

 Follow James Patterson on Instagram
@jamespattersonbooks

 Follow James Patterson on Substack
jamespatterson.substack.com

**Scan here to visit JamesPatterson.com
and learn about giveaways, sneak peeks,
new releases, and more.**